She Always Knew How

SHE ALWAYS KNEW HOW

Mae West

A PERSONAL BIOGRAPHY

Charlotte Chandler

APPLAUSE
THEATRE & CINEMA BOOKS
AN IMPRINT OF HAL LEONARD CORPORATION
New York

Applause Theatre & Cinema Books
An Imprint of Hal Leonard Corporation
7777 West Bluemound Road
Milwaukee, WI 53213

Trade Book Division Editorial Offices
19 West 21st Street, New York, NY 10010

Published by Applause Theatre & Cinema Books in 2010

Originally published in hardcover in 2009 by Simon & Schuster, Inc.

Printed in the United States of America

Book design by Dana Sloan

The Library of Congress has cataloged the Simon & Schuster edition as follows:

Chandler, Charlotte.
    She always knew how : Mae West, a personal biography / Charlotte Chandler.
        p.   cm.
    Includes index.
    1. West, Mae.   2. Motion picture actors and actresses—United States—
Biography.   I. Title.
    PN2287.W4566C43   2009
    791.4302'8092—dc22
    [B]   2008048182

ISBN 978-1-4234-8410-3

www.applausepub.com

To Mae

Contents

"Some women know how to get what they want. Others don't. I've always known how."

—MAE WEST

Acknowledgments

WITH SPECIAL APPRECIATION

Bob Bender, George Cukor, Tim Malachosky, and David Rosenthal.

WITH APPRECIATION

Michael Accordino, Linda Ayton, Marcella Berger, David Brown, Helen Gurley Brown, Charles William Bush, Fred Chase, George Christy, Bud Cort, Tony Curtis, Gypsy da Silva, Bette Davis, Mitch Douglas, Marie Florio, Joe Franklin, Steve Friedeman, Tom Gates, Cary Grant, Tracey Guest, Dick Guttman, Edith Head, Angela Herlihy, Peter Johnson, Jane Klain, Alexander Kordonsky, Deborah Landis, John Landis, Ted Landry, Johanna Li, Groucho Marx, Paul Morrissey, Jeremiah Newton, Dale Olson, Paul Novak, Arthur Novell, Marvin Paige, Dan Price, Anthony Quinn, Joan Rivers, Robert Rosen, Michael Sarne, Arthur Schlesinger, Dana Sloan, Carly Sommerstein, Jeff Stafford, Kevin Thomas, Brian Ulicky, Robert Wise, and Danny Woodruff.

The Academy of Motion Picture Arts and Sciences, the American Film Institute, Anthology Film Archives, the British Film Institute, the Cinémathèque Française, the Museum of Modern Art, the New York Public Library for the Performing Arts, Paley Center for Media, and the UCLA Department of Theater, Film, and Television.

She Always Knew How

Prologue

M Y FIRST THOUGHT was, women need a Bill of Rights.

"And then I thought, no, what women need is—a Bill of Wrongs.

"When I was a girl," Mae West continued, "I understood right away that there was this double-standard thing for men and women, not just in sex, but in everything. A man's world was one of freedom, a woman's one of limitations. I believe in a single standard for men and women.

"Many women's lives are defined by the man or men in their lives. I wanted to define my own life. I never thought of myself as a feminist, though many people have said I was. I never identified with groups. It seemed to me that I'm for people's rights, and women are people, too.

"When a man was courting me, he'd want to put a diamond on my finger, and as soon as he thought he had me, he wanted to put an apron around my waist.

"I made my way in a man's world. I lived in the world of show business, which was a man's world as far as where the power was concentrated.

"My mother told me you can't be too smart, as long as you don't let it show, especially with men. 'Men don't like a woman to be smarter than *they* are. Brains are an asset as long as you hide them.' My mother was born in a different time. Things were true in her time that weren't *as* true in mine. My mother was forced to live in what was a woman's world, while 'the Great World' was for men.

"What I'm proudest of is that I offered entertainment, not a message. But there was a message, too, only it was subliminal, hidden behind the wisecrack. Women told me I inspired them to stand up and walk on their own two feet, not just lie on their backs.

"I let people know that women like sex, too, and that's a good thing, not a bad thing, as long as you don't hurt anyone and as long as you are responsible about children. I can't say I had a mission, but it turned out that way.

"In my opinion, I lived a selfish life. If you asked me, that's what I would call it. I was dedicated to myself.

"But then, one day, a woman came up to me in a restaurant, and she said, 'Miss West, I just wanted to tell you how wonderful you are.'

" 'Well, thank you, honey,' I said, assuming she was talking about my work as an *artiste*. 'Is there something special you liked?' I thought she was going to name a few things, or maybe say something like, 'Everything.' Well, she surprised me. I was expecting something short, but she wanted to tell me all about myself. Fans often do that, but this was different.

"She said, 'You made a difference, a wonderful difference for all of us women.'

"Well, that made me think. I had to ponder. It made me look back on my life and what it all meant, and you know, I decided my trying for myself had turned out to be trying for *all* women.

"I hope she was right. Wouldn't my mother have been proud! My life had made a difference not just for me. That meant my mother's life had made a difference, because she was the important person in the shaping of who I am.

"Someday there'll be a woman president. I'm sure of that. Women have been leadin' men around for centuries. Myself, I never wanted to hold any political office, except maybe *vice* president.

"Can you believe that there are people who say that I must be a bad person because I play the bad woman so well? They believe the parts I play are me! They don't give me the credit I deserve as an actress, and a writer.

"The image I want to offer to my public is very important, but even more important is my self-image. That's my own image of myself.

"My advice to you is, throw away any bad pictures of yourself.

"And dress up in your own home, just to talk on the phone. It changes the way you *are, even* on the phone.

"You know who Mae West is? I'm Cinderella in modern dress— *sort* of modern dress—and I wear high-heel wedgies, 'cause those glass slippers are too fragile! The thing I know is, I wouldn't change my image for no one.

"I created myself. I developed myself. I didn't turn out exactly this way all at once, though I wasn't very different when I was a little girl, from the first days I can remember. But in the beginning, I did some tinkerin'.

"I've become legendary, but not historical. I'm contemporary.

"I'm proud of my movies, and I'm really glad I made them. They were wonderful in their time, but they are more important now because the grandchildren of the people who watched me in those films can watch me. Many of the people who saw me in the theater are gone, and the others will take their memories with them.

"I'm grateful to my parents, who got my timing right. The twentieth century, it's a century to treasure."

When Mae began her career, doors were opened *for* women. When she finished her career, doors were open *to* women.

Introduction

ON MY ARRIVAL the afternoon that Mae and I met, she held out her hand to me. As I took it, I scratched my palm on one of her diamond rings. Noticing what had happened, she commented in a matter-of-fact tone, "They're old-cut, very sharp. That's the best kind."

All of her fingers were covered with diamonds. She wore a diamond necklace, a diamond bracelet, and a diamond anklet. These, she explained, were just her "daytime diamonds." Holding out her hands so I could examine the stones, she said, "Look, they're all real. They were given to me by admirers." Her gaze settled on my own unadorned hands.

"Oh, my, you poor kid! You don't have any!"

For a moment she regarded me silently with amazement and pity. Then she brightened. "But you have some at home?"

I shook my head.

Her look of deep sympathy returned. She studied me for a moment, then said encouragingly, "You *could*, honey. You *could*. But you've gotta try, and you've gotta know *how* to try. There's nothing better in life than diamonds."

"Maybe that's what one has to believe in order to get them," I said.

"You're right," she said. "You put your finger on it. Everything's in the mind." She touched her forehead. "That's where it all starts. Knowing what you want is the first step toward getting it." She held out her hands for both of us to admire. "These diamonds here—they're my friends. Aren't they beautiful? The only thing more important is health."

I found myself aware of a distracting sound, something like the fluttering of the wings of little birds. Trying not to appear inattentive to what Mae West was saying, I could not resist glancing around the living room of her Hollywood apartment. But I saw no birdcages.

The sound continued at frequent intervals. Only after Mae had been speaking for a while did I realize that it was the sound of her heavily mascaraed, multilayered false eyelashes brushing her cheeks whenever she blinked.

Our meeting had been arranged by director George Cukor, who had known Mae since the mid-1920s, when they were both working on the stage in New York. She told me when we first met, "You can call me Mae, dear, because you're George's friend, and that's what he calls me."

Mae West was not anxious to give any interviews, especially to a woman. "I don't have anything I want to sell, so I don't like to give it away free.

"If you set your own price on yourself as free, you don't deserve to get anything. If you don't put a high value on yourself, why would you expect anyone else to put a high value on you?

"That's why I was leery of doing any television appearances, which I didn't get paid for. I didn't believe in giving away Mae West and downgradin' her value.

"I'm like fine wine. I get better with age. Now, I'm more me than I ever was, so you get a bonus."

But she could not say no to George Cukor. She was still hoping that she would write and star in a film that he would direct. He was the director she most wanted. The only problem that concerned Mae was that Cukor was "getting up there in age." That *she* was eighty-six at the time, Mae didn't consider a problem.

Cukor told me that the film he had in mind for Mae would have co-starred her with Natalie Wood, who was also a great favorite of his. It was to be the story of a young woman who goes to a clairvoyant. The young woman is Natalie Wood, and the clairvoyant, Mae West.

"The idea was really inspired by Mae's own belief in the extrasensory powers of certain individuals and what Mae liked to call 'The Forces,'" Cukor said. "She tells me she's had dozens of experiences with them and met all kinds of spirits, but none of them particularly interesting. Oh, well.

"Mae has some other ideas, and she wants to do the script, but she isn't working quickly enough for either one of us.

"If you'll pardon the triteness of it, I told her, 'Time doesn't stand still, Mae,' and you know what she said to me?

"'Not for *you*, George.'"

Mae said, "When I talked about it with George, I told him that I didn't want to be the young woman. I insisted on the part of the clairvoyant. He said, 'That's fine, Mae.'

"I told him I didn't want to play a part any older than being in my thirties. He said, 'The ages of the characters will not be specified. They'll be of indeterminate age, so everyone can just see.'

"So that sounded fine to me. I started writing my part."

Mae paused. "I want you to know, this is the last interview I'm ever gonna give."

"Am I *that* terrible?" I asked.

"No, dear. It's not you. You're very nice. It's just that I was already in retirement as far as interviews are concerned when George asked me to do him this little favor. So, I came out of interview retirement.

"These days, I'm not interested in meeting a lotta new people. I've met so many people in my life, I'm saturated. I'm not promoting anything or selling anything, so I don't have any reason.

"I've only got one of me, and I don't want to get spread too thin."

Paul Novak, Mae's friend who lived with her had opened the door for me. He asked how I managed to get through the Ravenswood's protective lobby and up in the elevator without being announced. I said that George Cukor had suggested I ask for Paul, assuming that strangers gave Mae West's name. His name would be the password. Mae liked this.

She already knew all the people she wanted to know, especially in light of the many hours she felt compelled to spend on her hair, makeup, and dress before she could see anyone, because of the importance she gave to first impressions. Her face was nearly hidden by its mask of makeup, but her throat and décolletage revealed strikingly fair, soft, and youthful skin.

I had cost her three hours, I was told more than once, but it would have been double that if I had been a man. If she were going to see anyone at all, a man would have been preferable any day, and especially any night, she let me know.

"They always sent a man," not specifying who "they" were. "I considered spending my time with girls a waste of time, so I didn't mingle with any." The only exceptions were her beloved mother and her sister, Beverly. Men were the ones doing the interesting things, she said, and they were the ones who had the power to enable *her* to do them.

For Mae, Hollywood had real unreality, and that was the way she liked it. To the end, she nobly resisted any assault on her fairy-tale castle. Her Hollywood apartment in the Ravenswood building was truly an extension of Mae West, not only reflecting her, but also enhancing her and probably inspiring her. She had put a great deal of herself into it, and in return had received a great deal back. The furniture was upholstered in eggshell-white silk and satin, and appeared virginal, as if it had just been moved in for my visit. Actually, most of the white and gold furnishings had been there since Mae first arrived in Hollywood, with time out only for reupholstering or cleaning.

Although Mae had owned a great deal of property, including a Santa Monica beach house and a San Fernando Valley ranch, she preferred her Ravenswood apartment to everything else, having called it home since 1932. She said that was where she felt the most secure.

She hadn't chosen the apartment. That was done by Paramount before she arrived in California. Her only stipulation had been that it be near the studio. Paramount selected the furnishings from its prop department, not realizing that what they did would have to last for almost half a century. Mae liked the results and, over the years, made few changes.

There were none of the ubiquitous house plants. "Plants use up too much oxygen," Mae explained erroneously, but with certainty. The apartment was cool because, as she said, "It's good for the furniture and the complexion. I like the air filtered and moving."

I wondered how her apartment was maintained in such pristine condition, wishing that the answer would be something I could apply to my own, but knowing instinctively that the sorcery could not be transferred. It seemed somehow natural that Mae West's furniture would not get dirty. Magic has a certain fragility; any answer would only spoil the illusion.

Mae did not like change. "There are people who change just to be changing—their hairstyles, their furnishings, even their faces. I'm not one of those people."

Once Mae had achieved perfection by her own standards, she

avoided further change, because she had never forgotten the life of the stock company and vaudeville when she had no control over her environment. "I did enough traveling when I was very young, so I didn't need to do that anymore. I got it out of my system, and I'm too finicky. I have everything I want right here, I never want to have to move."

Mae West's apartment was a home for her and by her that reflected not some noted interior decorator, but Mae herself. The accumulation of memorabilia, gifts from fans she couldn't throw away, together with treasured family souvenirs, indicated that the private Mae West was a more sentimental person than her public character pretended to be.

The celebrations of herself on display throughout the apartment—the nude marble statue and oil paintings of Mae West at the moment of her greatest success—evinced no false modesty. They also signified that in her mid-eighties she was not afraid to be in competition with her younger self. She was still optimistic and had plans and ambitions for the future.

The nude statue of her, which was uninhibitedly displayed on the white grand piano, was one of Mae's prized possessions. It represented one of those rare instances when Mae cast modesty aside and allowed reality to triumph over imagination, especially over male imagination. It was done by a sculptress. "I wouldn't have posed for a man," she said. "He'd have never had time to finish the job. Besides, I think a lady is entitled to a few secrets.

"I had murals of naked men on the walls of my beach house. Great art. Nudity in art isn't sex, it's art.

"I wish I could've shown you my beach house. But I sold it. I miss it.

"About 1950, I bought the greatest beach house in Santa Monica, by the architect [Richard] Neutra, who was a refugee from Vienna. It had the most wonderful water views, and people loved to go there and lie in the sun. I kept plenty of extra swimming trunks around, all sizes and shapes. For myself, I kept the drapes drawn all the time when there was sun, to keep it out. I was asked why I wanted a twenty-two-room beach house when I never set foot on a beach.

"Well, it was a beautiful house, and people I cared about enjoyed it, and I enjoyed the inside of the house, and the outside as we drove up to it. Then, when I sold it because I wasn't using it much, I was kinda sorry.

"But I made a good profit on any real estate I bought. Well, I'm not exactly boasting because where I was buying in California, it wasn't easy to lose. Everyone wanted to come here, and they did.

"I never lost any money in art or real estate. Real estate and diamonds, those are the best investments. I always put my money into my own projects, something I was doing or something I could see. Money is sexy for men, but people don't find it feminine for a woman to talk about it. So, you don't have to talk about it, just have it. The real security is yourself. You know you can do it, and they can't ever take that away from you."

"Do you think money buys happiness?" I asked.

"No," Mae answered, "but money is a great love potion for an affair. It buys a good bed in a nice bedroom with clean linens and time to enjoy it all. If you have money, you don't have to worry about it, and worrying spoils your looks and your sexual concentration. Are you doing this whole book about me?

"No," I said. "There are other people in it, too."

"I don't usually like to share. What are you calling your book?

"I don't know yet. Do you have a suggestion?"

Mae thought for a moment. "You could call the book *Mae West and Others.* That's 'others' with a small 'o,' and I want to be the first. Being first is important in life.

When Mae interjected one of her celebrated epigrams or aphorisms to make a point, frequently she would change from a serious tone to the sultry delivery of Diamond Lil. Sometimes she would break up long words into several syllables, pausing between the syllables to create an exaggerated sensual effect and enhance any innuendos for emphasis. She called it her Brooklynese "slanguage." She was not afraid to use ungrammatical language or incorrect words to make a point, and she occasionally tossed her head so that the movement of her hair would punctuate her comments. Mae always preferred a longer word to a shorter word, if she could think of it in time. "Sometimes I think of the word too late," she said. "In writing you can slip it in, but in speaking, you can't get that same conversation back."

Always the mistress of illusion, Mae wore long dresses or flared-bottom pants designed to cover her stiltlike shoes. Her shoes had the highest heels I had ever seen, and the heels seemed higher than the shoes were long, her feet being quite small. They reminded me of the heels on Carmen Miranda's platform shoes I had seen exhibited at the museum in Rio de Janeiro, which I mentioned to Mae.

Edith Head had speculated that it was the height of those heels that had produced Mae West's famous suggestive walk. Head said, "In those shoes it was the only way she *could* walk! They were so heavy it was actually difficult for her to rise from a chair."

I asked Mae how she thought men would do if they had to live their lives in high heels.

"They wouldn't make it," she answered. "They'd be wiped out."

Mae loved clothes and was a collector of them. Her perfectly kept gowns were not just stored but seemed to have a life of their own, rather like a row of headless ladies standing there waiting for a party to rescue them from their boredom. The feathered boas and lacy peignoirs looked as though they had stories to tell if I could have interviewed them, but they were forever keeping all confidences. Mae's final fashion show was for her best and favorite audience, preening for herself, alone.

Later, when she was showing me her wardrobe and she encouraged me to try on some of the clothes, I was hesitant, but she insisted I model a black peignoir. "Doesn't it make you feel sexy?" she asked. Her words were barely spoken when she looked at me in disgust. I had put it on over my blouse and skirt. "You can't get the feeling like that," she explained. "You have to be naked underneath."

Perhaps Mae didn't like to give interviews to women because she couldn't act her part. With a woman, she had to reveal more of the private person, because she couldn't use the time to be flirtatious or playful. "With a woman, Mae West has to be there and can't just send Diamond Lil," she told me. "You'll understand if sometimes I refer to myself as 'Mae West.' On occasion, I even think of myself that way. More often, I think of myself as Mae. I'm on very intimate terms with myself, naturally.

"You know, there's more to Mae West than to Lil," she said. "For Lil, happiness was sex and diamonds. For Mae, it was work, but people don't understand how seriously she takes it.

"Not everyone cares the way I do about what I'm doing. Then, they sometimes get angry if you make them work harder. But you don't let anybody stand in your way. You've got to have standards. I wasn't just a lottery winner, you know."

I told her I *did* know. That was why I was there and had wanted to see her.

"If you know you did it yourself," she continued, "you're not scared. You know you can do it again.

"Economic independence is as important to a woman as to a man, maybe more important," Mae said. She had achieved a kind of financial independence, which was rare for a woman, "and I've done it on my own, not by inheriting it, not by marrying it, and not on my back, but by using my brain and talent. Every woman has to make certain she'll always have some change in her coin purse.

"You know, this material you're getting with me is worth a lot of money, so don't sell it cheap. If you don't get a good offer, hold out.

"If you set your own price on yourself as free, you don't deserve to get anything. If you don't put a high value on yourself, why would you expect anyone else to put a high value on you?"

"When you get a reputation for being funny, people start to laugh at everything you say. It makes it hard to try out your material and judge it. You ask for a cup of coffee, and people read things into that. I'm not a flippant person. There was a lot of serious reflection in what I said.

"I hope you're going to show me that way in what you write. You know, there was always something going on in my head. My head was always working.

"Did I have a serious side? Both sides of me are serious. It's pretty serious finding what's funny. I worked a lot during the Depression, and I understood it was important people laughed so they wouldn't cry. There were people jumping out of windows. There were people selling apples on the corners who'd never before had anything to do with an apple, except eating it. Guys who had seats on the stock exchange had seats on buses, driving them—if they were lucky.

"You know when I was most serious? When I laughed at myself."

Mae gave me a hard look and said, "There's something I've gotta tell you before we really get into it.

"If you want to smoke, you'll have to leave the room and go out into the hall. We don't keep any ashtrays here. I don't let anyone smoke in my presence. I don't breathe it, and I don't want it getting into the furniture. Let me know when you want to go out into the hall."

I assured her that this would not be necessary because I didn't smoke and never had. Her approving look indicated that I had passed an important test.

"Then you'll keep your soft skin," she said. "That's how I kept mine. I always use baby oil. Baby oil's good for the whole body. But the secret is it has to be warm, and you have to have a man put it on you—all over.

"You aren't wearing any makeup! Is it because I said you'd better come on time? Did you have to get ready in a hurry?"

"It wasn't because I didn't take meeting you seriously," I said. "It's because I never wear any makeup."

"Never?"

"No."

"Oh, that's a shame. You'd look good fixed up. Remind me before you leave. I can let you have some powder and lipstick."

She noticed my Hermès scarf, which I was wearing tied around my neck.

"Is that scarf because you're cold," she asked, "or do you have something to hide?"

I took it off.

"That's better," she said. "Now, if you'd unbutton a few buttons . . . Men like it if you show them a thing or two. I dress for women and undress for men.

"I can smell you're telling the truth about smoking, because if you smoked, your clothes and hair would smell from it, especially your hair. You know, I never liked being touched by a man who smoked."

Mae invited me to smell some of the powders and perfumes on her

15

vanity. She told me that she had always been extremely conscious of scents.

"My mother was responsible for my olfactory development," Mae said. "It wasn't so much *what* she said as the way she smelled. We all learn more by example, especially when we're very young.

"My mother always smelled so fresh and clean, like she'd just come out of a bath. I liked to smell her bars of soap. They were perfumed, but not too much. Everything my mother did was delicate. Her perfume just wafted.

"I was especially sensitive because I had great smell buds, like some people have taste buds, you know.

"The baby oil my mother used to rub all over my body was warm, and it had a wonderful aroma. I've never felt anything more wonderful than my mother's gentle massage. She had the softest hands in the world. I guess my baby oil was good for *her*, too."

I asked about taking a photograph with her, suggesting that Paul could take the picture.

"I wish I could accommodate you, dear, but I never have my photograph taken with a younger woman." At Mae's age, the category of "younger woman" included almost *every* woman.

"I never like to see myself in a picture, except surrounded by men. I only keep the best pictures of myself, you know. You should always keep the best picture of yourself in your own head. You should have beautiful pictures of yourself all around to look at. When you don't look your best, you shouldn't even look at yourself in the mirror. You should put on your most beautiful wrapper. You should look your best for yourself when you're alone. You can't afford not to look good alone or you'll stay alone.

"I'll be glad to give you some pictures of me, and I'll autograph them for you. That's something I take very seriously, autographing. Every person who ever wrote me for an autograph, or asked for an autographed picture of me, or sent me something to sign, every one of them got a genuine autograph from me. It was a lot of work, but those were my fans who were asking, and I always treasured my public. I signed every autograph myself, because I would never cheat my fans."

She signed some pictures for me and a copy of *The Pleasure Man,* which I had brought along. She signed them all "Sin-cerely." When I mentioned her little joke, she said, "I have quite a few little touches like that."

Her next query had the same tone of entrapment as the smoking suggestion. She asked me if I wanted to have a drink. I declined. She said it was a good thing because she didn't have any liquor.

Paul served us each a glass of water.

"Go ahead and drink your water," she encouraged me. "We only drink bottled spring water here. I wouldn't drink a drop of anything else."

I took a sip and put the glass down.

"Go ahead. Drink some more. We've got plenty."

I drank some more.

"Do you like it?" she asked.

I said that I did. "It's delicious water."

"If you want some, Paul will get ice cubes for you. Just say. The ice is made from the same spring water."

Over the years, Mae had received innumerable offers to do a commercial for any number of products. She always declined. "I don't do that" was her standard answer for one and all. Then, Poland Spring Water approached her.

"For years, I not only drank it, but I washed all my vegetables in it, and I bathed in it. I brushed my teeth with it, and I washed my hair with it. And I sprayed my breasts with it.

"I'd been drinking Poland Spring Water for twenty-six years, ever since I was six." Mae did four radio spots for Poland Spring Water.

"My mother was a health nut and my father an athlete," she said. "I never understood drinking alcohol. It isn't good for your health or your looks, and it cuts down on what you are. I never wanted to cut down on what I am.

"I guess I owe my good health to my mother. In those days, if you thought like she did, they called you eccentric, or odd. Now a lot of people believe the way she did, and they aren't called odd. Lots of fruit, vegetables, not many sweets, you know."

Mae kept looking at the gift-wrapped box I had set down on the table. "What's that?" she asked with childlike enthusiasm.

"George [Cukor] told me you have a passion for chocolates," I explained.

"I do have a passion," she said. "What kind of chocolates are they?"

"One is very healthy, with hardly any sugar. It has prunes and dried apricots inside because I was told you like healthy things. The other is a cream truffle."

Opening the first box, Mae almost destroyed the contents in her haste to get inside. Then she voraciously attacked the second box, nearly mashing a few creams. It was only after she had both boxes open that she made her choice. As if fearing someone might take the box away from her, she snatched two chocolate truffles.

"I like my pleasure," she said, composing herself and holding out the box to me. "You can have one, too, honey." She never let go of the box. Not wishing to deprive her, I selected one chocolate-covered apricot and began to eat it.

"The next time you come, I'm gonna give *you* some chocolate.

Have you ever eaten Ragtime chocolate? Hardly anyone does anymore. I know the last place in America that still makes it, and it's not far from here."

Mae indulged in one more and was reaching for a fourth when Paul Novak firmly took the box away from her. She looked petulant, but not displeased. Clearly, she was accustomed to and enjoyed having him watch over her. "I like my men to be men," she said after Paul had left.

"Pills, I never take them. I don't even take vitamin pills because who knows what's in them? If I don't know what's in something, I don't like to put it into me.

"I think what they say is true. If something isn't broke, why fix it? And I'm in wonderful shape, no pun intended.

"I was always indefatigable. I never knew exactly why. I always had this extraordinary energy that I had to do something with. They only just found out that I had a double thyroid. Always had it, but I didn't know it. Maybe that's been the source of my energy, especially my sex energy. When they told me I had a double thyroid, they wanted to take one away, but I wasn't doing that. I don't believe in tampering with what's going right.

"I would never, ever have my ears pierced. I took a chance of losing a favorite diamond earring, which I never did. But I wasn't having anyone make a hole in my ear."

I suggested that what the world considers odd or eccentric might actually be a person's good fortune, but there would always be those who valued conformity over individuality.

"It isn't what I do, but how I do it. It isn't what I say, but how I say it. And how I look when I do it and say it. Individuality is everything. Individuality, and enthusiasm, too.

"I could hardly wait for life. I wanted to run toward it with open arms. . . .

"Do you know what question I'm asked the most? About the mirrors on my bedroom ceiling. I say, 'I like to see how I'm doin'.' It's the truth. It's very exciting. You should try it.

"And the next question I'm most often asked is, am I always the Mae West everybody knows, or am I different when I'm alone?

"The answer is, when I'm alone, I'm the same Mae West. But you'll have to take my word for it, 'cause when I'm alone, there isn't anyone else here."

After my meetings with Mae, I was asked, "Did Mae West understand about protecting her myth, or did she believe it?"

The answer to both questions is yes.

Chapter One

———◆———

CHILDHOOD

(1893–1910)

I ACHED FOR IT, the spotlight, which was like the strongest man's arms around me," Mae told me.

"Do you want to know about my first love affair? It was when I was five. I made my debut in Brooklyn at the Royal Theatre.

"I fell in love on that stage. It was with my audience, and it's lasted all my life. That was the only love affair that ever really counted. No man could equal that. I could hardly wait to be on the stage—in the warm glow of the lights. Even then I'd never felt so alive. I heard the applause, applause just for me. I knew they really liked me, and I knew then there wasn't any other place I wanted to be. I've never been more secure than when I'm on stage. I had to have the spotlight more than anything else, shining full on me.

"I was lucky to know so early what I wanted to do and be in life. It saved a lot of time and going in wrong directions. I always thought I had a long time ahead, but I didn't have a guarantee, so I figured early it was better not to waste any time.

"As a child, I was always imagining my name up in lights. I would fall asleep at night seeing my name up there, all in lights. It was beautiful. I used to sit and practice my autograph for hours. I'd try one way and then another, until I got it just right. I'm the one who changed my name from May to Mae. It looked better to me that way when I was a little girl practicing signing the autographs. I didn't like that 'y' hanging down below the line. I don't like things hanging down, and I don't like anything downbeat.

"My father asked me if I'd like a dollhouse for my dolls. I said, 'No, thank you. Why would I need a dollhouse? My dolls live here with us in our house.'

"My mother looked down and smiled very slightly. She knew me so well.

" 'Then, what would you like me to build for you, Mae?' my father asked me.

"My mother and I answered in unison, 'A stage!'

"So my father set about building a stage for me to practice my acts on. My mother made the curtain. She could sew beautifully, because she'd studied to be a modiste. I wasn't allowed to see what my father was doing until it was all finished.

"My mother took me to see the stage. My father was standing proudly beside it. 'Do you like it, Mae?' he asked. From his tone, I knew he knew my answer.

"My mother drew open the beautiful white curtain she had made, and I went right up on the stage.

"I introduced my act, and I began by dancing and then I sang, both at the same time, which isn't easy, but I didn't get out of breath.

"I saw many, many stages in my life, but I never saw a more beautiful one than the little one my father made for a little girl.

"I wish I had it now, but I have it forever in my memory."

• • •

"My mother did everything I wanted. If I saw a doll, she got me the doll I wanted. Only that doll would do.

"Once we went to a store, and there were a hundred dolls. I didn't count. Maybe there were more. Everyone thought all the dolls looked alike. The one I wanted was on the highest shelf where no one could reach. They had to go and get a ladder and someone to climb the ladder.

"It drew a crowd. Everyone in the store thought I just wanted that one because I was difficult and spoiled. But I wanted her because she had a mauve dress, a beautiful mauve dress. I don't know where that color went. It used to be real big.

"I was four years old, but I knew I only wanted that one. They didn't see the difference. If you see the difference and other people don't, they think you're just being difficult. I always knew what I wanted, but it was for a reason, not just a whim.

"My mother never questioned it. She made them get a ladder and get me the one I wanted."

"Do you know where that doll is now?" I asked

"No. I wish I did," Mae replied. "Maybe the doll's with my mother."

Mae's mother, Matilda Delker Doelger, had come to America in 1886 from Bavaria, Germany, where she was born, with her parents and five other children, three sisters and two brothers. Matilda's father, Jakob Doelger, was related to Peter Doelger, a successful New York brewer. Jakob had met Matilda's mother in Württemberg, where he was a chemist in a sugar refinery.

"I remember people mistaking my mother for Lillian Russell. That was how beautiful she was. She was more beautiful than Lillian Russell, who people said was the most beautiful woman of her time. It was true, about Lillian Russell and about my mother, too. But my mother weighed less."

John West, on his father's side, was of English descent. His family had been in America for several generations. His mother had come from Ireland. West came from a family of Anglicans and Catholics. Matilda was a Protestant.

"The English side of my father's family came to America from a place called Tuckinghampshire in the eighteenth century," Mae said. "I was told he was descended from a long line of John Wests, going back to before the 1700s. So I guess he was pretty happy when my little brother, John West, Jr., was born.

"I think my grandmother on my mother's side was one-half or one-quarter Jewish. I wasn't paying attention. My mother mentioned it once, when I was with a Jewish girl from school. Mother didn't treat it as very important. I told George [Cukor], but I never thought much about it."

Mae's father, John West, had been a professional boxer, a bare-knuckles fighter. Known far and wide in Brooklyn as Battlin' Jack, he gave up prizefighting at Matilda's insistence. He operated a livery stable and then a private detective agency. Matilda had been a corset model, an accomplishment of which she was quite proud. Not only was it a tribute to the beauty of her figure, but she loved the idea of having had a career.

"When my mother worked as a corset model, she wanted to be a designer, a 'modiste,' she called it, and she thought in this position she could learn something about dressmaking. She was a wonderful seamstress. Her parents allowed her to have this job because it was made clear that only women would see her. What she'd really wanted to was to be an actress, but at that time, it would've meant being classified as a 'fallen woman,' even though my mother was a perfect lady. My mother was sexy, but refined. She had a wonderful shape, but she didn't flaunt it. She didn't have to. You couldn't help but notice it.

"*She* didn't *need* a corset."

Matilda and John West were married on January 18, 1889 in Brooklyn.

While the West family approved of the pretty German teenager, her mother's family did not approve of their daughter's choice. They had envisioned someone better educated, with a more promising financial future than Battlin' Jack, as their daughter's husband. They felt that their "Tillie" had chosen a husband for impractical reasons— romance and passion—and that she would regret it. Matilda's family considered their daughter too young to commit her future to a man whose prospects seemed so limited, no matter how dashing and charming he was.

"She did exactly the right thing." Mae told me. "Where would the most important person in my world be if they hadn't done just what they did? I wouldn't exist. I wouldn't be here at all. Or I'd be someone else, and there's no one else I would want to be."

Mae said that her mother never complained about her marriage. "She would never have done *that*. It would have been betraying my father. It would have been bad for my picture of their world. My mother wanted me to believe in their perfect romance, and some of the time they *did* have it, especially early in their marriage.

"She always told me I should not marry too young. She never said exactly what *too* early was. She never said that it was what she had done. She explained that marrying too early would interfere with my career. She always told me reasons for what she said. She never once suggested one day I would find my future with a husband and children. From before I was five, there was my career in the theater to think about."

Mae rose and went to the white grand piano, where there was a silver-framed picture of a beautiful woman.

"I want to show you my mother's picture. Isn't she beautiful?"

I agreed.

"She was soft and feminine, completely the opposite from my father. He fought in the ring and on the streets from the time before he was eleven."

Mary Jane West was born on August 17, 1893, in Greenpoint, Brooklyn. She was named after her Irish paternal grandmother, Mary Jane Copley, but she was never called Mary Jane. She was delivered by an aunt who was a midwife. This was considered more decorous than delivery by a male doctor.

"A big part of my luck was my being born at the right time," Mae told me. "I lived at just the right time for me. A big part of luck in life is you've got to get your timing right. A little earlier and they would've put a scarlet letter on my forehead or burned me at the stake. A little later, and I couldn't have shocked people anymore. Now people are shockproof because they've been overshocked. Blushing's gone out of style. When I was born, a lady could still have the vapors and swoon. Skirts had to cover ankles; but then, in just a few years, they didn't even have to hide thighs.

"My father never seemed disappointed that I wasn't a boy. Never any sign of it. Father was what you'd call 'a man's man.' He loved sports, like boxing, and he had a lot to pass on to a boy. He passed a lot of it on to me, like training with weights, which I loved.

"My father was a great believer in physical fitness, and he took a keen interest in me being physically strong. He believed in sports, like skating, anything that was fun, not just exercise for the sake of exercise. I learned to ice-skate at a tender age, but he 'specially wanted me to do gymnastics and acrobatics.

"I watched him and I wanted to do what he did because I admired him so much. I never knew anyone stronger, not just up to that time, but from then on. Maybe my own attraction to musclemen who don't just have muscles, but are strong, too, goes back to my own father. After all, he was the first man I knew.

"The thing he did for muscles and strength was weights, so that's what I wanted to do. My mother was worried that I'd hurt myself, and I think she was also upset because she thought I might get lumpy biceps, like the boys do.

"My father reassured her that he'd be watching me, and I'd never be handling those weights except under his supervision. I loved doing it. I loved it more than my father did. It was fun. It was fascinatin' to see how my strength grew. I never strained, but I was excited when I could lift heavier and heavier weights with less and less effort.

"It's important you know how to use weights when you do it, or you can injure yourself badly, permanently. I never got injured doing the weights, and they've been important to me all my life. The weights keep everything nice and firm, and nothing droppin' down.

"I was probably the strongest little girl in the country, and I built a beautiful body, with no lumpy muscles.

"Maybe my father was hoping for a boy to continue that long line of John Wests when Mildred, who later changed her name to Beverly, was born. When that didn't happen, he never said a word about it. Both of my parents seemed real happy with their new baby girl. It had been looking like I was gonna be an only child. Beverly hardly had any time alone with my mother because John Jr. turned up the next year.

"Everyone owes a lot to being lucky, and the most luck you ever get is being born at all. The odds are against you, and you've got to get good genes to be healthy and smart, and good parents to guide you and give you a decent environment and start your life. And if you look pretty good, that don't hurt none, either.

"What I loved about Brooklyn at the turn of the century was the faith people had in their future, and in the future of the country. Everyone believed the twentieth century was going to be the best one that had ever been. It sure was for me, better than I could ever have imagined it being.

"Now, I don't know what's coming. People don't have that enthusiasm they had at the beginning of the twentieth century. People seem different, like their rose-colored glasses got stepped on."

Throughout her life, Mae was interested in the significance of her astrological sign. When she learned that her birthday, August 17, meant she was a Leo, she understood everything. "It's the strongest sign you can have, and it explains something of why I like lions so much," she told me.

Born under the sign of Leo, with her rising planet being Venus, she believed her destiny was determined. "I would be strong like a lioness, or even a lion, and, at the same time, totally feminine."

Mary Jane was actually the second of the four children born to Jack and Matilda. The first, Katie, died in infancy. After Mildred was born in 1898, a brother, John Edwin, Jr., was born in 1900.

"My mother lost a baby girl just before me," Mae told me. "My mother was only a girl herself, a teenager, when she and my father had their first child.

"My sister only lived a few months, so I was especially precious to my mother. Maybe because of my mother's love of Katie, I started life with double love. She was so grateful for me. I was her whole world. She treated me like her precious jewel. She did everything for me, everything I wanted. She never even used a bad tone with me.

"My father and mother were both brokenhearted when they had

Katie only for a little while before she passed on. I *think* my mother felt a little guilty, like there was something she did wrong, but she didn't know what it was. My father and mother were young and healthy, so it didn't seem right they wouldn't have a very healthy baby.

"I don't remember my mother ever telling me about Katie. When I was very young, I heard about her when my mother was talking with some friends from the neighborhood.

"My mother had a lot of German-speaking friends, and these ladies were at our house drinking the strong black coffee with hot milk that my mother loved, and one of the women was crying.

"They were speaking in German. My mother was fifteen before she came from Bavaria to Brooklyn, and she saw German as her secret language. It never occurred to her that I understood it perfectly. Well, not perfectly, but enough to get a pretty good idea of what conversation was transpiring.

"I knew I was good at imitation, and I had a good ear. I had a natural talent for singing, and I think speaking languages might be related. When you're very young, I think languages come easily, sort of naturally. I'd picked up the German I knew without trying.

"The lady who was crying was telling the others about her baby dying. That's when my mother started talking about Katie having trouble breathing and how hard she'd fought to breathe and how much she wanted to live. That was when my mother started crying. After that, my sister Katie seemed very real to me. All my life, I remember her like a living person.

"Then, another woman told about losing a baby, and they were all crying. I guess I was about four. I never forgot that kaffeeklatsch.

"My mother served my meals on fine hand-painted china which had come from Germany. I was so young when she began using the dishes, I don't remember when she didn't. She only used the dishes for me, never for my sister and brother, because she didn't think they would be careful enough, and she really loved those dishes. Even when they were grown up, she couldn't trust her dishes with them. They broke things. They didn't have my aesthetic sensibilities and artistic appreciation. They would have been 'just dishes' to them. And they didn't notice or care that I was served on special dishes. Even my father didn't get served from those dishes. He understood. He didn't want to use those dishes. Too much of a responsibility. I didn't have to be told they were very precious and valuable. I could see it with my own eyes, and I could see how my mother touched them with love.

"Not everything had to be said between my mother and me. We understood each other.

"I didn't have to think about being careful. I just naturally was. I never broke one saucer or one cup or one dish.

"I'm a person who eats with my eyes. The food has to look beautiful and appetizing to me, or I lose my appetite. My mother understood that. She was a wonderful cook, and she made everything look beautiful on those wonderful dishes. Now, Paul [Novak] does all of the cooking for us, and he's a wonderful cook. I tell him what I want and he does it just the way I like it. Sometimes he has to practice a little because he didn't learn from his mother the way my mother learned from my grandmother."

"I'll tell you a secret, honey, a kind of confidence. There were times in my life, not many, but a few, when I wished I could go back just for a day or an evening to the time before I was world famous, when I could go anywhere and not be recognized. There is a difference between being noticed and being recognized. I could never go anywhere and not be noticed.

"Before I was two years old, my mother used to dress me up in beautiful clothes, and she would dress up, too. She loved to dress up.

She would have looked beautiful in rags, but she kept her lovely clothes and mine in perfect condition.

"I guess we made quite a picture when we went out on our promenade. My mother told me the neighbors and friends and strangers and shopkeepers and clerks in the stores would all say, 'What a beautiful little girl you have!' And she would smile that smile that could light up a block.

"I remember my father said some of the men in the street used compliments about me to try and start up a conversation with my mother. But she wouldn't talk with them. She would smile, or nod, and move on quickly. My mother always had perfect manners."

"I admired a lot about my father, and I looked up to him, but I wasn't as close to him as I was to my mother. I knew he was a good father. What I didn't like was he smelled of cigar smoke, and the smell of cigar smoke made me sick, as long as I can remember. He never smoked his cigar in my presence, but the smell of his cigar never went away. You know how some people have more sensitive taste buds, well I've got more sensitive smell buds. I found myself moving away from him. He didn't seem to notice.

"He had this terrible temper, but never with my mother or us children. He was gentle with us. It's a funny thing, but all my life, it seemed I was being attracted to men who, in a lot of ways, resembled my father. I guess I was like my mother that way, too."

"I was a perfectly healthy child. I was so healthy I didn't even know what it meant to be sick. I didn't have toothaches, and I never had cavities. I didn't know how a toothache felt, or a tummy-ache. I was naturally healthy, but my mother watched over me all the time, and my father, too. My father gave up boxing, more or less, but he stayed in training. Both my parents believed in eating only fresh food, fruit, vegetables, no cans, no packages. I had this fabulous energy, and my parents did, too. I never saw them get tired. My father was a very physical person. He never could sit still very long. My mother was very even and her energy was never jerky, but she always had it to draw on.

"My father liked his food, all fresh, and that was the way my mother's mother taught her to cook. My mother's mother was French, or partly French, French Alsatian, something like that. Her name was Christiana Bimier. I think my mother's cooking had a French accent. She cooked very American for my father, who enjoyed it that way. She was proud of her accomplishment and, at the time, we took her delicious food for granted, but she was very careful for herself about portion size."

Matilda liked to eat, but she cared even more about her beautiful figure.

"I thought my mother enjoyed cooking. Maybe it was just she never complained. She had what you might call a sunny disposition.

"Something I wondered about is, she never talked about me learning to cook. And I never talked to her about it. I wasn't interested in knowing how it was done. Even as a child, I never confused liking to eat with liking to cook. I enjoyed going out to restaurants with good food, but I never confused that with wanting to buy a restaurant.

"I was too busy working on my career to want to learn to cook. I guess if my mother never suggested showing me how to do anything in the kitchen, maybe it was because she really wanted to get out of the kitchen herself.

"I never did learn to cook. I didn't have time.

"I owe it to my parents that I got such wonderful teeth. I owe it to my mother that they stayed in condition, because she wouldn't let me eat candy when I was a child, when my teeth were just beginners. She told me I could have some, but not until I got my first teeth, because your first teeth determine what your second teeth will be. That way you give your final set of teeth the best chance to be healthy. After that, you and your teeth are on your own. I have every one of mine.

"After I got all my final teeth, I indulged a little. My first choice of an indulgence has always been chocolate. I believe it's healthy, contrary to some popular misconceptions. I hope one day it's proven healthy. I always feel my best when I eat chocolate, and when you feel your best, it shows. You look your best.

"Personality being everything, teeth are very important. They determine whether you will be a sunny person, with a good smile, or someone hiding in the shadows, lips sealed together so people won't see your teeth.

"You know, I never had a cold—well, anyway, not more often than once every ten years. I thought it was kind of a defeat when I had one, and I felt ashamed. A performer can't afford colds.

"I made up my mind not to have a cold. People don't understand the power of the mind." She touched her forehead. "Everything's right here. Everybody's busy thinking about what's in other people's heads. It's your own you've got to live with.

"Imagination can make you happier. People don't have to use their minds to torture themselves. I never understood why people use their minds to store unhappy thoughts. It's not easy to shut out thoughts of bad stuff once they get into your head, so the best thing is to try and stop them from getting in. I think you've got to take as good care of your mind as you do of your body. Just like you put oil on your body and take bubble baths to keep it soft and in good shape, you don't want to clutter up your mind with negative thoughts and bad news.

"When I grew up, I wanted to take care of my mother and spoil her the way she had done for me.

"She always started out talking to me saying, 'Dear, would you please do this,' or she'd say, 'Would you do this for Mother?' She had such beautiful manners, and she understood I could never be forced. Even a wrong tone of voice upset me terribly. I've never liked arguments. They ruin everything. They ruin eating. They disturb your work. They aren't good for making love. They can get into your head, so you hear the bad words more than once. And you might say something you're sorry for. I never argued. My mother was the same way."

Mae's mother was careful to see that "baby May" was tucked far back in her baby carriage, with the top sheltering her from the rays of the sun. When Matilda took the little girl for her first walks, she tied pretty bonnets under Mae's chin, and as soon as Mae could carry her own parasol, her mother had one made for her, using the same material that was used in her own. Matilda avoided the midday hours of the brightest sun in order to protect Mae's soft white skin, as well as her own.

"The sun is a great enemy to a fair and delicate complexion," Mae said. "My mother knew that, and she was very careful to have us stay out of the sunlight. She was way ahead of her time in everything. We walked in the shade. She wore big hats that were like small parasols, and I got one, too. Sometimes we carried our parasols. She had a bigger one, and I had a smaller one. A parasol is a very feminine thing, and practical. They went out of style, but I think they should come back, especially now that there's more emphasis on what the sun can do to your skin, not only to its beauty, but its health.

"A lot of sun damage is done years before it shows up. The damage has been done."

Mae showed me her hands. "Look—no brown spots. It wouldn't have been much fun wearing my twenty-two-karat ring, if I didn't have good-looking hands. They're the same as when I was a girl. My hands are twenty-four-year-old hands. No, I take that back. Twelve-year-old. And it isn't just your hands you want to protect. The rest of me is just like that, too."

Mae opened the top of her blouse to reveal fair, unwrinkled skin. "Here—look. Just like baby's skin. Feel it." It *was* soft, like a baby's skin.

"I never allow bright sunlight to come into my home. When I see pictures of sunbathers, I think, 'Poor things.' The delicacy of her complexion is more important to a woman, but men should care, too. They should do their best to look good, too.

"Those out in front of us get the benefits of our taking care of how we look, but the person inside of each one of us gets the greatest benefit."

"My parents were sitting at the table and whispering. Well, my father wasn't exactly whispering, which is how I happen to know about it. And he wasn't exactly sitting there, because my father was up and pacing. He was very physical, and he didn't like to sit still for too long, especially if he got agitated, which he often did.

"My mother was calmly explaining about some money she got from her family. She always spoke calmly. It was her way of calming my father. I was in my bed, and I didn't have to get up and look in to see that my father wasn't pleased.

"He said, 'I don't want any money from your family, so use it for yourself and Mae.' This was before Beverly was born. That was the only time I ever heard them discuss it specifically, but personally, I think it happened a lot.

"Us children always got everything we wanted and nobody ever had to look at a price tag. We had what we needed, with no worry. No worry is important. My mother often didn't ask the price for a dress or shoes or a hat, especially where a hat was concerned. She'd just try them on, and everything looked good on her.

"Mother just walked out with whatever she bought. The bill must have gone to my father because I never saw any bills go to my mother.

"My father was not driven by ambition. He was pleasure-loving. He believed more in being happy, but he was always a good provider. Imagine what he would have been if he tried!"

"I used to love shopping with my mother. I'd be all dressed up the way she was for a promenade. We never went shopping without dressing up, because it was a special occasion, and we both enjoyed sharing the experience. When she would ask me which dress I thought looked best, I would say, 'All of them.' She would laugh, and select one or two.

"She always showed the dress first to my father before she wore it, to see if he liked it. He always did. She would ask him to choose one. He would say, "Buy them both. They all look good on you." He always encouraged her to buy more dresses. My mother had the tiniest waist, and even after four children, her breasts were beautiful."

Mae was a careful child, as her mother told her later, and she never spilled anything on her dress. She wished to be as meticulous as her mother, who was her model in all things. Her mother also told her that when Mae was as young as two or three, she would reject a dress to wear that day if it was wrinkled.

Mae realized later that some mothers might have been "put out by having such a fussy child," but not hers. Matilda was proud that her daughter was so discerning.

"I've always liked ecru," Mae said. "That's a color, you know. It was a color my mother always wore. Those warm flesh tones are sexy, while restrained. But they are a little fragile.

"Mauve was one of mother's favorite colors, too, and it's one of mine. It's easy to find harsher versions of colors, like purple and pink, which are easier to dye. I had a wonderful dress when I was a girl. It's difficult to describe the color. The closest I can come is pale peach. Boys called me 'Peaches' back in those days when I was about twelve. Maybe the dress had something to do with it.

"Anyone who knew me well as a very small child, remembered me as being what you might call 'clothes-conscious.' My mother told a neighbor that my first words were, 'What am I going to wear?'

"My mother's words were a little bit of an exaggeration, you might say, but I've always been interested in clothes; like my mother, I spent a lot of thoughts on them. People spend a lot of time considering how they will spend their money, but not on how they will spend their thoughts, which is even more important. Some of my interest was for my character, some for my audience, and some of it was just for me. Nice clothes made me feel good."

Mae remembered what she loved to do as early as four, to look in store windows. Everyone, including her mother, believed that "little May" was looking at the merchandise in the stores. It seemed strange when she looked into the windows, not just at dresses, dolls, and cakes, but at rakes and shovels. Matilda soon learned what so fascinated her little girl.

It was Mae's own reflection. Mae knew it was an exceptionally pretty girl she saw there in the glass looking back at her.

Her mother did her hair with care, whether for an afternoon's shopping promenade or for just a quick trip to the store. When she went into one of the shops with her mother, or they met acquaintances of her mother's on the street, everyone reaffirmed what Mae already knew.

"Matilda, you must be so proud. May is beautiful."

Mae continued to look at her own reflection in the shop windows. "It was a sort of foggy image with no sharp edges, and I preferred its softness to the harder reflections in regular mirrors. That was true when I was a little girl and a teenager. It stayed true.

"Take a look now, dear, at the glass on the tables there," she said to me. The tables had mirror tops. "You can see your own reflection. Get up and take a look." I did, although I already knew what I looked like.

"I was very lucky to have the parents I did. I was very proud of my father, so strong and handsome, and I had the most beautiful and best mother who ever lived."

On the white piano, Mae had pictures of her parents in old silver frames. "I lost a lot of pictures when the basement flooded," she told me. "It was terrible. I lost a part of me."

She paused before continuing.

"I was an only child for a long time. I was lucky that way. I had my mother, as my companion and friend, totally devoted to me. I had a sister and a brother, but they came along later, and it wasn't the same for them. I had my mother alone for the first five years. My sister and brother had to share her with each other and with me.

"By the time they came, I didn't need so much from her anymore. I'd had the good start and the advantage that I always knew what I wanted.

"I was never jealous of my sister and brother. In my whole life, I've never envied anyone. I was too busy thinking about myself.

"Even so, I still got most of the attention after Beverly and then my brother, John, one year later. That's just the way it was, the bond between my mother and me, for as long as one of us was alive.

"I think an only child has a lot of advantages because of having all the attention of the parents. I've always felt like an only child. I had the chance to perfect my personality. Even what's natural needs a little developing.

"My sister, Beverly, had a clubfoot. She never wanted anyone to see it. She didn't have my self-confidence. I had enough for both of us, but I couldn't share it. I wish I could have, because I had plenty to spare.

"I think Beverly had two handicaps. One was her foot, and the other was me.

"She was ashamed of having this deformed foot. My parents never said anything about it or made anything of it, but she always had me to make the comparison with. And my mother, too. We both had beautiful feet.

"From the first as a little girl, I had very pretty feet. I remember my mother exclaiming over them when I was very little, and kissing them and saying how beautiful they were. My feet were perfectly formed and my mother used to look very happy as, after my bath, she would massage them with warm oil.

"I always had shoes that fit perfectly and were never too small. She paid a lot of attention to making sure I got a lot of new shoes, so shoes that were too small wouldn't deform my smallest toes. She had me wiggle my toes in the shoes for her.

"As soon as I saw my sister was drawn to show business, I tried to help her, putting her into my shows. I really wanted to help her, but not perform with her."

"My father had a livery stable after he gave up boxing because my mother didn't want him to get hurt. He told her, 'I don't just know how to hit, but I know how to duck,' but that wasn't enough to make my mother happy. My father wanted my mother to be happy. He melted before her gaze, and that was well after the honeymoon.

"His stable had carriages and coaches with horses, and sleighs for the winter. My mother and I enjoyed carriage rides and sleigh rides. It was a very good business until it wasn't. The automobile happened. Some people told my father the automobile was a passing fad, but he was smarter and knew better, and he looked around for another business he would enjoy. It was important he enjoyed what he did, because he was a very enthusiastic person. He couldn't be tied to an office all day, or he probably would have lost his temper and ended up in a brawl.

"I remember once a man looked the wrong way at my mother, and my father took care of him. My mother had this beautiful figure, tiny waist and a lovely bosom, but not as big as mine. I don't think my mother noticed that look, but she sure noticed what my father did.

"My father walked up to the man, and he hit him with his fist. Just one blow, and he knocked him down. The man wasn't knocked out, but he just lay there. He knew better than to get up and maybe get hit again. My father wasn't going to hit him again, because he knew the man had learned his lesson. My father could have knocked him out, but didn't want to hurt him, just teach him a lesson and embarrass him. My father was a natural boxer.

"When he was going to hit that man, my mother said, 'Oh, no, don't do that. Oh, you mustn't do that.' But she spoke softly, as she usually did. She didn't really try very hard to stop him. Not that she could have stopped him, but personally I think she liked it. It made her feel appreciated, protected and feminine.

"After the stable, my father opened a detective agency. There was a waiting room, and I used to sit there on one of the chairs. My legs didn't reach the floor yet.

"I would play with my doll and make up stories for her. She became a detective and solved mysteries I made up. I didn't want to disturb my father while he was working. Besides, I liked to watch the people who came to see him, and speculate on why they were there. I would scrutinize them.

"I would see the men change their deportment as they were called in to see my father. They were all men. I guess women didn't go to detective agencies in those days.

40

"When they left, I'd go in and give Father my opinions of them. I was always right. He'd go home and say to my mother, 'How could Mae know so much about people? She's had no experience in the world. She's so sheltered. But she can read them.'

"Mother said to him, 'I told you. That's how Mae *is* about people. Mae's been doing that from the first moment she could talk, and before. She knows right away about people. She likes them or she doesn't. And you want to listen to her.'

" 'Mae, you have the greatest intuition about people,' Father said to me, and that made me proud.

"I was very introspective. I judged people that way all my life. If I didn't like you when you came in, I would've told you to go.

"I like to use bits and pieces of my life and my observations of the people around me for my writing, and then I doctor them up. There was this one play I'll tell you about that I had germinating in my head for years.

"It was an idea I started but never finished because I decided the part I was writing for myself didn't do me justice. I was a lady detective. I think the idea began with my doll and me in my father's detective agency office.

"It was based on my memories of when I used to visit my father. I was going to have a detective agency fall into my lap, an inheritance or something, and I would be a detective like Sherlock Holmes, but wearing beautiful dresses, and maybe a cape. My lady detective would've operated in the nineties, at the turn of the century, or just after that, because the long skirts and fancy dresses would've been a good contrast with her uncommon sense. She would've been operating in a man's field, in a man's world, in her long dresses. Men would have been poking fun at her, and she would've had to win their respect by being the one who got her man, and a few extra men, too. She'd use brains rather than brawn.

"Someone told me to read an English writer named Christie, Agatha Christie. I would get ideas. That was just what I didn't want to do, to use somebody else's ideas. I had enough of my own. I never had trouble getting ideas.

"I never had much patience for reading, even just a newspaper. I did this thing called skimming. I read the headlines, and if something caught my fancy, I might read the first and the last paragraphs, which pretty much gave me all I needed to know. I found out later that was what my father did.

"I liked to read the funnies. That's how I learned to read, reading the funny papers. I learned to read early because I wanted to know what the words with the pictures said. *Little Nemo in Dreamland* was my favorite. He had wonderful dreams about lions and tigers. I loved *Happy Hooligan* next. He wore a tin can for a hat. And I always read *The Katzenjammer Kids*, Hans and Fritz, and *Hee Haw and Her Name Was Maud.* They were funny. The funnies ain't funny no more. They take themselves too seriously and expect us to. That's no fun.

"Reading was a matter of time and how you spend it, and I needed all my time for my work. I found out reading could help in my work sometimes. It would've been a different story if the newspapers had entertained me, but I found them kind of depressing, except for the funnies. And, like I said, even the funny papers aren't as funny as they used to be. I never changed. It was the funnies that changed.

"School kind of got in my way, you might say. I'm all for education, but I wasn't getting it at school. They told my mother, 'Mae's an average student.' Can you imagine? *Me,* average? I never was 'average' anything!

"I'm not very grammatical, because I'm only a third-grade graduate. And I didn't exactly graduate. I sort of retired from it. It's not something I'm proud of and not something I'm ashamed of. It's the way it is. I knew right away school wasn't what I wanted to do. I decided that when I was in the second grade.

"I used to be embarrassed about the little bit of education I had, that I didn't go to school more and that I didn't pay attention when I was there. But I'm not embarrassed anymore. I was afraid educated people wouldn't judge me very well and would look down their noses at me. Then I started to meet people who had gone to college and graduated, and some who had stayed in college for years—doctors, lawyers, scientists—and they were asking for *my* autograph. Imagine that!

"Some of the best universities started havin' tributes to me— UCLA, USC—and it wasn't just the football teams that wanted to come up and see me some time.

"You know what I learned? Education and intelligence aren't the same thing.

"It was impossible to make me do what I didn't want to do. I didn't have tantrums and make a fool of myself. I believed in retaining my ladylike composure, like my mother, and not letting my emotions show. I'd just go into myself and get quiet, but that wasn't necessary with my parents.

"They didn't care much for school themselves. They both came from families that valued education and boasted educated people, but my parents were black sheep in their families when it came to school. They felt pretty much the way I did about school, not having been too interested in it themselves, especially my father. And they had a lot of faith in my talent, especially my mother.

"I hope you won't write I was dumb. I speak perfect Brooklyn-ese. It's not the King's language. It's the Queen's language. I guess you might say I had a lot of *in-*formal education.

"I preferred living to reading about living, even before I'd learned to read. I'd learned to read before I was five years old, but life beats fiction any day. My life did.

"After my stage debut at five, my mother played a game with me she made up. She called it 'Synonym.' She had a big fat dictionary, so heavy she could hardly pick it up. I liked to carry it around for exercise and building my muscles, like my father did with his weights. Mother would take a word, and she would look for as many words as she could find that meant the same thing. Then I would say them with different intonations, rolling them around on my tongue, giving emphasis to a certain syllable till I got the best word for my act.

"I was always partial to long words. A long word always seemed better to me than a short one. They're more mell*ifluo*us, if you know what I mean. The game was constructive, and I enjoyed it. I enjoyed anything I did with my mother. She enjoyed our game, too, and I think it helped *her* English."

"We had this real cozy home, you know. Did you ever see those things they put over teapots to keep them warm? They're sort of an English thing, and it's called a cozy.

"Well, that's how it was for us as children. You couldn't have lived in a more wonderful place in the world than Brooklyn was in those days.

"We had the most wonderful white lace curtains. Sometimes in the morning, before I'm wide awake, all these years later, I think I see those white lace curtains on my bedroom window. Then, when I'm fully awake, they're not there anymore.

"I don't know how my mother kept them so perfect all the time. She had a woman who came in, but the curtains were always hanging there. Later I figured out the only possible answer. My mother must've had more than one pair."

Mae remembered the beautifully decorated interior in those pastel colors so rare at that time, when interiors were all done in dark colors. "Most people lived in dark houses, which was the accepted style of the time. They had dark walls, and everything was in dark colors. My mother was very affected by beauty and color, and she always liked light colors, so inside our house was the lightest and the brightest and the prettiest in the neighborhood. Everyone who came over was struck by it."

Matilda found it more cheerful to use white and cream, ecru and yellow, and an occasional accent of mauve or lavender. There were fresh flowers from their garden. Her pastel dresses matched the interior of the house. The fabrics were silk satin, fine cotton, always the best. Matilda believed this kind of home affected how the people who lived there felt, emotionally and physically. She knew that *she* was greatly affected by "pretty things." Her husband was well aware of her taste, but far from being displeased, John West was immensely proud of his wife. Jokingly, but affectionately, he nicknamed her "Champagne," or sometimes "Champagne Til." She enjoyed a glass of champagne.

"Now I understand there's the economic thing, too, to think about," Mae continued. "My father was the security our family took for granted. Money was never discussed. I guess that meant that money was never a problem in our house."

One morning, young Mae was posing in front of the mirror in the hallway of her Brooklyn home. Some women who were neighbors had gathered in the parlor for a kaffeeklatsch. The coffee cake and rolls were German, Matilda's homemade specialties. Because some of the women were German, some Irish, and some American-born, the conversation was in English. Mae, who wasn't paying any attention couldn't help hearing what one of the neighborhood women said about her mother: "Matilda is a wonderful businesswoman."

Mae, who was only about seven at the time, remembered being startled and thinking, What a strange thing to say about her mother! Many years later, as the bit of conversation Mae had overheard drifted back to her, she understood that in addition to her mother's beautiful exterior, figure, and face, she had a brain. Mae had been guilty of believing the popular fallacy, that a beautiful woman wouldn't have a fine sense of business, too. It had surprised her at the time, because it wasn't at all the way she thought of her mother. Looking back, she understood how true it was.

"I remember my father whispering to my mother about whether I should be having a stage debut while I still had my baby teeth. I didn't see what my baby teeth had to do with it. My act didn't include biting anyone.

"I always had very good hearing, but when my father whispered, it was like a roar, so it wasn't hard to hear him. He was worried I'd get scared on stage and freeze or cry, but it never happened. I was never shy about showing off my talents."

Battlin' Jack argued that a paying audience could protest, rudely, vociferously, if they didn't like an act, even if the performer was only five years old. It was still a time when performers were looked down on by many, though not in Mae's home. Both her parents were performers at heart.

"My father wasn't as sure as my mother about me going on the stage so young. He thought maybe I could wait till I was seven or eight. But I couldn't. So, he said, 'Let her have a chance, and we'll see how she does. But if she gets stage fright, she'll have to wait till she's older.' Can you imagine? Sometimes even one of your own parents doesn't know you. Stage fright! I didn't know the meaning of the word. Still don't.

"My mother didn't listen to my father. She knew I could do anything I wanted. As a child I had perfect confidence. Maybe that's why I wasn't ever afraid of anything. Earthquakes don't worry me. Even now, the only time I give a thought to earthquakes is because of the mirror over my bed.

"I was happy on boats. It never bothered me that I can't swim. Once when I was a little girl, I was at the beach, and I heard someone screaming. There was this little girl drowning. There wasn't anyone else around, so there was nothing else to do. I jumped in and pulled her out, and got her back to shore. I didn't think about it before I did it because there wasn't any time.

"Afterwards my father was really angry. 'How could that child have done it when she couldn't swim?' he asked my mother. 'You gotta watch Mae. You never know what she's gonna do.' It was the only time I ever heard him raise his voice to her.

"I wouldn't have been afraid to be an astronaut. I would've *liked* walking on the moon. Imagine making love weightless."

"My mother made almost all of my dresses until the time of my theatrical debut," Mae told me. "That was a very important dress for Baby May. I hadn't gotten rid of the 'y' in my name yet.

"We went to the best place in Brooklyn that had theatrical costumes. My mother and I both saw the dress and chose it at the same moment. It was a pink-and-green satin dress with gold spangles, if you can imagine that. I had a large picture hat, the kind Lillian Russell had become famous for. She wore really big picture hats, but mine seemed bigger because my head was so small. I remember it had white lace on it, real lace, not the machine-made kind. The hat had tiny pink flowers and green leaves and pink ribbons and matched my dress, and pink slippers and stockings. My mother and I were both very particular about the hat. The outfit made me feel wonderful.

"At home, my mother had me practice my song 'It's Movin' Day' while I was wearing my costume. I hesitated. 'Shouldn't I keep it brand new for the show?'

" 'Oh, no,' my mother said. 'When I was modeling corsets, I always liked to put them on before and walk around in them so I knew them like old friends and felt comfortable. It's very important that you and your dress become one, so you don't have to think about it when you're performing.' What my mother said made good sense to me, as it always did."

Baby Mae began her stage career by appearing at amateur shows. Her mother booked her, brought her on time, and, during cold weather, held her daughter's muff and scarf while Mae performed. Battlin' Jack was almost always there, too.

Matilda also suggested that "Baby May" prepare another song, "Doin' the Grizzly Bear," just in case an amateur before her sang "Movin' Day." If this happened, Mae's first onstage moment might be a letdown for the audience. Mae would then miss their most enthusiastic response, that wave of love that gives a performer an extra boost of adrenaline.

Matilda didn't mention her greatest fear. What if laughter greeted her daughter when she began to sing the same song as the amateur before her? Even if Mae sang it better, her feelings could be hurt and her confidence undermined.

Mae's debut took place at Brooklyn's Royal Theatre. "It had seven hundred seats and charged, people *paying* to see you," Mae remembered with obvious pride. "Well, they weren't exactly paying to see *me*. They got me for free along with the show they'd paid for."

Matilda stood in the wings just out of sight of the audience in case Mae needed reassurance. It was more likely that Matilda would need Mae's reassurance. John West sat in the second row of the audience with some of his friends. He brought a small but enthusiastic claque of his buddies with him as extra clappers.

Mae sang, as planned, "It's Movin' Day," a song about a woman who can't pay her rent. Mae had a big voice, which she said surprised the audience, coming from such a tiny figure. Not only was Mae young, but she was small for her age.

"The audience had paid for the professionals, but they got us amateurs thrown in. They could leave after the main show if they wanted to, but no one ever did. The audience really liked the amateurs. Sometimes, it seemed they enjoyed that part of the show most.

"There would be this sound of a horn and drumbeats, and then the emcee would come out and call for 'a big hand for the talented amateurs. And show your appreciation with generous offerings.' That last part meant the audience was supposed to throw coins on the stage. Personally, that seemed to me a little demeaning.

"I watched the last of the professionals. He wasn't too good, but I was fascinated by the spotlight that followed him off. I could hardly wait to feel it on me. I asked one of the stagehands if it would come back for me. He said, 'It'll pick you up when you get out there.'

"I went out on stage, but the spotlight didn't come back for me. I stopped and waited. Nothing. So I stamped my foot and looked up and said, 'Where's my spotlight?' I was thinking I wanted to say, 'My father's Battlin' Jack, and if you don't give me my spotlight right now, I'm gonna tell him to go after *you*.' I didn't do that, but I *was* disappointed, and my disappointment turned into anger.

"I could see Father sitting there in the second row, right in front of me, waiting anxiously for my act. Father was leaning forward on the edge of his seat. He was nervous for me, like he probably never was when he was in the ring. Mother stayed in the wings. She was very fair, but now she looked even paler than usual.

"Some of the audience thought my nerve was part of the act. They laughed and applauded. I was defiant.

"Then, my spotlight arrived. It engulfed me. It was a very grown-up spotlight. It felt wonderful. Nothing in my life ever felt better. Nothing.

"I went into my act. I loved to sing and dance at the same time. I never got out of breath, like even the grown-up performers did. That was my special trick, but I don't know how I did it."

Mae danced a variation of kicks and turns, which came from her brief ballet and tap dancing training, while she sang. The applause started before she had finished singing.

"It made my little heart beat fast. The applause was the most wonderful sound. During my number, the audience started throwing coins on the stage. They threw so many with such enthusiasm, it got a little dangerous, but I didn't let it perturb me and disturb my performance.

"I didn't pick up the coins. I wouldn't. My father said from where he was sitting, 'Mae, don't you know that's insulting? The people will be insulted if you don't pick up the money.'

"I didn't care. I wasn't picking it up. I pretended I didn't hear him.

"Two of his boxing buddies were sitting with him, so he had them go up on the stage and pick up the money. They turned their derbies upside down and filled them, not to the top, but about half full, which was pretty good. The audience kept throwing coins.

"My father was happy. He was the one who'd had his doubts about me going on the stage so young. He saw my debut as a test which put a lot of pressure on that performance, but I didn't know it. Anyway, he forgot all about having his doubts.

"It must have made my mother a little nervous, having my father give her an ultimatum about my career. But not too nervous, because she had perfect faith in me. In her ladylike way, she persuaded my father to go along with her.

"When I came off stage, he tried to get my sympathy for his two friends and their derbies.

" 'Mae,' he said, 'you should at least have thought of those two handsome and expensive hats. They got ruined by all those coins.'

"The conversation was concluded when I came back with 'Buy them new derbies. And I won first prize.' "

Mae described herself in her first stage appearance as "impudent. That's related to impish," she said.

"I got ten dollars and that beautiful gold medal from the Elks Club that was sponsoring the show. I don't know if the medal was real gold or not, but it sure was precious to me.

"Five dollars was the second prize, but I wasn't interested in that. I always wanted to be first, never second. Real early, I understood the difference.

"My father lost any doubts he had about whether I was ready for a career. He was so proud; his chest, which was very well developed, stuck out even more than usual. He was my escort as I went out on the amateur circuit. He got all dressed up for it. After a while, he seemed to believe that my going on the stage was *his* idea! My mother didn't correct him. She and I knew the truth, and I didn't say anything, either.

"We began going regularly to the amateur nights with my appearances. I just about always got first prize. I don't remember it not happening. And there was no one, besides Mother and me, more enthusiastic than Father. He loved seeing me perform, and he loved seeing me win. He had a winner's mentality as a fighter. Very competitive. He was very popular with men, and a lot of his friends and acquaintances turned out to see me. Father was frequently recognized at the theaters we went to. He was very well received, and people wanted to shake hands with Battlin' Jack.

"My mother was always there, carrying my muff and scarf, during the winter. My father carried my little suitcase with all my paraphernalia—costumes, makeup, dancing shoes, everything I needed.

"I loved appearing on the stage, but almost as much, I loved watching and learning from the star acts. I noticed that the most desirable places on the program were just before intermission or next to closing, never first or last. Openers and closers were throwaway acts. I only wanted to be the star.

"I think amateur hours make great shows. The audience seemed to like us amateurs a lot, and it would be a good show for television now. Meanwhile, pretty quick, what I was thinking was it was time for me to go professional.

"I always changed things in my parts. By the time I was seven or eight years old, I would see a piece of business that could be added. Sometimes I'd add lines of my own. I put fresh things into my act to keep my own interest. If you don't keep your own interest, it shows. I used to write myself extra material so I could do fresh stuff for my encores. You've got to believe in yourself. I knew the theater was my destiny, and I always worked hard. That's all I wanted to do, was to work. I knew I didn't want a life of dull routine.

"I was always ready for encores. I was thinking about my encores from before I was six. I had to be prepared for the best that could happen. It was the way I lived my life. It was my personality. And I wasn't thinking about two or three encores. I was thinking about seven or eight. And that's the way my life turned out. I believed it and I worked to make it true.

"There was something that fascinated me when I was about eleven," Mae told me. "I was interested in where babies came from. I asked my mother a few times, but she got off the subject and distracted me, which wasn't too hard in those days, when I was little. But the thought stayed in my mind, reinforced by my mother not answering me directly. She was always very alert to my questioning mind, encouraging me to question everything. The thing about babies and where they come from was something different. That made me more curious.

"When I was about eleven, I asked a girl who lived near us in the neighborhood. She was a year or two older than me, and she looked intelligent to me. Maybe that was just because she wore glasses. That was a misconception people had, that if you wore glasses you were more intelligent. Well, *I* never had to wear glasses, and as you can see, I'm intelligent enough.

"The girl's mother was a doctor. There weren't so many women doctors in those days. I figured her mother knew the answers and would've clued her in.

"Well, she didn't know any more than I did, and she was interested, too, but not as curious as I was. I was a celebrity in my neighborhood because of my show business success, so I think she wanted to be ahead of me in something. She said her mother had a library of books that told everything.

"Her mother wasn't home, so we went to work. Sure enough, we found books with pictures that told it all. I could hardly believe what I saw, but there it was. Shocking.

"What hurt most was the thought that my mother and father had done such a shocking and repulsive thing, at least four times, maybe more, because there were three of us children, and there was Katie. That was at least four times.

"I never told my mother what I found out. It would have been too embarrassing for me and more embarrassing for her. It seemed ugly and disgusting, especially when I thought about my father and mother doing it. I was sorry I'd looked at those books.

"After a while, the way I felt changed. It went away. I understood. *More* than understood. My mother was right not to explain things too soon."

• • •

"I didn't mix much with other children. I was deeply involved with myself. My mother was my best friend, and we had such an understanding that I didn't care about friends my own age. There was nothing to learn from them.

"My mother and father decided I ought to have some companionship my own age, so my mother invited some girls from my class in school to come to our house. We had this nice big house, and my mother cooked and baked wonderful things, so everybody liked coming over.

"The food was great, but the company was boring. They didn't have anything to offer, and I never liked wasting my time when I was a child, even when there was so much time ahead of me. There was so much to experience and learn and see. I knew that early. I didn't see time as a commodity to waste.

"The girls didn't have sophistication or experience. They only went to school and didn't work. They only played, and they seemed pretty silly to me. They didn't know what they wanted to be when they grew up. I guess they would've said wives and mothers if you'd pressed them for an answer.

"There weren't any boys there, so maybe I would have found boys more interesting, but I don't think so, not boys the same age as me. They would've been too young for me.

"Show business is the most wonderful education you can have, so I was ahead of my years. I was working and learning about life, which was very exciting. I was happy when they finally ate all the cookies and cake, and went home.

"Amateur nights were a lot of fun, but it only took, maybe, just the first one before I began thinking about turning professional, and then about how long after that it would be before I'd be a star.

"One night I was appearing at the amateur night on a Saturday at a very good theater, the Gorham. I won first prize, the ten dollars, and I was starting to feel like I wasn't exactly an amateur anymore.

"There was a regular stock company at the theater owned by a fine actor, Hal Clarendon. He was watching me from a box. He came backstage, and I was excited that he'd come to meet me because he was impressed by my act. He held out his hand and came toward me, but he walked right past me and shook hands with my father.

"He said, 'Battlin' Jack, what an honor to meet you.' Then he turned to me. He looked down at me, and I expected him to say the usual, about how great my performance was. But he had a better compliment for me.

"He addressed me as 'Miss West.' I don't think anyone had ever called me 'Miss West' before, so I knew something special was in the offing.

"He invited me to join his company. My parents were speechless, but I wasn't. Before my father could speak for me, I said, 'Yes.' I was thrilled, but I didn't want to appear overanxious, and I didn't want to appear that I wasn't anxious enough, or that I didn't appreciate how wonderful the company was.

" 'Thank you,' I said. 'I accept.' I said it in a nice clear voice because I wanted to be sure he heard me.

"By that time, my father, who was never speechless, found his voice and said, 'I accept for my little girl.' Well, I wasn't *that* little.

"I was very happy and my parents were, too. On the way home, we were all talking at once, like the birds do."

From the time she was eight until she was eleven, Mae appeared with the repertory company, playing child parts. Her favorite was Little Nell. "I was the child who enters the saloon looking for her drunken father." When they did a show that didn't have a part for her, she watched and learned. Sometimes she traveled with the company, but much of the time she lived at home.

"I had a tutor, so I learned to add and subtract, and spell. That was so when I pushed grammar around, I knew what I was doing. A lot of the time, I do it for effect and because my characters didn't go in for a lot of schooling.

"I learned a lot of French from a tutor who owed my father money for boarding a horse. That was interesting, but not very useful. I never liked spending my time learning just to be learning. I thought time should be spent for a purpose. I liked to practice the accent, because I knew a good accent might come in handy for playing a part. I couldn't see how French was going to come in very handy, but I liked learning anything I thought could propel my career. I knew, very early, that someday I was going to be a star.

"From time to time, I dropped by school when it suited my fancy. It wasn't enough to suit the teachers' fancy. The last time I saw the inside of a public school, I think I was twelve, maybe thirteen. They didn't keep such a tight watch on you in those days. There was more freedom. Education was more optional.

"I was lucky I was small for my age, so I could play a child longer than most, but at twelve my figure was developing along the lines of my mother's, and I couldn't pass for a child anymore. I was forced into temporary retirement and I had an involuntary interlude with only sporadic opportunities.

"I found a new way to fill my time. Experimenting. I always enjoyed male company more than female, except for my mother. I would go out with six boys, and maybe there'd be one other girl. We'd go skating or sledding, and kissing. My mother said not to stay out later than ten. I never did. She didn't worry, because she trusted me.

"I noticed every boy's kiss was individual. Each had his own kiss print, just like a fingerprint. Each one had a different technique. They weren't very experienced. They were just finding themselves.

"One day, a tattletale girl cousin of mine reported me to my father. I never placed my trust in girls, before or after. It was what she heard at home, I guess, that I was staying out late and playing with boys. My father went into a rage, but my mother calmed him down. She could always do that. She said I could be trusted perfectly. And I could. I never would have done anything that would have made my mother unhappy.

"There'd be all these boys hanging around, and I'd start to think I liked one of them better than the others. Well, my mother wouldn't say anything much against him, but if she saw me liking one too much for my own good, she would point out some little flaw he had, like big ears that stuck out or something. Then I'd see it right away. So I'd like another one, and she'd just mention lightly some little fault he had. That gave me the idea early, which was very important—there wasn't just one.

"I loved the world of vaudeville, and during the time I wasn't performing, we went to shows. I studied it, and I enjoyed it. My parents loved it, too. They weren't in the theater professionally, but they were theatrical.

"There was small-time vaudeville and big-time vaudeville. You know what the difference was? The difference was in the breaks. Some of the best people didn't get the breaks.

"My father had a niece in vaudeville who was older than me. She had hair to her ankles, but she wasn't only long on hair, she had talent. She made it to the *Ziegfeld Follies*. You can't just climb to the *Ziegfeld Follies* on your hair, like Rapunzel in the fairy tale. That only works in fairy tales.

"It helps to see someone you know have success. You see it can be done by a person who's mortal. At fifteen, I went back on the stage, and again on the road, briefly.

"My whole education was the theater. And that was great. I saw Billie Burke and Tyrone Power, the father of the movie star. My mother took me a lot of times to see Eva Tanguay. When I told my mother that I liked Eva Tanguay very much, she said she was one of her favorites, too. My mother and I always had the same taste.

"She told me Eva Tanguay spent a thousand dollars a month on gloves and stockings. I didn't care about gloves and stockings, but I loved clothes, and it was wonderful to think of having so much money to spend on clothes.

"My mother and I went backstage to meet her. She was nice to us, and she and my mother had an affinity.

"Miss Tanguay was called the 'I-don't-care girl.' I've been told I have an air of nonchalance about me. Maybe a little of that came from watching her, but I think I had it anyway. It wasn't true, though, because in my heart I was the 'I-*do*-care girl.'

"After I was a star, Eva Tanguay was sick, and didn't have her money anymore, and I was glad I was able to help her out. I gave her money to pay her rent and see doctors.

"Bert Williams was my favorite entertainer when I was a child, and I wanted to meet him. I said that to my father. Both my parents listened carefully to everything I said.

"One night my father came home and said, 'Mae, I have a big surprise for you.' Father seemed pleased with himself. 'Bert Williams is here. I've brought him home to have dinner with you.' I rushed in, looked at this man, and screamed, 'It's not! It's not!' I went up to my room and cried. I was terribly upset, not because meeting Bert Williams meant that much to me, but because I thought my father had tried to fool me.

"My mother told me my father wanted to go up to me, but Bert Williams stopped him. He said, 'I'll do it.' He stood outside my door and started to sing. Then I knew and came right out of my room, and we all had dinner."

Mae had instantly recognized his unique voice and style. "Do you know why I didn't recognize him? He was too light. He was a black man, but he was too light. On stage he wore blackface for his act. I didn't know that. He used burnt cork."

Williams was from the West Indies, and he was too light-skinned for the stereotyped character the times required he play, so he darkened his face before each performance.

"He was a great star, but they used to make him use a separate entrance. Can you believe that? He died a long time ago, before I came to Hollywood.

"I never cried, but I cried that night because I couldn't bear the thought that my father had lied to me. I never cried again except when my mother was taken. I had no reason to cry. I got everything I wanted. I just had to say what it was.

"Bert Williams worked with all-white casts, and later he went to the *Ziegfeld Follies.* He was a big star, but he had to face all kinds of unfair segregation problems in those days because of being black. I wish he could have been in my pictures. He was an immense talent, and I admired him so much."

It was a time when a black man would not have been invited as a dinner guest by many white people. Segregation was the assumed way in New York and Brooklyn at that time, if not as extreme as in the South. Black entertainers stayed in separate hotels, sat in a separate section in the theaters, and were not afforded the same privileges routinely enjoyed by everyone else.

Mae's father was not someone who approved of any of this. He had great respect for black boxers he had known and had friends among them. He believed each person should be judged on his own and accorded the respect he deserved, the color of his skin having no bearing on it. This was the attitude he imparted to Mae, by example. "In that way, you might say my father was color-blind."

"Audiences are wonderful teachers," Mae said. "You learn how to handle a disruptive cough, or sneeze, even a coughing fit. Well, you don't learn how to handle it as much as you learn how to shut it out, to appear to shut it out and not get all broken up by it.

"You can be prepared if you know that a cough in an audience can be contagious. It often is. If one person coughs, someone else feels a cough coming on, and there you go.

"I created my own style. You have to understand your audience, but what's more important and much harder to do, you have to understand yourself. I'll give you a personal example.

"I like to come out and get a big reaction. That gives me what I need to have, the best energy. I needed that wave of energy. So, I made it my style to always come out strong and get the big reaction that I loved.

"Personality is the most important part of what makes a star. I'm gonna tell it to you so you don't miss it. Write it down:

"Personality is the most important part of what makes a star."

She paused to make sure I had it, and then went on.

"You can try to train your personality. It's possible to take it out in the world and exercise it. Try it out. See which aspects of you are the ones people like best and respond to. We all have various facets, like diamonds. There's no book that really tells you how to train your personality. It's just trial and error. Most of it's Mother Nature.

"You know, we're all typecast in life. And if you don't know exactly how life has typecast you, people soon let you know. But you have to remember, if it isn't exactly what you would have chosen for yourself, you *can* make some alterations and get a better fit."

"It's funny how you remember important moments in your life, and they weren't the ones you planned. I mean some of them, the innocent memories, not preplanned ones, turn out to be the most memorable. You can't just say, 'Today I'm going to set out to have a good memory,' but you can try.

"I'll tell you one day I remember. I'll never forget the day diamonds caught my eye. I'd seen diamonds before. My mother had a few tiny ones, but they didn't have enough facets to fascinate me, if you'll pardon a little pun. Those tiny diamonds my mother owned never seemed like diamonds to me, even though they were real.

"I looked in the window of the best jewelry store in Brooklyn, and it was all sparkling. I was drawn to it, and I led my mother to that window. She couldn't understand what I was so excited about.

"But she knew if I was so interested in what was in that window, it must be something special. She was always open to my feelings and opinions. She would say to my father, 'We have to listen to Mae.'

"She told me that those diamonds were very expensive. They weren't really the very best diamonds, and I had a feeling even then that there were greater diamonds elsewhere. I decided on the spot that as many as possible of the best were going to be mine. I made my plan right then and there that I was going to start collecting, as soon as possible.

"'Which one do you like, Mae?' my mother asked me.

"I remember like it was just yesterday. I said, 'All of them.' And I meant it.

"'No, Mae. I mean which one do you like best?'

"I knew right away. 'The biggest one,' I said.

"My mother explained to me very carefully, she always explained everything to me very carefully, 'It's not just size, Mae. It's also quality. You have to see the difference in the quality.'

" 'Can *you?*' I asked her.

" 'No,' she answered truthfully, as she always did, 'but *you* will because you are going to have lots of diamonds someday, Mae, if that's what you want. You have to know what you want. No one can have everything, so you have to try for what you want most. And you have to start early. If you go in the wrong direction, sometimes it's too late and you can't go back.'

"I didn't quite understand all of what she was saying, but I knew what she was saying was important to her, so that made it important to me. Looking back, maybe she was a little wistful.

"Then, she asked me if I would like to go into the store, so I could see the diamonds more closely.

"I said, 'Oh, yes.' I clapped my hands. I was so excited. What I really wanted to do was to touch them. They looked like they would feel wonderful to touch. And then, what I wanted to do was to try some on and see how they looked on me.

"I remember my father saying to me when I was about four, and I was showing him my new dress that my mother and I had bought that day, 'You know, Mae, You're just like your mother. Everything looks good on you.'

"My mother took my hand, and we went into the jewelry store.

"Mother had never been in that shop, but the man in the store seemed very pleased to see her. She was always smartly dressed and such a beautiful woman. She looked like she could buy all of the diamonds in the store, or some man would buy them for her.

"He said, 'May I show you some jewelry that—'

"Before he could select anything from the showcase, she said, 'We would like to see a few of your diamonds.' Only diamonds. He didn't pay any attention to the 'we,' because he didn't understand that *I* was the *real* customer, *potent*ially.

"He asked my mother what size diamond she would like to see, and she hesitated. She didn't know the terminology. For her, 'karats' were vegetables that improved your eyesight. She always encouraged me to eat my carrots, but I have to tell you, from that day on, when I discovered diamonds, handled them, and saw them on me, I was more interested in karats with Ks than with Cs.

"In the store, I piped up, 'I want to see the largest diamond you have.' Well, you should have seen the look on that gentleman's face. I assumed he was a gentleman. It was like in the funny papers. I thought he was going to faint, and it would say, 'Plop!' above his head.

"Mother wasn't at all surprised by my self-assurance. She was used to it. She would've been surprised if I *hadn't* surprised her.

" 'Yes,' she said, backing me up, 'we'd like to try on the biggest.' He brought out a diamond that was the size of a marble, not just a marble, but a shooter marble. It was attached to a black velvet ribbon you could tie around your neck.

"The first thing I wanted to do was to touch it. I really wanted to hold it, but I settled for touching it.

"It felt cold, but it made me feel warm.

"My mother took it as though she was going to put it on, but instead, you know what she did? She hung it around my neck, tied the black velvet ribbon, and then she held up the hand mirror that was on the counter so I could see myself.

"I was speechless. And that didn't happen much. 'Mae, you look beautiful,' my mother said. It was true. I knew it, but I didn't say anything. 'Diamonds suit you.'

"The diamond did look wonderful, and it felt so comfortable there on my perfectly flat little chest.

"My mother took it and held it against her beautiful bosom. I didn't know that one day my chest would look like hers and that the diamonds would be displayed the way they were on her. I just *knew* that someday I was going to have diamonds, and I knew I wanted to buy some for my mother, as soon as I could.

"As we left the shop, I said to her, 'As soon as I earn money, I'm going to buy you a diamond.'

"She said, 'Don't you worry about me, Mae. I'm not the diamond type. But you are.'

"My mother wore pearls. She had a single strand of them that had been in her family. I think it was her grandmother's or *her* mother's. I don't know if they were real pearls, but she treated them like they were very valuable. She also had a pearl choker. It looked wonderful on her. Hardly anybody in the world could have worn that. You had to have the neck for it, and she did, like a swan. It was old-style, like they were in the middle of the nineteenth century. That one had come down to my mother through her family, too.

"Do you know who it was who bought me my first diamond? It was my mother.

"When she saw how I loved diamonds, she bought me one. It was the smallest diamond I ever saw and the diamond I loved most in my whole life. It didn't matter that it was the smallest one I ever owned. The quality was perfect, like everything my mother ever selected.

"I never wore it because it was so small I was afraid I might lose it. Then, one day, when I was traveling in show business after my mother had died, I couldn't find it. I looked everywhere. I was frantic.

"Finally, I was too exhausted to look anymore. It was impossible to find it. I was heartbroken.

"Then, I thought about what my mother would say, and it was like I heard her voice in my head:

"'Mae, don't feel bad. You didn't lose anything. That diamond was only a token of my love for you, and you always have that. You don't need the diamond to know how much I love you. You haven't lost the diamond because it's a symbol, and that can't be taken away. The real diamond served its purpose in its moment. Now, enjoy your bigger diamonds, and your life.'

"That was all, but it was enough. My mother always knew just what to say to make me feel good and take away anything that hurt. It was worth a skinned knee when I was a little girl to have her take the hurt away.

"Later, my father bought me a bracelet with some tiny diamonds. He wanted to make me happy. And he did. The bracelet didn't really have any valuable stones in it, but they were valuable to me."

Chapter Two

INGENUE

(1911–1921)

M Y CAREER IS everything," Mae told me. "Always was. I never changed. Inside, I feel like the same little girl I was. But it was the way I grew up outside that men liked.

"My only experience with being too old for something I wanted to do occurred when I was twelve. I was too shapely to play a child anymore, no matter how loose the dress was. So I was pretty much retired for a few years before I could get back into action."

Mae was anxious to return to the stage, and she was impatient to get past that awkward transition for an actress, between childhood and being an ingenue. Her father suggested that she might be "growing up too fast, anyway," and he thought it was a good idea she stay home for a while.

Matilda might have prevailed, as she always did in decisions involving Mae's career, but this time she agreed with her husband that Mae needed some rest. Even Mae felt a little tired, but she wanted to rest for a few weeks, not a few years. Her idea of rest was creating and learning some new routines.

A trusted friend of the West family came to them with an offer. He had a vaudeville act and wanted Mae to appear with him. Jack and Matilda felt their daughter could accept, if that was what she wanted. Mae didn't hesitate a second. She was thrilled. She would be back on stage, the place she felt most alive.

"Then," Mae recalled, "I found out that this man, who was in his thirties, was going to try to pass, on stage, for twelve years old, with the help of a red wig. I was to play his girlfriend. It was hard for me to play twelve, when I was fourteen. You can imagine what it was like for him, but he was able to get bookings. I'd find the key to my part and make something out of it, no matter what. I was determined.

"It didn't always take a lot of determination. In one scene, we're both supposed to be twelve-year-olds. He shows me a worm, and I'm terrified. I screamed. That always got a big laugh. I never knew why.

"I learned something important. You learn more from doing something that comes hard for you than from doing something you could do in your sleep. I always try to plan a good 'get-off' for when I leave the stage. You can't relax and take it easy or you lose the audience. You have to keep surprising them. You have to surprise yourself and not bore yourself, I kept telling myself. Boring yourself is terrible for you, and worse for the audience, because it always shows through.

"I saw that we were doing the same show every time, but each audience was different, and the audience is a character in the show. An important character. I never forgot that.

"At the time, and in my memory, it seemed like my time on the road with the act was almost a year, but it was really weeks, not months.

"When I got home, after our bookings dried up, I found my

brother, John, was deathly ill with pneumonia. I hadn't been told. My parents decided to let me be on stage and not worry me because there wasn't anything I could do. It was terrible for our family. I loved my little brother.

"But John had a wonderful woman as his private nurse, and she and my parents pulled him through. When she was leaving because John was cured, I met her son who came for her, Joe Schenck.

"He was handsome and musical, and he became my beau. He was gallant like a knight and sent me flowers, and he brought his band to my house, which my parents enjoyed, too."

"I can interview myself, you know," Mae said to me. "I know all the questions."

"And all the answers, too?" I asked.

"No, I have to be spontaneous or I'd bore myself. I only have my one life to draw on, but fundamentally, that's a pretty special life."

I asked her which questions she has most often been asked.

"Well, they used to ask me all the time, 'How come, Mae, you never married? Was it because you couldn't find the right person? Because you never found Mr. Right?'

"It wasn't because I didn't find the right man. It was because I kept *finding* him. The right man kept turning up. I found *too many* Mr. Rights.

"Of course that was before people found out about Frank, my five-minute husband. He was a singer-dancer, and handsome. He was my early teenage blunder. It was a secret marriage. I wish it had been a secret from me.

"I had love affairs before I got married. Plenty. But I never had a sex affair before I was married at seventeen, going toward eighteen.

"Necking, hugging, some restricted touching . . .

"I guess that's how I happened to get married. I was never confused about all that again.

"We never shared a room or any place, because I didn't want my parents to know, and because I need a lot of room in bed to stretch out in. I can't sleep with anyone. I always slept alone.

"At night when the lovemaking is finished, even if it's well past daylight, I always go to sleep, alone. I've never slept at night with anyone else in my bed.

"I didn't know it then, but I wasn't the marrying kind. I was asked why did I get married at seventeen. I certainly can't remember now. I guess it was just this physical thing. I told Frank that when he came back from a road trip and wanted to set up a domicile and have me be domestic. I said, 'Frank, it was just this physical thing,' but he said it wasn't that way for him, that it was so much more, that he loved me.

"I always took marriage very seriously. It just wasn't for me. I don't believe in being married and not keeping the contract."

Frank Wallace and Mae had first met briefly in vaudeville in 1907. They met again in 1909 when Mae was touring. Wallace was billed as a jazz dancer.

His real name was Frank Szatkus, and he was the son of Lithuanian immigrants. His father was a tailor in Queens, New York, who could barely subsist with his family on what he earned. To earn a little extra money and tips, he played the violin at weddings and parties. It made the difference in putting enough and better food on the table.

Frank's father loved performing. He discovered that it was wonderful being paid to do something he loved doing. He shared this enthusiasm with his son, though Frank knew he was expected to get a job and marry a sensible girl who would have a lot of babies. Frank's parents had made that clear to him.

All that didn't matter to Mae. "I thought he had a big personality, but most of his personality was in his feet. It was jazz dancing, and he was a jazzy dancer." For a while, Mae and Wallace appeared as a team, "but the glow wore off, and I wanted to be on stage and single.

"Frank was a young song and dance man all the girls were enamored of. I found him attractive, myself. All the other girls falling for him and going after him didn't hurt. I guess I was always kind of competitive, like my father. Frank and me, we both admired the black style of singing and dancing, and we were doing ragtime before it got respectable.

"Girls in the show and ladies from the audience used to pass him their phone numbers. Just having a telephone was still a big deal then, especially if you didn't have a party line and have to wait your turn. They'd put their numbers in his pockets. But he wasn't that kind of fellow. He'd empty his pockets and throw them away.

"What they didn't know was Frank only had eyes for me, but that soon became pretty obvious. He was always looking at me with eyes filled with longing. Well, that didn't bother me. I was used to it. I liked his talent, and he sure was swell in the looks department, which always had a big effect on me.

"He was sort of young, but that's not a big problem because time takes care of that one. He didn't have a line, and he was sexually innocent and shy. But that was okay with me. I didn't know as much myself as I thought I did.

"Most women don't like a man who seems overexperienced, like he's done too much practicing. Men don't know that. They think a woman likes a very experienced man. I think it's fun to teach a man something, so he discovers a part of himself he didn't even know was there, and finds out about his own powers. He never forgets the one who helped him learn that.

"I prefer a forty-ripened man, a man who's been around. I've heard men say that they were afraid of the responsibility with a girl who was a virgin. But I always thought that initiating a virgin man was a privilege. A certain lack of expertise can have its own kind of charm, and they learn fast. It's fun to be able to teach a man something.

"With Frank I was still interested in exploring. I wasn't seventeen yet, and Frank wasn't quite twenty-one.

"We started out doing routines and practicing together. He asked me if I would like to be partners with him and work together. It sounded good to me, but I told him I'd have to ask my mother. I would never have made a professional commitment without asking her. I didn't think I would ever have made a personal commitment without her, either, but you never know. You have to be careful of impulse, especially when you're just seventeen.

"Mother met Frank, and it wasn't that she didn't like him, but she was always worried if I seemed to like just one fellow, instead of a lot of them, and she felt I was too young to do anything that would get in the way of my career and influence my whole life. I told her we were going to be a team only on stage. I'd never lied to her. I thought it was true when I said it.

"We were good together, and audiences liked our impassioned way. So did Frank. He asked me to marry him. I told him I didn't want to be married, not just not married to him, but I didn't want to be married to anyone, only to my career.

"So, on April 11, 1911, we were married in Milwaukee. He was twenty-one, and I wasn't quite eighteen yet, the age in Wisconsin for marrying without the consent of your parents. I told him he had to promise me he wouldn't tell my parents until I said he could. He didn't know how long that promise would have to last. I didn't know, either, but he kept his word for a long, long, long time.

"I knew my father would be disappointed, probably angry, except he could always be talked out of being angry by my mother because she was so serene. His boisterousness was no match for her serenity. But this time, she wasn't going to be serene. She would be heartbroken, disappointed because I'd married so young, and heartbroken because I'd lied to her.

"Well, it wasn't exactly a lie. I just hadn't said anything. That would be the same as a lie between my mother and me. I had betrayed our special relationship. But I couldn't tell her. I was too ashamed. I wasn't ashamed of Frank. Well, maybe I was, it's true, but I was more ashamed of me. I couldn't explain to her why I'd married Frank Wallace because I couldn't fully understand it myself. You know, I could never once in all the years that followed imagine having been known as Mae Wallace. His real family name I couldn't even pronounce, and neither could anyone else. Can you imagine? I can never be anyone but Mae West.

"I told him we couldn't live together because I couldn't tell my parents, and besides, my mother wanted me to be a single in a new act. We were separated sometimes by our work, and I found I liked that best.

"I did tell my sister, Beverly, the truth because I knew she would understand and wouldn't judge me, and I could trust her to keep a secret. She understood how word leaking out could hurt me professionally, and she knew about how hurt our mother would be.

"I didn't care about getting a divorce because I was afraid if anyone found out I got a divorce, they'd know I'd been married. And I didn't need a divorce because I *knew* I would never marry again.

"When I told Frank again I felt it was just 'that physical thing,' he said he felt more for me than that, professing his love forever.

"I didn't want to let him down hard, so when I heard of a good career opportunity for him to get a booking far away, that would take him on the road, I used my influence to help him get it. I was able to help arrange for Frank to go on the road for a year, with my nudge. We never got together again. My choice. I never let him back into my life, and I've got to say for him, he kept our secret for many years.

"One thing being married did for me was, if I ever had a weak moment again, I couldn't get married because I already was. I had a protection. For me, it was the best of all worlds.

"At first, I just felt it, but I quickly got to understand it. It was simple. I couldn't be a sex symbol and somebody's wife, too.

"A woman who is married and has children, in my opinion, can't be a true sex symbol. As long as I was single, I belonged to *every* man. At least, he could *think* there was a possibility.

"Marrying Frank was one of those days when 'Miss West' should have stayed in bed—alone," Mae told me. This was one of those occasions during our conversations in which she referred to herself in the third person. It was as though she wanted to distance herself as much as possible from the youthful indiscretion that she had come to regard as such a terrible decision.

"I understood I didn't want a hubby, because I already had a hobby—me."

After a few months of their secret marriage, Mae and Wallace separated, at the end of 1911. He kept his promise of secrecy until the mid-1930s when, needing money, he sold the story to the *New York Daily Mirror*.

During 1911, Mae appeared briefly and for only a few performances in two Broadway shows, *A La Broadway* and *Vera Violetta*. The latter is remembered for bringing Al Jolson to the attention of the public.

By this time, Mae had sung and danced her way through numerous vaudeville tours, as well as being a stock company veteran. By the age of eighteen, she had served her apprenticeship on the stage and was already a seasoned performer with a distinctive style that she herself had created. Her name was becoming her own. She was already writing dialogue and sketches for her evolving onstage character.

"From the first, I never had much patience with performers who walked off stage complaining about bad audiences. 'They were dead, real zombies,' they'd say.

"It seemed to me that the audiences had paid their hard-earned money and given up their time, and they'd come to have a good time, so if they didn't have a good time, there was something wrong with us, not them.

"I was proud that I could coax, tease, cajole, beg, work with all I had to get my audience to have a good time.

"I was traveling around so much, sometimes I'd wake up in the morning, and I'd have to think, what place am I in? But even if I knew I was only going to be in a place one night, the first thing I did, no matter how tired I was when I got in, I started moving the furniture around, so I could make it more homey, like it was my home. I didn't have a lot to work with, but I always tried, because where I live is important to me."

Appearing at the Columbia Theatre, after a Sunday concert, Mae was seen by two of the great New York producers of the day, Florenz Ziegfeld and Ned Wayburn. Each sent word he would like to meet with her. She saw Ziegfeld first. Her dream seemed to come true when he told her he wanted her to be in one of his shows.

"He thought I would be happy to grab the opportunity without even asking about the part. Well, he was right. I didn't ask about the part. But what concerned me was the theater, actually the stage of the theater. I told him it wasn't right for my intimate style, and I didn't think I could work well in that type of house. He was pretty surprised, because no one ever said no to him. But I *knew* I couldn't do well for him, or for me. I told him I'd love to work for him in the *Follies* in another theater. But he didn't give up easily.

"He invited me to visit his theater during the day, when I could be alone on the stage and try it out, to get used to it.

"I thanked him, but I never took him up on the offer.

"I went to see Ned Wayburn. He told me he wanted me to be in a new show he was doing. My first question surprised him, too. 'What theater?' I asked. He told me it would be at the Fulton on West 46th. He was curious about why I asked. I didn't answer his question in a direct way. I answered with another question. 'Could I look at the theater?' He thought it unusual, I know. I ran out and went straight to the theater. The door was open and nobody stopped me. I looked the place over.

"I felt at home right away. It was just my kind of theater. I'd won first prize in a lot of amateur shows in intimate theaters it reminded me of. I didn't need to go on the stage. It was made for my style. It had a lot of gilt and boxes that hung over the stage. In that style theater, everyone would be able to see me, and I could make contact with them.

"I went back to see Ned Wayburn, and I said yes. Then I asked him about my part. He said I would be playing an Irish maid. I thought to myself, There are Irish maids and there are Irish maids. He showed me my part. I liked it right away. I was very familiar with the Irish, starting with my partly Irish father and his Irish family, and his Irish friends in our Brooklyn neighborhood. I think there were as many Irish people in the area as there were in Dublin. It sure seemed like it.

"I saw the possibilities. I said to Mr. Wayburn, 'Is it okay with you if I make a few changes here and there, in my character, and some of her lines?' I was dying to write them in, right that moment, there in his office. But he sort of pulled back.

"He said politely, but firmly, 'I think we can wait until rehearsal, Miss West.' I took my cue.

"Meanwhile, I went home and began working out my part. I loved the song, 'They Are Irish.' It needed some more choruses. I was supposed to do it with two comedians, a vaudeville team I liked. They would be plumbers, but everything went wrong with their plumbing stuff, and that was the comic part of it.

"At first, I was a little worried because I wasn't getting enough rehearsal time, but I decided it would be to my advantage because I would have an excuse for not getting all my stuff into the skimpy rehearsals and I'd be able to sneak it in when it counted.

"On opening night of *A La Broadway,* Wayburn asked me if I had an encore prepared. I answered yes.

"I had several. I couldn't imagine going out without many encores ready to go."

Mae's first number earned her seven encores. She delighted audiences by singing each encore in a different ethnic accent. "It was a showstopper," Mae said.

The Irish maid was supposed to have been played in a straightforward manner, but Mae embellished the part, giving the character a different personality. The character became bright, but lazy. As written by William Le Baron, the maid was to have been placed in a wealthy home to take notes for a writer about a rich family's actions and manners. He could scarcely recognize the scene-stealing Irish maid he had written, but he wasn't angry because the show was a hit. He received a lot of the credit for it.

In 1932, in Hollywood, Mae met William Le Baron again. He would be the producer of several of her films.

When the play ended, Flo Ziegfeld, who had attended, threw a rose to Mae. Mae, who had at the age of five refused to pick up coins thrown on the stage, picked up that rose. She said she kept it pressed in a book for quite a while. Mae was told that sitting in the house seats were Lee and J. J. Shubert.

"It seemed everyone wanted to take me out that night, but I made my choice. I left with my parents. I most wanted to share my happiness with them.

"People judge you by the value you put on yourself—in show business, in sex, in life. But in my first show I didn't even sign a contract. The show was a tremendous success, and people said to me, 'Now you can hold 'em up and get plenty.' I didn't care. I just wanted to be the star of a hit show."

Mae drove only once in her life. About 1915, while in her early twenties, she went out with her father, who planned to teach her how to drive his new Model T Ford.

One of the great achievements of Henry Ford was designing and producing a car that, for the first time, allowed women to drive. Before the Model T, most automobiles came with a professional driver, always a muscular man. The Model T was not only cheap enough for Everyman to afford, but simple enough for Everywoman to drive.

Mae had been enthusiastic and confident, even overconfident, about her ability to learn how to drive, she admitted to me some sixty-five years later. All that ended, however, when she took the wheel, released the handbrake, stepped on the low-speed pedal, and pulled down the throttle. What followed was not smooth acceleration, but a bone-rattling series of lurches, jolts, and jerks.

There never was a second lesson. While the first was still in progress, her father informed her that one lesson was one more than enough and she would have to get another car and another teacher, or she would have to get another father!

"That was the end of my driving lessons. Father never wanted to be in a car I was driving again, and he never was. And *I* didn't want to be in a car I was driving, either, so I never learned to drive. There was always somebody to drive me. But I did enjoy, every once in a while, buying a nice car for someone else to drive me around in.

"I always bought one kind of car for myself, a Cadillac limousine, except once for my forty-second birthday I bought myself a birthday present, a Duesenberg. You probably don't know what that is."

I said that I did. "An expensive luxury car."

She said, "They don't make them anymore. That's where the expression, 'It's a doozie,' comes from."

Matilda hoped Mae might like to try out a sister act with Beverly, but the idea had no appeal for Mae, much as she wanted to please her mother. In 1916, at her mother's urging, Mae finally agreed to be a team, or sister act, with Beverly.

Mae had resisted the idea for quite a while, but there was nothing in life that she found more difficult than saying no to her mother. "Doing the act with Beverly was a one-way deal," she told me. "I had everything to give and nothing to gain at the time." Mae persuaded her agent, Frank Bohm, to represent Beverly, and he was able to arrange employment for the entire summer.

During the summer of 1916, Mae and Beverly appeared together in New York at the Keith's Fifth Avenue Theatre as "Mae West and Sister," a vaudeville song and dance act. Beverly played it straight, and Mae performed with suggestive humor.

The act had a certain success, although Mae did not enjoy the idea of being one part of a sister act. Mae liked to appear solo. If not solo, it had to be with men who were only featured players.

Audiences liked Beverly. Her handicap, the clubfoot, was not noticeable, and she was more of a singer than a dancer. "She had a natural, lovely voice," Mae said. She did not, however, have Mae's strong stage personality.

Mae said Beverly was staying out late, and she could not control the actions of her younger sister, except by threatening Beverly's place in the act.

Finally Mae felt compelled to inform her mother that Beverly had to go home. Mae knew that her mother would never want anything to hurt Mae's career.

One of the worst aspects of having an act with a close relation, Mae felt, was if the act didn't succeed, it was a worse breakup, and the personal relationship would sour. "Bad feelings in a family is terrible."

"How do you fire your little sister?" Mae asked me. "I did, and it didn't seem to make a lot of difference to her. I suppose she didn't like it, but it wasn't something really big. I guess she couldn't understand how much a career in show business meant to me, and I couldn't understand how little it meant to her.

"It wasn't so easy to help Beverly, because she didn't want success on the stage the way I did. I wanted it more than anything else. She wanted it along with a lot of other things. She could let a romance with a boy distract her. Later, it was a romance with a man. Still later, it was alcohol, and she smoked. But I kept faith with my mother, and I did my best for Beverly.

"I think what she wanted was all of the rewards of success, the attention, the clothes and shoes, the car, and I wanted the work.

"My mother understood, Beverly never said anything much about it, and I don't think our relationship, Beverly's and mine, was any the worse for us. We still had time left on our booking. I learned how to do a quick change so I could do both sisters, one at a time, of course.

"I'm not the maternal type," Mae told me, "but I know my mother hoped I would do what I could for my younger sister. All my life, I watched out for her like I knew my mother would have wanted me to. I even wrote a part for one of her husbands in one of my shows.

"As soon as I was successful in California, I got a lovely ranch in the San Fernando Valley for my sister, so she would always have a place to live. She likes horses. I do, too. And my brother liked them.

Most girls like to shop. I do. Beverly never had to come to me for money. I anticipated. I paid her a salary. I never asked her how she spent her checks, but she sure had a lot of clothes. It was a good thing she had plenty of room at the ranch. I put her on my payroll, to keep her out of trouble.

"I liked keeping my limos as long as I could, but Beverly liked having new cars, so I obliged. I was glad they made her happy."

In 1916, Mae had a torrid affair with a fellow performer. She identified him only as D. "He was a great performer, and on the stage, too."

"D was a great passion in my life," Mae told me. "He was very hot-blooded. He was someone I could lose my mind with. I had mixed feelings about totally losing myself that way. It's the greatest sex. No doubt about it. Mindless sex. No talk. Transported. The trouble is, it's hard to come out of it. And the appetite grows with the eating. You find yourself thinking about it and getting yourself in the mood for it when you need your mind clear to think about other things. Sex can make a jumble of your thoughts.

"He just had to look at me and I was ready, because I knew he was ready. I was lucky I had an invisible wedding ring on my finger. It was invisible for the whole world, but I could see it. Being already married saved me from making another mistake in a weak moment, blinded by passion, which can be very blinding.

"There was one time when D was having one of his jealous rages. He had them so much, the intervals between them kept getting shorter, so it was like one continuous rant.

"On the one hand, I liked his being so possessive, but it started to get suffocatin'. And he was always ready to get physical with his fists with other suitors. 'First-Blow D,' I called him. At the time, I didn't think of it, but later, I did some ruminatin', and I came to the conclusion that he was 'Battlin' D,' and that he reminded me of my father.

"He'd rush in to defend my honor, which wasn't in any need of defending, without any fear of consequences to himself. He would take on two or three, any number. I remember once he did that in this café where we were, and he felt I'd been insulted when I just felt I'd been flattered by some aspirants for my favors.

"D looked at me and asked my permission before creating a scene.

" 'Mae,' he said, 'would it trouble you any if I went over and hit their heads together?'

"I was a little coy about it, and just said, 'You go and do whatever you think the situation calls for.'

"So he did. They were dented, but I don't think they were permanently damaged.

"It reminded me of that incident I told you about when my father hit someone and knocked him on the ground, just for giving my mother the eye. My mother felt she had to say, 'Oh, you shouldn't have,' to my father. Well, that was another day and age, and I didn't feel I had to be demure like Mother must have felt she had to be.

"Another surprising occasion occurred when I was coming into the theater with this big, handsome, well-built guy, and we were looking at each other kinda cozy-like. After the gentleman dropped me in my dressing room and went on his way, D barged in. He didn't stop to knock. Of course, he *never* stopped to knock. Seeing me was always urgent for him.

"This time, he was breathing smoke, but naturally not smoking, which I didn't allow. There was nothing I could do about someone breathing smoke who didn't have a cigar or a cigarette. I tried to calm him down, or excite him in a more constructive way, but nothing I could do worked. His eyes were blazing.

"He was suspicious of me and what I'd been doing.

"I said, 'Don't you trust me?'

"He said, 'No.'

"He was right.

" 'If I see that man again with you, I'm gonna sock him on the jaw so hard, I'll knock him out,' he said.

"Just then, there was a knock at the door. My friend had left something behind, besides me.

"I said, 'Come in.'

"He said, 'I'm sorry. I forgot my coat and hat.'

"That often happened to my gentleman callers, who were so taken with me, they left something behind. I think sometimes they did it so they would have an excuse to come back. It was a good thing D hadn't noticed the hat and coat because he would have gotten even angrier, if that was possible.

"The gentleman, and he was that, when I failed to introduce him to D, introduced himself.

"He said, 'I'm Jim Corbett.'

"It was 'Gentleman Jim' Corbett, the former heavyweight champion of the world.

"I saw the look of recognition on D's face. I don't have to tell you the rest of the story. D didn't throw a single punch. So I guess his passion for survival was greater than his passion for me.

"D went to my parents, and he asked for my hand in marriage. My father said, 'Why don't you ask Mae? She pretty much makes up her own mind on what she does, and we don't tell her what to do. It wouldn't be any use.'

"D said he had asked me about one hundred times, and I didn't answer or said no. Then D asked my mother, thinking she'd be more of a pushover for his masculine charms, with which he was over-endowed. But he didn't know my mother.

"She said, 'Mae has to think. She should have a few more years before she marries anyone.'

"The passion was draining, and I felt that I needed to save my sex energy for my work. It's the same energy, you know.

"Sex and work have been the only two things in my life, but if I ever had to choose between sex and my work, it was always my work I'd choose.

"I decided that D was too possessive, too jealous and obsessed with marrying me, and I didn't like him involving my parents. I couldn't modify him, so I decided I had to give him his walking papers, and the only way I could do that was to give myself *my* walking papers.

"My mother was worried about me and very happy to see me break it off. I always preferred to avoid any unpleasant scenes. I left for my bookings and didn't leave a forwarding address. I didn't say good-bye, and that troubled my conscience. I talked it over with Mother. I told her I wanted to call D.

"She asked me, 'Why?'

"Just to say goodbye wouldn't make it better. The only reason to call would be if I wanted to continue the relationship. Mother always understood me.

"If I called D, I was afraid of myself. If he spoke with me, I thought I'd go back to where we were. I didn't call.

"The next time I heard from D, it was a long time later. He called me in 1945, and he said he'd like to see me. We met.

"He said, 'You haven't changed, Mae. You didn't get older.'

"I enjoyed hearing him say it, especially because I knew it was true.

"He looked pretty good. He hadn't held up as well as I had, but he was still an attractive man.

"When he called me, I was curious if the old feeling would still be there. I couldn't tell from the phone. I was so shocked to hear from him, I wasn't really tuned in. It wasn't till he hung up that I started to get in the mood. I looked forward to seeing him. I figured he would be surprised to see I hadn't changed in all that time.

"I wasn't anxious about what he'd been doing. I was living in the present. I wanted to check and see if my own heart beat faster when we were physically together.

"It didn't. I didn't feel much of anything.

"So I guess it's not true what they say about absence making the heart grow fonder. It doesn't.

"I was wondering if he'd been thinking about me the whole time. If he had, he must have gotten pretty tired.

"There was nothing awkward about us being together. It wasn't like old times, but we'd had good times. He wasn't bitter about the way I'd walked out on him.

"He said he understood why I had to break it off that way. He understood there was no other way to break off something that was too hot to handle for both of us.

"I'd wondered if it might be dangerous for me to see him, 'cause I was afraid he'd go into one of his violent rages. It seemed he'd mellowed. I sort of missed the passionate old D.

"Then I found out he'd come on a mission. He said he'd written an article about our time together, and he wanted to publish it, but first he wanted to make sure it was okay with me.

"It wasn't.

"He said he brought it with him, and would I like to see it before I said no.

"I said our time together was private, just for us, not for strangers to read about.

"So he said, 'Then I won't publish it. Here it is, Mae. It's yours.'

"He kissed me just on the cheek and he left.

"I didn't read the story he'd written until later that night. It was pretty good. It was very private. It was kind of exciting. For a minute there, I wished I'd asked D where he was staying.

"I tore up the story.

"I never heard from D again."

Arthur Hammerstein had seen Mae at his father's theater and decided she would be perfect to play Mayme in *Sometime*, a play he was producing. Mae was thrilled, recognizing this as "a great break."

On October 4, 1918, Mae opened in *Sometime* at the Shubert Theatre in New York. The play starred Mae opposite Ed Wynn.

Just as she was luxuriating in her good fortune, New York City was struck by the worldwide influenza epidemic of 1918. People were terrified by its virulence. The strange aspect of the epidemic was that, unlike earlier ones, young people were more likely to be stricken than the elderly. The first assumption was that it was spread by young men in the military who suddenly found themselves confined in close quarters. A great many of the young soldiers were stricken. Later, it was thought that the influenza that had struck the population in the 1880s immunized those who survived and were still alive in 1918.

Fear kept people at home. They stayed away from restaurants, movie theaters, and stage performances. It was during the height of all this that *Sometime* opened. Many shows were closing, but *Sometime* opened successfully and survived to enjoy Armistice Day on November 11, when *all* the theaters closed that night as celebrants jubilantly filled the streets.

While Mae had been performing in Chicago, she went with a group of actors to a café, the Café Elite, catering to black people who liked to dance. It was there Mae saw a couple dance the Shimmy-Shawobble. Mae said she became very excited watching the man and woman stand in place "while they shook like jelly." It was sensual. It was passionate and, Mae thought, "a little funny." She couldn't get it out of her mind.

The next day at the matinee, on impulse Mae used it in the show. The audience applauded it wildly. It was a sensation. She repeated the dance for the evening performance. The effect was the same.

Mae referred to the dance as the Shimmy, and it became popular among those few who could do it, as well as among the many who liked to watch it. It attracted great attention. There was criticism, and there was curiosity.

Sometime ran on Broadway for 283 performances, though Mae was no longer Mayme when the bans were finally posted. A road trip was set, and the show was already sold out in many theaters and gave every indication of being a success on the road, too. It had been a successful venture, and Hammerstein told Mae it would have continued to run longer on Broadway with her in the part.

Mae, however, did not believe in repeating the same show too long, no matter how great the success. She said, "I believe you can get stuck in success. It's not as bad as being stuck in failure, but it can lead to being stuck in failure."

Mae left because it seemed to her that it was a good idea to depart while the show was thriving, and more important to her to go on to something that offered her the opportunity to enlarge her horizon. "If the truth be known," Mae told me, "I got the wiggles if I stayed on too long doing the same thing. Actors told me that if they played the same part for a long time, it got to feeling real natural for them. For me, it was the reverse. If I stayed on one stage playing one part for a long time, it got to where it felt real *un*natural. Henry Fonda told me that for him, every performance of a play was like a different show. He was a handsome guy, but I didn't know what he was talking about." It also struck Mae that more good opportunities would be offered to her "if I left while I was on top."

Mae was disappointed, however, to find out that when she was free, no one noticed. "All the raves were just words," she told me. "You don't want to let words confuse you. Words come cheap."

No line formed to cast her in projects that were beyond even *her* imagination. She had to let people know she was free. Even then, there was what she called "waitin' time." One thing did not just lead to another, Mae learned. It was a painful realization. Fortunately, she was a genuine self-starter.

"My mother introduced me to her lawyer, Jim Timony, a former football player and a prominent attorney. That turned out to be a big thing in my life. Jim was still young, and he was interested in politics. Everyone agreed that he had a fine future in law or politics. There were people saying that someday he might become the mayor of New York City. He owned a baseball team and field in Brooklyn, a racing car, and he flew his own private plane. He was also a great devotee of the theater, and he specialized in theatrical law."

James A. Timony was thirty-one, Mae, twenty-four. After graduating from Brooklyn Law School, he took an office at 42nd and Broadway, where he specialized in theater clients and real estate investments. Mae observed that he was "very well connected."

"It was clear he was attracted to me. We had dinner, and after that, he called me every day. My mother thought he was a wonderful man, and she said, 'Mae, dear, he's quite infatuated with you.' I didn't need my mother to tell me that.

"I've always wondered how much my mother foresaw of what was to be.

"As far as my attraction to him goes, I've always liked a big, strong man. Like I say, a hard man is good to find. And I don't have anything against him being smart, either. After my mother, I considered Jim my best friend. He became my second-best friend."

Mae did some vaudeville, taking the Shimmy with her. Audiences on the vaudeville circuit were more shocked by it than had been the New York audiences. There were those who loved it and those who hated it, and those who weren't certain. Mae dared to risk rather than to bore, and some criticism did not break her spirit. Then, she agreed to do the Shuberts' *The Mimic World*.

"Some of the actresses said they didn't want to appear in a show with me. I've never been so flattered! They were worried about being overshadowed. And they were right.

"So, Mr. Shubert said to me, 'There's only one answer, Mae. We'll do a show with you as the only woman.' I loved it."

Mae opened on August 17, 1921, at the Century Promenade in *The Mimic World of 1921*. Her co-star, Cliff Edwards, later became the voice of Jiminy Cricket in Walt Disney's *Pinocchio*.

The Mimic World was a revue with many sketches and some lavish production numbers. Mae included a skit she created for herself, "The Shimmy Trial."

"The idea was, I was brought before a judge and accused of doing a libidinous dance that unduly aroused people, and the judge didn't know what the Shimmy was, so I demonstrate—a very enthusiastic demonstration."

Chapter Three

◆

BROADWAY

(1922–1931)

"VOLSTEAD WAS A tough act to follow," Mae commented.

The Volstead Act of 1919, the Eighteenth Amendment to the Constitution, established national Prohibition. Beginning in 1920, the production, sale, and consumption of alcoholic beverages was banned in the United States.

Instead of curbing alcoholism, as intended, Prohibition inspired it. Forbidding alcohol made it increasingly tempting and popular. Moving from smoky saloons to swanky salons called speakeasies, drinking became fashionable. After Prohibition took effect, many "speaks" sprang up in the Theater District. They were openly advertised in *The New York Times*. Women were welcome.

There were other changes around the same time. Women got the vote, and everyone, or almost everyone, was able to buy an automobile. Grand movie palaces were springing up, befitting the new product of Hollywood. Movies were becoming enormously important in the lives of people all over the country. Negro jazz music was heard everywhere. Previously taboo subjects, such as sex, were being discussed openly, often by women, who were often holding cigarettes.

As skirts got shorter, the list of aspirations of women grew longer. "Women's liberation" wasn't a phrase yet, but women were starting to liberate themselves. World War I had produced, among other things, the brassiere, invented by a Frenchman, which allowed women to work more freely as they replaced men in wartime factories.

In this bold new world of the future now, *The Mimic World* seemed dated and old-fashioned. It closed after twenty-six performances at the Century Promenade Theatre on Broadway. "I don't know if Prohibition had anything to do with it," Mae said. "Maybe it was that terrible war, 'The Great War' they called it. I don't know why they called it 'great.' There was nothing great about it except it was a great waste of the lives of young men, on both sides. Then, there was the memory of the Spanish flu epidemic. Maybe it was just all that change in the air. Anyway, audiences seemed restless. There was a pervasive feeling of the wiggles. I could sense it. I could even feel it, a sense of it myself."

Mae went back to vaudeville. She had extended one of her sketches into a short one-act play, which she called *The Ruby Ring*.

At the same time, Mae had ambitious plans. She had become fascinated by Freudian and Jungian ideas about the conscious and unconscious importance of sex, and she wanted to use them in a legitimate drama she wrote and in which she could star. Her first effort, *The Ruby Ring*, was a one-act play about "a girl who knew how."

The Ruby Ring (1921)

Outside a ballroom, two girls, Alice and Irene, talk about their friend, Gloria, who seems to get all the men. Gloria manages to escape the crowd of male admirers gathered around her, and she senses her girlfriends' envy. She boasts that with "the right method" she can make any man propose to her within five minutes of their meeting. She offers to demonstrate her prowess with five different men. The other girls are skeptical, but curious, and Irene is willing to wager her ruby ring that Gloria can't accomplish this seemingly impossible feat. Gloria wins the ruby ring.

Mae thought enough of her play to copyright it with the Library of Congress. Then she adapted it into a vaudeville sketch, which she called "How Different Types of Vamps Put the Bee on Their Heavy Johns."

Her pianist was a young man recruited by Timony named Harry Richman. He also portrayed, when necessary, her "heavy Johns." The act was successful enough to tour vaudeville circuits for two years. Afterward, Richman became performer Nora Bayes's accompanist, and then a popular singer in his own right.

In the play, Mae "vamps" a college boy, a businessman, a cowboy, an older man, and a college professor. Since none of them can resist her charms, she wins the ruby ring. The vaudeville sketch was done in the style of a lecture with songs, double entendres, and some quick costume changes—Mae West specialties.

As Mae's vaudeville and revue popularity rose, so did her aspirations. She wanted to be a star of the legitimate stage.

Her next writing effort, *The Hussy*, was a three-act play. To help her write this longer work, Timony hired Adeline Leitzbach, a writer whose 1918 play, *Success*, had been made into a film starring Mary Astor. *The Hussy* is described on its title page as "A Serio-Comedy Drama." Mae was inclined toward this type of description. She, of course, was to be "the hussy."

The Hussy (1924)

Nona Ramsey and her brother, Thomas, are boarders in a suburban middle-class home. The house belongs to Mrs. Clinton Somerville, who shares the residence with her two grown children, Jean and Clinton Jr., and a young female ward, Nancy Baynes.

Jean hopes to marry Robert van Sturdevent, who is a millionaire, but he is attracted to Nona, who encourages him. For this, Mrs. Somerville calls Nona "a hussy."

Nona rationalizes her desire to marry the rich young man because of memories of an impoverished childhood when she and her brother often went hungry and ragged.

Mrs. Somerville hires a private detective to prove that Nona is a woman of loose morals. Nona disappoints Mrs. Somerville by rejecting a large offer of money for sex.

Robert informs Jean that he has lost his inheritance, causing her to lose interest in him. Nona, "the hussy," accepts him for what he is, with or without millions, because she loves him.

The Hussy was never produced, but it bears many of the characteristics of Mae's later style. Diamond Lil had not been conceived yet, but Nona is very much like Lil. Although judged immoral by hypocrites, Nona, like Lil, triumphs in the end, her unconventional morality accepted.

Mae continued to be encouraged by her mother and Jim Timony. Matilda always believed her daughter was going to be the brightest star on Broadway. As Mae's career progressed, her greatest pleasure came in rewarding her mother's faith in her. Sometimes Mae's gratitude was expressed in a small but meaningful gift, such as a hat.

"As soon as I could afford it," Mae told me, "maybe a little ahead of when I could afford it, I started buying hats. My buying was always ahead of my wearing. I could never wear all the hats I bought, but I never let that dampen my enthusiasm.

"I'll tell you about the greatest hat I ever bought, the one that meant the most to me.

"My mother loved hats. I've never known anyone who loved hats as much as she did. One day in New York I saw this hat, the most wonderful hat in the world, and right away I knew it was made for my mother, and that she could wear it with her favorite black lace dress. She had a black dress with lace sleeves, long tight-fitted lace sleeves, and black lace up around the neck. It was mauve. As I've said, mauve is the most wonderful color. I don't know why you don't see it around anymore.

"I can see that hat in my mind just as clear today as I did the day I was holding it in my hand in the store. It was turned up on one side so you'd be able to see Mother's blond hair. The crowning touch was the feather, the greatest ostrich feather you ever saw. The hat cost eighty-five dollars, which was really a lot then. I'd never seen a hat that expensive before. But I knew I had to have it for my mother. I didn't hesitate a second. I would have bought it whatever it cost.

"I took it home, and I couldn't wait for any special occasion. I just rushed in the door and gave it to her. She couldn't wait, either. She put it right on and kept it on for a long time. She just didn't want to take it off at all, she loved it so much, just the way I knew she would. It was worth everything—that look of pleasure on her face. That's what money's for, when it's really worth something—to buy someone you love so much happiness. That meant more than any diamonds.

"I always loved hats just the way my mother loved hats. I loved buying them. I loved wearing them, but looking back, I think I enjoyed the hunt, finding them and being able to buy them, most of all. Some of them I didn't even wear once, but it was worth it. I was definitely a hat wearer, but I was even more a hat collector.

"I still have just about all of them I ever bought. I can go into the bedroom and try them on by myself all afternoon and be happy. Other people collect paintings to hang on their walls, and I've known some who bought more pictures than they had wall space to hang them on. For me, hats are works of art. I own more than anyone could wear, but show me a great hat and I can always make room.

"The funny thing is I live in California where nobody wears them, and many of my hats have never been out of my bedroom. Some people thought I ought to see a psychiatrist, but why spoil a good thing?"

In 1924, the Shuberts had announced they were looking for a play to star Mae West. In 1925, Mae's vaudeville tours ended, and she temporarily withdrew from show business. She was reading plays, looking for a vehicle that would be suitable for her.

"It was my mother who said, 'Mae, it's your great opportunity. There's only one person in the world who can write the best play for you:

"You!'

"I never had any ambition to be a writer. I only wanted to perform. I wanted to be on a stage with the biggest audience. I didn't want to be all alone in one of those garret places, trying to get inspiration. Being a writer seemed to go with being educated, and school gave me a headache.

"Being an actress and a writer both—that's the best thing you could be in life because you can be anyone you want to be. You just write yourself the part, and then you play it. That way you can skip the dull stuff. And when you get tired, you can be somebody else. And besides, I don't like sitting around doing nothing. I like to keep active. I'm like a boxer who's got to stay in training for the big one.

"So I became a writer because I needed material.

"I didn't like the material I was getting, and I liked to write my own character. My mother said to me, 'All you need to do is write the other characters, too.'

"There's my mother's confidence in me again. Well, why not? And she was right again.

"My mother always had perfect confidence in me. I can't put into words what that meant to me. She believed if I set my mind to something, I could do it and do it well. Well, why not? She was encouraging, strong and soft at the same time, never pushy, not at all like those stage mothers you hear about. She never pushed me any way except the way I wanted to go, so that doesn't count as pushing. She said, 'Dear, you always create your own character. Now, you have to take the next step. You just have to write something for the people around you, too.'

"Well, why not? Writing a whole play sounded like I'd have to work at it, and it would take at least a few weeks. Boy, was I wrong!

"I told her my problem was I didn't have an idea, and she said, 'Oh, that's not a problem. It will come to you.' My mother was an optimist, and she was always right where I was concerned."

Just after that, Mae was in her car, and the driver drove along the waterfront. "I saw a prostitute of the lowest order. She was carousing with a couple of sailors. She was all crumpled-looking, wilted like old salad, except for a turban replete with bird of paradise feathers."

Wherever she was, Mae began writing on any scrap of paper around. Jim Timony, at that time her lawyer-manager and lover, in that order, was astonished by her fervor. Mae had discovered that writing a play took more than a few weeks. "After that," she told me, "I always smiled a little to myself when people told me they were going to write a play or a script or a book in a few weeks. But I never said anything to them. They'd find out quick enough for themselves when and if they actually got started." Mae worked with Adeline Leitzbach, who was uncredited. Only after the completed play had been typed by Timony's secretary did Mae give it a title: *The Albatross*.

A writer later sued Mae, claiming that she had "borrowed" from his own *Following the Fleet,* a one-act play that Timony had bought as a vehicle for Mae in 1924. He contended that she had distorted his original moral message, but Mae was very proud that her play did *not* contain a moral message. His suit was dismissed. Mae decided that it was a good thing she had a lawyer as a lover or she would have needed to keep one on retainer. "The price of fame and success as a writer of plays," she said.

Mae's mother and Timony decided to produce *The Albatross* themselves, because they saw great promise in it, and because no producer had accepted it. Director Edward Elsner was the only one of several experienced directors they approached who liked it. That qualified him as the perfect choice. As soon as he read it in her hotel room, he was enthusiastic. He particularly liked the second act jazz band on stage, a feature all the other directors had hated. He told Mae that she had written a great play, and she agreed.

Mae changed the title to *Sex*. "I don't think I had a winning title. People were always asking me what an albatross was. When I changed the title to *Sex*, nobody asked me what it was. It was a simple title for a complex subject." Many years later, Mae defined sex for film critic and friend Kevin Thomas as "emotion in motion."

In spite of, or perhaps *because* of, the title, a scant few showed up for opening night in New London, Connecticut. Those who did mostly purchased balcony seats. Mae looked around the theater, and then she told the people in the balcony to move down to the best seats.

She considered closing after only one night because she didn't want to lose the money her mother had invested.

"My mother wouldn't hear of it. 'No, Mae,' she said. 'Give the word a chance to get around. You'll see.'"

Mae did see. When she arrived at the theater the next day, there was a line of more sailors than Mae had ever seen before in one place.

She could see they were excited. "They were about to be more excited. It was only a matinee, but the word had gotten around."

The problem was quite a different one from the night before. There weren't *enough* seats. " 'We'll have to have standing room,' my mother said, 'and the sailors won't mind standing.' They were a wonderful audience, and by that night, everybody was coming to the theater."

Initially, Mae used the pen name "Jane Mast" as playwright. Jane was her grandmother's middle name, as well as Mae's middle name, and Mast combined the first and last two letters of her own first and last names. She explained it was because she didn't want "to show off." The New York opening did not take place in the Theater District, but on the Upper West Side at Daly's 63rd Street Theatre, near Central Park, on April 26, 1926. Reviewers shunned *Sex* until it became too much of a cause célèbre to ignore.

Sex (1926)

The play opens in a Montreal brothel. It is operated by Margy La Mont (Mae West) and Rocky Waldron (Warren Sterling).

One of the younger girls, Agnes (Ann Reader), confesses to Margy that she is saving up to "get off the game." Margy would like to "go straight," too, if she could find the right man.

One evening while Margy is away, Rocky brings back an intended blackmail victim. The woman, Clara Smith (Eda von Buelow), is a thrill-seeking Southampton socialite. After drugging her, Rocky steals her pearls.

When Margy returns, an old flame is waiting for her. He is Lieutenant Gregg (Barry O'Neill), an officer in the Royal Navy. He wants her to join him in his next port, Trinidad.

They find Clara unconscious. As they revive her, police detective

Dawson (Gordon Burby) enters. Having seen Rocky leave with a suitcase, he is suspicious.

Clara accuses Margy of drugging her and then stealing her pearls. Dawson threatens to arrest everyone, but Clara bribes him.

Act 2 opens in the Café Port au Prince dance hall in Trinidad. Musical numbers are accompanied by an onstage jazz band.

Margy rejects Gregg's offer to retire with him in Australia. She has found a "clean, wonderful love" with young Jimmy Stanton (Lyons Wickland). Unaware of her past, Jimmy, having asked Margy to marry him, wants to introduce her to his parents in Southampton.

Agnes arrives in Trinidad, ragged and bereft of her hopes and dreams. As Margy and Jimmy prepare to leave for Southampton, Agnes drowns in the bay, a routine suicide.

Act 3 takes place in the living room of the Stanton mansion in Southampton. Jimmy's father, Robert Stanton (Pacie Ripple), receives Margy warmly, but his mother does not. She is Clara "Smith."

Jimmy brings home Gregg, whom he knew in Trinidad. Gregg repeats his offer to Margy, but she is determined to marry Jimmy, in spite of his mother.

Then, Rocky appears, threatening to expose Clara. Margy surprises him, armed with a pistol. She will expose him as an escaped convict unless he leaves and never comes back. Clara is grudgingly grateful to Margy.

Realizing she cannot escape her past, Margy tells Jimmy the truth, and leaves with Gregg.

"The reviewers not only shunned the play, but they shunned the title," Mae remembered. "When they finally *had* to review it, some of them didn't even mention the name of the play, and just called it 'that Mae West play.'"

Whatever the critics said or *didn't* say about *Sex*, it continued playing to full houses for almost a year. Then, on February 21, 1927, during the play's forty-second week, the theater was raided by the police.
Sex was denounced as "immoral" by the Manhattan district attorney.

While Mayor Jimmy Walker was out of town, the acting mayor,
Joseph McKee, ordered the raid. Mae posted bail after spending the
night in the lockup at the Jefferson Market Women's Prison.

The play reopened after Timony obtained a restraining order in the
State Supreme Court. A jury would have to determine whether *Sex*
was, indeed, "immoral."

"It wasn't so easy," Mae told me. "There really wasn't anything obscene in *Sex*. Racy, but never dirty, that was my specialty. Sexy, but in
good taste.

"There wasn't any nudity, and the language had less profanity than
some other Broadway shows. What they objected to was that it told
the truth. Prostitutes aren't the only ones who are in the sex business.
A lot of very respectable dames sell it, too, and for a high price, like
marrying a man for his money. And who's buying it? Men, of
course."

During the trial, Mae occupied herself by studying the expressions
on the faces of the jury and the onlookers rather than concentrating
on the legal proceedings. "I called my play 'a comedy drama,' but it
wasn't anywhere near as funny as that trial. The judge accused me of
showing contempt for the court, and I told him I was doing everything in my power *not* to show contempt for the court. I don't think
it helped my defense none, but I couldn't resist the temptation. I
should have saved the line for a play. I learned you'd better leave a
good joke at home rather than trying to be funny in court."

Mae was found guilty of producing an immoral theatrical performance and sentenced to $500 or ten days in the women's workhouse

on Welfare Island, now Roosevelt Island. The facility had originally been used as an isolation hospital for contagious disease patients. Its most famous tenant had been Mary Mallon, better known as Typhoid Mary.

"I was told I could pay the fine and get out of going to jail, but I made up my own mind. I decided it would be more interesting to go to prison. I was always fascinated by prisons and mental institutions and wondered about them. I wasn't going to be deprived of *that* experience. I saw those as ten very valuable days, a kind of working vacation."

Mae looked forward to an adventure, to exploring a side of life she hadn't previously encountered. She was curious about the life of a woman in prison and especially about the kind of women who went to prison. She thought that it could offer her material for her writing.

Matilda went to the courtroom every day. Timony told Mae that her mother had said to him, "If only I could serve her sentence for her."

Even her mother, who understood Mae better than anyone else, had not comprehended how much Mae was looking forward to going to prison. Mae had known men who had been in prison, who had served time, but never a woman. The men's stories had caused her to become more interested in the plight of the prisoners.

Mae valued her freedom highly and never easily accepted people telling her what to do. She became more stubborn if ordered to do something. She anticipated a certain amount of difficulty in having to conform and adjust to prison rules and regulations.

"I remember a teacher calling me re-*cal*-citrant," Mae said. "But I decided I was going to *attend* prison." She spoke in a tone more appropriate to going to school.

Her new experience began in the courthouse, where she remembered being treated very politely as she waited to be taken away to begin serving her sentence. When she first heard the sentence, it hadn't seemed very long, but as the moment to start serving it approached, "I had a few qualms, if you know what I mean." She was treated with respect and everyone addressed her as "Miss West."

She was taken to a room where she met some other women who were making the same trip she was. "There was one woman who seemed about seventy," Mae observed, "all worn-out, too old to be sent to prison, even if it wasn't a tough prison. It was technically a 'workhouse,' and they said we wouldn't be doing 'hard time,' whatever *that* meant. I wondered what *soft* time was."

When she talked with the woman, she learned that she was only forty, that she had been an orphan and didn't have any family. She had been all alone for more than twenty years and didn't have anyone with whom to talk. Her clothes were rags.

The woman's crime had been taking a pair of used shoes from a bin on the street without paying. Someone saw her, and she was too weak to run away. It was clear that she really needed the shoes.

"What was most terrible," the woman had told Mae, "was the shoes weren't my size. Too big was bad enough, but they were too small."

A young man Mae assumed was the prison driver led them away to their fate. "I was left behind," she said. "The plan was for him to come back and drive me there alone. I said that I could go in my own car, or I could go by taxi. The young driver was so disappointed.

"But the rules said I was supposed to go in the black car for prisoners, and there wasn't anybody there with the authority to change the rules, so I made the trip alone in the wagon. That made the young guy who was supposed to drive me pretty happy. He probably ate dinner on that one for years, I suppose, telling people what it was like taking Mae West to the slammer."

At the prison, Mae was greeted as a celebrity. Only in one respect was she treated as an ordinary prisoner. "Very ordinary, I thought at the time," Mae said, "but looking back, I think I got singled out.

"Would you believe, they made me strip. Naked. As naked as the day I was born. They said, 'Take off all your clothes,' and I said, 'I thought this was a respectable place.' They said they *had* to do it because it was the rules. I guess the other women did it in a group. I was solo. I preferred that.

"Anyway, it wasn't in the rules that they had to *look* that hard, was it? They kept me naked for what seemed longer than the required time. And every one of them took a mighty good look. Curiosity, I suppose.

"They had something to tell their friends. I gave them an eyeful, and they could give their friends an earful. I could feel their eyes running up and down my body. Maybe they were making comparisons. If *that's* what they wanted, they got the punishment they deserved.

"I've always been rather modest. I never liked being naked in front of women. I prefer men. I was there alone with all those women gaping at me in a way I reserve for just a few men in my life. Even then, I like to have the lights low. It always seemed kind of embarrassing with women, having dresses fitted in the dressing rooms, and in the theater, even in front of my sister, Beverly. The only woman I was never embarrassed in front of was my mother.

"They left me standing there a while, so I just sat down on the only chair. It was pretty embarrassing, I must say, though I think I put on a pretty good show for 'em.

"I'd brought my own silk lingerie to wear under the prison dress. I thought it would make me feel more like myself. The house-issue was so rough, it would have given my delicate skin a rash.

"There was this hag of a woman guard, and she piped up with, 'Where do you think you are? Saks Fifth Avenue?'

"I said, 'This rough stuff will give me a rash. I'm allergic.'

"The warden was a very decent man and understood my predicament. Later, he said to me, 'Miss West, I can't see any reason for you not to wear your silk panties, since it's a matter of your health. And you have an allergy,' he added.

"So, I slipped on my slip, too, and I saved the prison some money."

Mae was assigned a private room. "I was gonna get me a concrete bedroom.

"There was a wire screen on a window that offered a view of the Manhattan skyline from the East River. I have to say, the prison I was in was a very clean place. I'd heard stories, though, from men I knew who'd served a stretch in men's prisons. They said they had roaches there that were so big you could walk them on a leash.

"When I was inside and thought about leaving there, I thought about everything I would be doing as soon as I got out. *Everything!* When I first heard my sentence, I thought, 'Ten days, that ain't nothin'. A breeze. Ten days seemed hardly enough to get the feel of it.

"When that door closed behind me, I heard the sound of it closing and all of a sudden ten days seemed forever. I felt panic. A doctor, when I told him later, said it was routine claustrophobia. I never had 'routine' anything! Anyway, I got control of myself. I never wanted to surrender control of my emotions. Even in sex, I never wanted to do that, not completely anyway.

"I figured I was going to spend my spare time while being incarcerated scribbling. They couldn't keep you working all the time, even in the joint. I wouldn't have enough time there to write a book, but it would be enough to get perspective for a book. Or a play. Kind of a sequel to *Sex*. I thought it would be funny if the judge gave me the material for a play to be the sequel to *Sex*.

"But I couldn't do it. I couldn't move the pencil on the paper. Then, somebody told me it was against the rules to write in prison, and I'd have to show what I was writing to some 'higher authority.' I didn't feel like reading, either. Being there sure wasn't conducive to anything constructive or enjoyable.

"I wanted to help the girls there, but I couldn't do much. A lot of them had made just one mistake. They all wanted to meet me. They admired me. They weren't jealous. What I wrote was ahead of its time, and I took the chance of going to jail with what I put on stage.

"Being a writer, I was always listening to how people talk and especially *what* they talk about. You might think that in prison I'd pick up some pretty unusual stuff, but that wasn't how it was at all. They just talked about what every woman talks about, you know, clothes and shoes and things like that, stuff they wanted. In prison, women get shopping-deprived.

"Mostly they talked about what they didn't have, and that was usually a man. The unhappiest knew they didn't have a certain someone waiting for them on the outside. The few who thought they had a man waiting couldn't be all that sure.

"Part of the punishment of being incarcerated is taking away your love life. The girls said the guards seemed more interested in preventing them from finding some way of satisfying themselves than they were in anything else.

"One of the girls told me how they used to look forward to sausage for dinner. Then, the guards found out they weren't eating the sausage. So the cook started chopping up the sausage before it was served."

"The most terrible thing about the whole experience was some of the sad images I saw. I have always tried to keep my mind clear of bad things and to avoid filling it with bad images, 'cause once they're there, they don't ever go away completely.

"I think what I went through served some purpose, to help make a difference. I knew from the beginning that it could serve a purpose only if I made something happen. It's a wonderful thing if you know what you do makes a difference. My celebrity made that more possible.

"It was easy to make a few of the girls feel better. When the warden let me walk past the cells, I heard their screams of 'Mae! Mae! We love you. What do you think of our home? Do you wanna stay?' "

The warden, who had thought it would be a good idea to bring her through to provide some cheer, was astonished by the bedlam caused by just the sight of Mae West. Everyone on Welfare Island had heard that Mae West was coming there to serve her sentence, and they were all waiting for her.

The warden determined that Mae posed no danger and could be domiciled in his residence, along with six other women inmates who worked there. Cooking was already taken, as were serving, heavy work, and ironing. Mae said she didn't know how to cook anyway, so she was assigned chores like dusting the warden's law books in his library. "I was a pretty good duster, even though I'd had no previous experience."

Mae had brought along one of her favorite pictures of herself to help cheer her.

"What surprised me most," she said, "was the women prisoners weren't bitter. Bitterness is a terrible thing. Bitterness makes wrinkles. Outside and in. And once you get 'em, it's irreversible.

"One of the younger inmates was an attractive woman, pretty even in her prison dress. She wasn't really a woman, still a girl, and she told me her tale of woe.

"She was all alone in the world, and she had no one to care about her or to care for her. Her crime, she said, was prostitution. I asked her why she did it, a girl like her.

"She said she hated that life. She only resorted to it because she didn't know what else to do. I asked why she didn't get herself a job, a respectable one. She said she couldn't get one. No one would ever give her a chance because she didn't have the right clothes. And they always wanted to know what job you had before they'd give you one. How do you get started? It's the old chicken-before-the-egg or egg-before-the chicken thing.

"She said she tried, but she could never save enough, because before she could shop, she got too hungry and ate her dress by spending what she had saved on food. I couldn't imagine what it was like to be hungry. Once in a while for the sake of my figure, I gave up a second slice of chocolate cream pie, which was a sacrifice, but I knew that wasn't anything to do with real hunger.

"What did *I* know about hunger? I'd tried a little dieting from time to time, not that I ever really needed to, not for life or for the stage, but later for the camera, because the screen packs on about ten pounds, you know. So I had to think a little about it. And sometimes Paul [Novak] doesn't want me to have butter or marmalade, and especially not both together on my morning toast, and I have to kind of watch the chocolate situation.

"But I understood that it's a different kind of hunger when you impose it on yourself because you want to look your best and the kind you *feel* because you haven't got any money to buy food. Knowing you don't have any money for food has got to make you even hungrier. The girl was a desperate soul.

"She'd been back and forth several times. Five or six, she said. Can you imagine? She couldn't even remember the number of times. How could you lose count of a thing like that? I knew I'd remember my one time for all the rest of my life, no matter how long I lived.

"She told me about what happened to her the last time around.

"She held out as long as she could, and then she hit the street. She was always a little shy about approaching men, but if she stood there, they approached her. This particular evening, a very good-looking and well-dressed man greeted her. She said whatever it is she was supposed to say, and they agreed on the price of her sexual favors.

" 'Are you hungry?' he asked her. She answered that she was. 'Why don't we have dinner first?' he asked her. 'My treat,' he reassured her.

"They went into a nearby restaurant, a very nice one, but not too fancy, because she wouldn't have felt comfortable in her shabby clothes.

"He was very nice and encouraged her to order everything she wanted. 'It was lovely,' she sighed.

" 'And then what?' I asked.

" 'He arrested me,' she said. 'He was a detective, and that's how I ended up here.

" 'After a few arrests, they're on the lookout for you. You have to go farther away to where you aren't known. But I didn't have carfare or the strength.

" 'It's not all bad here. The food's terrible, but they let you have all you want, and you never go hungry. On the last day of my sentence, I always eat up so I'm as full as I can get, and that keeps me going for a few days on the street.' "

"The worst section in the place I visited," Mae told me, "was the one that seemed the jolliest. Some of the girls," Mae referred to all of the women there as "girls," "were really young, some of them were pretty, they were bouncing around with energy, and some of them were giggling.

"I said to the warden who was taking me around, 'What are they in for?' He said in this dark tone, the exact opposite of theirs, like we were at a funeral, 'They have venereal diseases. Most of them are going to die.'

"I asked him, 'Do they know?'

" 'They know.'

"When the girls saw me, they got even more animated. 'Hi, Mae. We love you, Mae!'

"They were warmhearted kids. *Too* warmhearted, I guess.

"I mingled for a while, and they told me about one girl who looked like she was about fourteen and a hundred and two at the same time. She was Chinese, and her father had smoked opium in front of her when she was a child. One day, she tried his pipe and got hooked. Poor kid.

"I never understood how people could want to escape from their lives into drugs and to make themselves less.

"Sex is beautiful, but these girls didn't know any better and let sex become their enemy. They were careless and they didn't get good advice. Tragic."

"I was so sad for these women, I forgot about myself. I was so overcome with sympathy, I forgot to have self-pity. But I was different, because I knew I was going to be specially watched over and given better treatment than the others. They couldn't afford to let anything happen to me. The press photographers had gathered, they told me, and they were pushing and shoving to get in position to get pictures of me. I could hear them as they increased in number. The reporters were usually courteous, but the photographers were dangerous when they began pushing and shoving to get that shot.

"They treated me with a lot of respect, I have to say, and if they got too *boi*sterous—that should be spelled B-O-Y-sterous—I'd just say, 'Hold off, boys. You don't wanna damage the merchandise.'"

Mae believed herself well protected by the presence of the press.

"They laughed and moved back. I could feel they were totally in my corner.

"They take extra care of celebrities because they can't afford to lose any, or have anything happen to 'Miss Mae West' when she's in *their* hands, if you'll pardon the expression."

"I got a million dollars' worth of publicity. I got an experience that changed my life. I thought it was going to give me material I could use in plays and movies, but I never imagined the kind of promotion and press I'd get. It was a million dollars' worth, when a million was really a million. But the most important thing turned out to be the way it changed me.

"I know it made me open my eyes and appreciate my life even more, though I can't say I was ever short on appreciation for what I got in life. I was lucky from the first moment I was born and opened my eyes in bed with my beautiful mother. I only knew love and that was worth everything.

"I never forgot all those unlucky girls who didn't get the start in life I did. It's a terrible shame the way the law is too ready to pounce, and that there isn't more attention paid to rehabilitation, getting these girls on their feet. It they were on their backs when they got out, it should've been for pleasure, not for pay.

"The warden suggested that I come and see them all, sometime. He said I brought inspiration to the girls, I was a role model, or however they said it then, an example. I thought that was nice, and I said I'd be back. I meant it when I said it. But, you know, I never did get back . . .

"I confess I didn't think about it at the time, but you know what really haunted me over the years? It was the innocents. What about the girls who were innocent who were there? A lot of them claimed it, but some of them really were, and we had no way of knowing which ones were telling the truth.

"Some of those girls were there just because they couldn't prove their innocence. It's supposed to have been a matter of the system proving the person is guilty, but it doesn't always work out that way.

"Years afterward, I found myself waking up in the middle of the night and thinking about some girl who might have been innocent. By then, she wouldn't've been a girl anymore, except in my dreams, Those girls never got any older in dreams, but always stayed the way they were when I saw them. Dreams are like that.

"I guess that whole experience affected me more than I knew.

"When I was serving my time, I had this *brilliant* idea.

"Every man and woman should serve a sentence of compulsory prison service.

"If every man and woman spent time there, just a day or two, they would reform the system right away. What's more, people would be pretty careful about what they did, so as not to end up there themselves."

One of Mae's backers for *Sex* was an Englishman named Owney Madden.

"Some people called him a gangster," Mae said, "but with me, he was always dolled-up. He wore white gloves. When he wore them inside places, sometimes someone asked him if he was cold. Well, no one who knew who he was ever asked him that question, or any other. But when he was with me, he was very polite. He would answer them, it was because he was sensitive to germs, but I always thought the real reason was because he didn't want to leave fingerprints.

"He had a beautiful Duesenberg. It was rumored that this car was bulletproof, but it was never tested when *I* was in it.

"He owned a participation in the Cotton Club, where Duke Ellington appeared. I sang a song about him in *Belle of the Nineties*: 'He's a bad man, but he treats me good.'"

Mae said she broke off the "*close* friendship," but kept the friendship because she never wanted to be involved with the mob.

It was through Madden that Mae met George Raft.

"His family name was Ranft, but he changed it to Raft," Mae said. "Like me, he had a German mother, and his father was from Germany, too. George was a Hell's Kitchen boy. In case you don't know what that means, it ain't no restaurant. It was the toughest neighborhood in New York City. I was a carefully brought-up girl from a very refined Brooklyn family, so you might say it was the immediate attraction of opposites.

"Raft was driving for Owney Madden, picking up and delivering money. He was someone they could count on to deliver the same amount of money he picked up. He was on a lower rung, but it was obvious he was going places, although at that time he was a driver without drive. He seemed satisfied with where he was, and he didn't have a thought to the future. He lived in the present.

"I like livin' in the present myself, but I couldn't ever not be sentimental about my early days, and I like to reminisce. And I like to look forward. I consider both of them, looking back and looking ahead, to be elements of the present.

"The only bad thing about looking back is if you look back with regret and want to change things in the past, which is too frustrating. It's foolish because it can't be done, so you have to skip that kind of thing as much as you can.

"I thought I could instill a little ambition in this good-looking, *very* masculine kid. So, I offered him a part in *Sex*. Well, he was interested in sex, but not in *Sex*. He didn't like the idea of being on the stage. I remember he said, 'Mae, I'm just not cut out for it.'

"Then, the next thing I know, he was on his way to being a movie star after he'd changed his name to George Raft."

Mae's next play, *The Drag*, was billed as "A Homosexual Comedy in Three Acts by Jane Mast." As with *Sex*, Edward Elsner was the director. The theme of the play, Mae told me, was "live and let love."

"I'm really proud of the way my gay following feels about me," she said. "I think they know I'm *with* them.

"I've always had a big gay following. Some of my biggest fans. They're entertained by me, but they also know what I'm trying to do for them.

"A lot of people gave me bad reviews because they said I glorified the homosexual, and they were punishing me. I wouldn't say I 'glorified' them. That's a little strong. But I didn't think they should be discriminated against. I wanted to tell a good story, and some homosexuals were part of my story.

"I had homosexuals I knew tell me that their dearest desire in life was to 'marry' their lover of the same sex. It didn't satisfy them just to live together, as if they were married. They were more anxious to be legally married than a lot of man-woman couples I knew. Certainly, more anxious than *I* ever was to be married.

"The freedom I wanted was to be able to live my private life in private, and the legality of a marriage didn't provide a guarantee that you were going to love someone all your life, or vice versa.

"I see marriage as essential for having children. That's different. Bringing children into the world is a tremendous responsibility. Children have to be provided for as much as possible.

"I'm talking about the male homosexuals because they were the ones I knew."

After two preview performances in Bridgeport, Connecticut, *The Drag* opened on January 31, 1927, and ran for two weeks. "The reviews were lousy, and the houses were totally sold out," Mae said. "I made $30,000."

A private performance was staged in New York for city officials, so they could judge whether *The Drag* was suitable for Broadway audiences. They were joined by twenty-five doctors. Their verdict was unanimously negative, as Mae heard the report.

The Drag (1927)

The first act opens in the library of Dr. James Richmond's New York mansion. It is afternoon.

Dr. Richmond (Elmer Grandin) advocates treating homosexuals with understanding, while his lifelong friend and brother-in-law, Judge Robert Kingsbury (A. Francis Lenz) regards them as degenerates who must be controlled by strictly enforced laws. The judge's son, Roland (Jay Sheridan), called "Rolly," is married to Richmond's daughter, Clair (Margaret Hawkins).

Two men, overtly homosexual, request an appointment with the doctor after office hours. One of them, David Caldwell (Allan Campbell), is pathologically depressed. His friend, Clem Hathaway (Leo Howe), has brought him there for treatment. David is so agitated, the doctor sedates him and leaves him in his office to rest.

Clair casually tells her father that she wants to make a European trip without her husband, Rolly. Clair explains why to her Aunt Barbara—Rolly has no interest in having a physical relationship with her.

Rolly readily agrees to the European holiday.

Clair has been seen at a social event with handsome Allen Greyson (Marshall Bradford), one of Rolly's business associates and an architect.

David groggily stumbles in from the office. He and Rolly instantly recognize each other as ex-lovers. The doctor reenters the office to find them struggling and assumes his drugged patient has become violent. Afterward, Richmond tells Rolly, "Thank God you're not what he is."

Act 2 opens in the Kingsbury residence drawing room, later that afternoon. Parsons (George Du Val), the butler, admits three obviously effeminate men who have come to plan a weekend party with Rolly. When Allen Grayson arrives, Rolly asks his friends to behave themselves. Allen has come to talk about an industrial building he is designing for the Kingsbury works.

After the other men have left, Rolly explains to Allen that he married Clair: not just because the two families encouraged it, but because it provided a convenient cloak for his homosexuality. Rolly tells Allen he is in love with him and hopes that Allen feels the same way toward him. Allen is appalled. He has fallen in love with Clair. He threatens to quit, but Rolly persuades him to reconsider.

Allen, no longer feeling an obligation to respect Rolly's marriage, proclaims his love to Clair. She is not displeased.

Act 3, Scene 1 takes place in the drawing room of the Richmond mansion, which has been converted into a small ballroom. A drag ball is in full swing, with bizarrely attired tranvestites and an onstage jazz band. Accompanying the solo songs and dances is a great deal of suggestive banter.

When the party gets too rowdy, Rolly sends the merrymakers home and goes upstairs.

A shot is heard off stage. Parsons enters, clearly shaken. He phones Judge Kingsbury, telling him that his son, Rolly, has been shot.

A police detective and Judge Kingsbury have just arrived at the opening of Scene 2, on the morning of the next day. Parsons tells of the argument Rolly had with Allen, and of his later seeing Clair in the arms of Allen. Allen becomes the prime suspect.

Dr. Richmond arrives with David. Dr. Richmond tells them that he is the killer, and David admits it, revealing that the judge's son had been his lover. The doctor pleads with the judge to be compassionate.

The judge, wanting to avoid the scandal of his son and the two families being linked to the homosexual world in a murder investigation, tells the inspector to report the shooting as a suicide.

"To tell the truth," Mae said, "at the time I had the idea, I was more interested in the big theatrical scene, the staging of forty men dressed as women, having a ball at a ball. What a great scene it was going to make!

"My play treated a part of life the way it was, and I didn't want to conjecture.

"I wasn't as interested or aware of the particular problems of my characters until I started writing about them. That's when I started to feel close to them and to feel what they were going through."

Reviews of *The Drag* during its two-week Bridgeport run ranged from unfavorable to scathing. Mae was accused of exploiting a serious theme to justify theatrical vulgarity. George Cukor thought differently.

"I saw *The Drag* and was impressed," he told me. "It needed a lot of work, but it was never dull.

"People said Mae wasn't sincere. They accused her of using a sermon to justify a burlesque show. I disagree.

"What was important was people were thinking, and thinking for themselves, not just canned thinking, pre-thought thoughts thought by others.

"Mae's heart was in the right place, at the right time."

"I learned two things for myself about playwriting," Mae told me. "My Platinum Rules, I call them, and I don't mind sharing them with you and your readers.

"Write about what you know, and entertain people, in reverse order.

"They say you can learn a lot by going to plays that were a success on Broadway. That didn't work for me, because I didn't want to be a copier. People could say a lot of things about me, but they couldn't say I was a copycat.

"Plays that fail, those are the ones to see. I began going to see shows people had invested a great deal of money and heart in, and they believed in what they were doing, and they'd guessed wrong for the audience. I tried to see where they'd guessed wrong. Those were expensive mistakes, and I tried to learn what I could, so I wouldn't make the same ones.

"Do you think you're going to have a best-seller?" she asked me.

"I hope so," I answered.

"You hope so, but do you *believe* you will?"

"No."

Mae disapproved. "If you have that attitude, how are you going to succeed, even with *me* as a subject?"

Mae's next venture was *The Wicked Age*, "a satirical comedy in three acts." In it, she plays a contemporary teenage girl. Her grandfather is played by Hal Clarendon, in whose stock company Mae got her theatrical start.

The Wicked Age (1927)

John Ferguson (Francis Reynolds), the town promoter, wants to hold a bathing beauty contest in Bridgeport, New Jersey, a quiet seaside area. Firmly opposing the idea is Robert Carson (Hal Clarendon), the town's most respected citizen. He doesn't want to change the quiet dignity of the town. He is voted down, however, and the contest takes place. Carson's teenage granddaughter, Evelyn (Mae West), is elected the first beauty queen.

Evelyn, known as Babe, a likable but overconfident "jazz baby," enters other beauty contests, including the one at Atlantic City, and wins them all, becoming a national celebrity. With her earnings from product endorsements, she buys a mansion in New York and becomes part of the Roaring Twenties fast-living scene.

She comes under the influence of a profligate French count (Robert Bentley), who introduces her to many new vices, among them, cocaine. Babe becomes an addict.

Her girlish buoyancy changes and she becomes abrasively unpleasant to everyone.

She is visited by a mysterious old woman who tells her that she was once a wealthy sought-after beauty. Then, when she lost her looks and her money, no one wanted her anymore. She warns Babe that this is her future, too, if she doesn't change her ways.

As the old woman's prediction seems to be coming true, Babe is saved by a wealthy young man, Jack Stratford (Raymond Jarno), who has fallen in love with the real person he perceives beneath her drugged exterior. He also helps to bring the count, who is a murderer, to justice.

Once again, Edward Elsner was the director, and a jazz band was featured on stage.

The reviews were no more unfavorable than they usually were for a Mae West play, but they were wrong in predicting its commercial success. The play opened at Daly's 63rd Street Theatre on November 4, 1927, and closed after nineteen performances.

Mae believed the real origin of "the magical title" that came to her, Diamond Lil, had its origin in the nickname her father had for her mother. West called his wife, Matilda, "Til," short for Tillie.

Matilda West didn't drink hard liquor, but she was particularly fond of champagne, and her husband would call her Champagne Til.

Thus, Diamond Lil's name really owed a great deal to Mae's beloved mother and also to Mae's father.

"When I was writing *Diamond Lil*, I had to get into character. I wanted to be inside Lil, writing from the inside out. I might put on a dress Lil could've worn. Or I'd put on a silk satin slip, and sometimes maybe a gown and a peignoir.

"But the big thing is I put on some diamonds and made sure that I was wearing them so they touched my skin. The feeling was very sensual and inspirational.

"I'd worked out a lot of stuff. I'd created my heroine. I had the lines, a lot of plot, some characters. It was going real well. But I was missing my leading man. Lil had to have a leading man, and I hadn't been able to imagine him. He had to be someone Lil could fall for big.

"So I went out one day, and I had my driver drive all around while I let my imagination go free. But it wasn't any use. It just wasn't happening. I had him drive in the Bowery.

"Then, I looked out the window, and I saw this shack, a real dump. I don't know what attracted my eye to it. Something. I mean it was *really* ramshackle. And there was this big American flag flying overhead. It was almost as tired-looking as the little building it adorned. I told the driver to go as slowly as he could.

"Then, I saw *him*. This really handsome man came out of the doorway. He had *everything*. Well, he *seemed* to have everything. He was pretty well covered up, so I couldn't get as good a look as I'd've liked. He was wearing this uniform with a cap. He wasn't a chauffeur. I recognized it. It was the Salvation Army. I was always attracted by the Salvation Army because I heard it was in my genes, that a West ancestor of my father, in England, was one of the founders of the Salvation Army.

"The captain in the Salvation Army walked straight to my car. I felt he was looking at me. I was certainly looking at him. He took off his cap. He had wonderful dark hair. I have a preference for dark hair in my men. I think it goes better with my blondness.

"He turned and started back to the shack. My driver had kept going, and we couldn't see him, so I said, 'Go back quick.'

"I wanted another look, but he was gone. He was gone so completely, for a second, I thought he was one of those aberrations. I thought to myself, Why did he come out at just that moment? What made him do it?

"Well, I know now, and I guess I kind of started to know then. It was pretty clear. There really was no other possible answer.

"It was The Forces. I was feeling a supernatural presence.

"I wrote," Mae said, "that after the success of *Diamond Lil*, Lil and I together climbed the ladder of success, wrong-by-wrong. But one thing I want people know. I'm all of Diamond Lil, but she's not all of me."

Diamond Lil (1927–1928)

During the 1890s, Diamond Lil (Mae West) is the powerful mistress of Gus Jordan (J. Merrill Holmes), a corrupt Bowery ward boss who is the owner of a dance hall, which is also a brothel and the center of profitable vice. She herself manages many of his illicit operations, everything from shoplifting to the trafficking of drugs. She has no moral compunctions about what she does, only that a woman in her social position has no other means of survival. She is satisfied with her lot until a man comes into her life and challenges her happy amorality.

He is Captain Cummings (Curtis Cooksey) a Salvation Army officer who has opened a mission in the Bowery to save the downtrodden. His main attraction for Lil is that he seems able to resist her charms.

There are several subplots, including Lil's attempts to save a young woman from a life of exploitation by men, the death threats of an ex-lover who has just escaped from prison, the menace of an ambitious rival's takeover of Jordan's dance hall, and the ever-present danger of law enforcement officials who cannot be bribed.

At the end, the dance hall is raided by the police. Captain Cummings turns out to be "the Hawk," a policeman in disguise who has been spying on Jordan's unlawful operations. When Lil defiantly holds out her hands for him to handcuff her, Cummings takes her hands into his own and informs her that *he* hasn't made the conquest, *she* has.

"Before 1929," Mae reminisced a bit wistfully, "America was like a big candy store.

"There was this wild bull market going on, and the chorus boys and girls were getting richer every day, the doctors were rich, everybody was rich—on paper.

"Sometimes the actors could hardly remember their lines, they were so busy adding up their profits in their minds, even when they were on stage.

"I didn't have money in stocks because that kind of paper didn't seem real to me. I never understood why they called them 'blue chips.' They weren't chips and in a few years they were just good for bad wallpaper. I always liked investing in things I could see and touch and enjoy. I wasn't so rich I didn't have to make choices. I was still putting some of my own money behind my career, and whatever else I had went into diamonds. The country was on the gold standard. I was on the diamond standard.

"If the market in diamonds fell out of bed, I could always wear them. They'd always be just as beautiful.

"But I couldn't help but be pretty upset for all those people. Poor things. They were rich, and then they were poor. Really poor. I hope they enjoyed their happiness when they thought they were rich. You want to enjoy happiness when you have it. Then, after that, no one can take that away from you."

While Mae was still appearing in the wildly successful *Diamond Lil*, rehearsals for her next play, *The Pleasure Man*, were held after her performances in *Lil*. Even though she would not be appearing in *The Pleasure Man*, she attended every rehearsal, which necessitated a long drive from the Broadway Theater District to the Bronx.

"My best lover," she told me, "was a Frenchman who would pick me up in his car after *Diamond Lil* and take me over to the other theater to rehearse *Pleasure Man*. I always was interested in foreign affairs. One Saturday night we were at it till four the next afternoon. A dozen of those little rubber things. Twenty-two times. I was sorta tired. Like I always said, 'It's not the men in my life, it's the life in my men.'

"He said he'd never done it more than twice in a night, and that only a few times. It shows you, you never know what you're capable of until you do it.

"I'm sure he never achieved anything like that again, because he would've needed me, but I think the memory of that night gave him enough satisfaction to last a lifetime. Over the years, I've had a few giggles over it myself.

"I'll tell you, dear, when I was a girl, it was generally believed that sex was a man's thing. Men were open about what sex meant to them. They could afford to be frank. That's frank with a small 'f.'

"Men are simple beings. Women are the complex ones, and the secretive ones. We're taught, without anything being spelled out, by example. The 'o' word was not supposed to be part of our vocabulary. I felt it before I knew what to call it."

The Pleasure Man opened at the Bronx Opera House on September 17, 1928, and then moved to the Boulevard Theatre in Jackson Heights. It was not reviewed by the New York papers. Variety reported, "That West girl knows her box office."

The Broadway opening at the Biltmore Theatre on October 1 was featured in the newspapers, but not in the conventional manner. Police raided that performance and the next one a few days later. Each time, Mae put up bail for all of the almost sixty cast members.

When it became apparent to Mae that the city intended to prosecute her under the penal code for indecency, which would expose everyone in the cast to the possibility of prison terms, she closed the show after only two and a half performances. Mae said. "Only the lawyers would get rich."

The Pleasure Man (1928)

Most of the action takes place on a theater stage and backstage in the dressing rooms. Upstage, several dressing rooms stand next to each other, their fourth walls open to the audience. Several stories unfold in these dressing rooms, the main one being that of Rodney Terrill (Alan Brooks), a handsome matinee idol.

Terrill is an unrepentant womanizer. He tries to seduce any woman he meets, married or single, never mindful of their own feelings for him and the damage he might do to them and their lives. One girl, Mary Ann (Elaine Ivans), comes to him and tearfully tells him she is pregnant and she expects him to keep his promise to marry her. Terrill scarcely remembers her and certainly not such a promise. She has an abortion.

When she dies after the abortion, the girl's brother, Ted Arnold (Edgar Barrier), the house electrician and a medical student, sets out to castrate Rodney with a scalpel. He succeeds, but in the process kills him. When he is told that what he did was not only murder, but obscene, he replies:

"Men can fight dirt with dirt and still fight for what's clean. I know what I did was right, and I'm glad, glad!"

Mae never gave up on *The Pleasure Man*. She continued to hope for another stage production. In 1975, she rewrote the play as a novel. By that time, the theme of castration was not so shocking; Tennessee Williams had already used it. Mae also had hopes for a *Pleasure Man* film.

"You've got to keep the right thoughts in your mind," Mae told me in 1980. "People think that sex has to end at a certain point. It doesn't have to end, unless you think it does. It can go on as long as you do. Same for work. I'm never going to stop working. Nothing's brought me more happiness than my work. My work's always been my whole life. I have projects now. I still want to see *Pleasure Man* made into a film. I did it as a book, but it's really a play.

"I wrote it in 1928. It had an advance ticket sale of two hundred thousand dollars when a dollar really was a dollar. But the police came carrying nightsticks and arrested everybody in the show, while I was a few blocks away in *Diamond Lil*.

"It's a story that's as true as ever. It's about Rodney Terrill, a man who used women.

"There were people who said *I* used men. Well, maybe my character did, sometimes. But I didn't use men. I enjoyed them. Anything I did, I did because they wanted to. And they wanted to again.

"Rodney Terrill was never particular about what women meant to themselves, only about what they meant to him. I've seen lots of women get into that position. I felt sorry for them. I'd never let it happen to me. I had a lot of sympathy and understanding for the romantic innocence and the high expectations of the pregnant young Mary Ann, who can't believe Rodney won't marry her. I always respected honest emotions. I couldn't bear her being disappointed.

"The character I identified with is Helen Webster. I wrote that part for myself. I still want to play it. She's not a pushover. And she won't have anything to do with married men. She's like me. Even in a play or a film, I don't have anything to do with a married man, if I know it. I got fooled once, and there might've been times I didn't know about."

Mae told me that she wanted actor Laurence Harvey to play Rodney Terrill in the film version of *Pleasure Man*. "I thought he'd be great. He was a really attractive man. He was fascin-atin'. It wasn't just that he was good looking. He had something extra. Maybe it was a look in his eyes. You felt he knew special, secret things, and you wanted to find out what they were. He had real style.

"The Pleasure Man was a cad. That goes without saying. But attractive, yes. He had to be, because women were falling all over themselves over him. I, myself, couldn't understand it, because I couldn't understand how women could be such fools; but I had to believe it, because I'd seen it.

"So many women think a man holds the key to their happiness, and it's true only because women make it so. Men are all alike, except the one you've met who's different. Women feel he holds their happiness in his hands.

"I always liked having a lot of men around. On a rainy night it's like having more than one book to choose from, only better. Men's thoughts and ambitions were like mine. If you were out in the world doing interesting things, it would be men you'd meet. It was a man's world, and you'd be with men because men were the ones doing things.

"I found one man who had beautiful hair, another had great muscles, and another one . . . umm. I didn't see why I should deprive myself of anything, so a lot of men was better for me than just one man. That way I could enjoy what was great about each one, but I wasn't tied to him. I didn't have to waste any time worrying about what he didn't have and trying to change him.

"I'm a one-man woman—one man at a time. I enjoy a forty-ripened man who's been around. Of course, there's fun in teaching a young man. All of my ideas about women are what men's ideas are about women because all I know is what men told me. I never mingled with too many women.

"Men were so surprised by me, I knew there must be a lot of women out there doing it badly. Or maybe not doing it bad enough. Women spend too much of their lives saying no. Most women are so used to practicing no, they get to stay home and wash their hair on Saturday night. They expect a man to answer all their problems for them. There's nothing better than a man's shoulder to lean on, but you don't want to lean too hard.

"*The Pleasure Man* was put out of other people's misery," Mae said.

"The New York critics had a field day with *The Pleasure Man*. The only thing bad they didn't say about it was that it was dull. What I know is, people can have dull at home, but on stage they want excitement. And you've got to keep surprising audiences.

"The play shows some homosexuals in drag. I fought for gay rights before it was the thing to do, before it became fashionable. In the twenties, the police were really hard on them, and I did my best to show how wrong that was.

"I always tried to treat everyone with understanding. I remember once when one of the major performers [Lester Sheehan] in *Pleasure Man*, who plays Queenie, was having a kind of tantrum at rehearsal, and everyone was all upset.

"I went right over to him and I said, 'Queenie, dear, what's wrong?'

"I spoke to him in a respectful and sympathetic voice, and he said, 'I just want to scream!'

"I said, 'Well, why *don't* you, dear?' I said it like it was a perfectly natural thing to do. He let out one terrific scream, and then he was just fine."

In May of 1929, while performing, Mae had some trouble with abdominal pain, which occurred as frequently as once a week, and then more often. Sometimes the pain recurred more than once a week and it lasted several days. As there were more days with the pain than without it, Timony and Mae became increasingly worried. As her closest friend, Timony was even more worried than Mae.

Mae admitted to me that, although she was worried, she was more afraid of doctors and especially of hospitals than she was of the pain.

When Timony succeeded in persuading her to go to the doctor—doctors, in fact, since none of the doctors was able to find anything wrong with her—the various doctors, each on his own, made the same suggestion. Mae should go to the hospital for tests. Timony took her there, where the suggestion was made that exploratory surgery was necessary.

"That was more exploration than I was interested in," she told me. "I think I set a new speed record getting out of there."

She left carrying some of her clothing, not having bothered to put on any undergarments, "only enough clothes to not break any laws pertaining to decency.

"Do you know what they wanted to do?" she called back to Timony, who, having been an athlete, was right behind her. "They wanted to cut my skin, to give me a scar. I'd rather die than be disfigured."

They set out to find another way. Timony found Sri Deva Ram Sukul, known as the Sri. He was an Indian mystic.

Mae explained her problem to him. He said it would not be difficult to cure her. He chanted a Hindu prayer. Then, with both of them standing, he behind her, he pressed on her stomach with his hands for two or three minutes. Then suddenly he released his hold.

He assured her that she was cured and told her that she would never be troubled again by that pain.

That was not enough for Mae. She wanted to know what had been the cause of her agony, days and nights of anguish, and terrible fretting about her career.

The Sri knew the cause. "Envy," he told her. "Someone who envied you put a curse on you, all because of her terrible envy."

That made sense to Mae.

Matilda was diagnosed with terminal cancer of the liver. Her husband, Beverly, and John were told. Matilda was also told all of the diagnosis except for the word "terminal," but she had a pretty good idea of her limited future without the confirmation, because she knew how she felt. She understood that she would not be getting better. She did not want Mae to know how bad it was.

Mae's father made efforts to tell Mae the truth, but he couldn't speak the terrible words. Knowing Mae's bond with her mother made it more terrible to have to tell his daughter the doctors had said there was no hope. Jack West believed there was always hope. He'd been in many fights in which he was the underdog. After all, doctors didn't know everything, and they didn't know the strength of Matilda's will. His wife certainly was a strong-willed woman. Underneath her demure femininity, she was not a person to give up easily. Still, Mae had to be prepared for the worst.

Mae felt she had just the answer to brighten her mother's spirits. She had to admit her mother was ill, but happiness was important to getting well. Mae believed if she could cheer up her mother that it would be a step on the way to Matilda's recovery.

Mae remembered how she and her mother giggled together when Mae was a child and her mother was almost still a girl. No one else knew at what they giggled. Some of the time, they didn't know themselves.

"I wanted to tell her every good thing that ever happened, every treat, so we could giggle together, and my pleasure made her pleasure greater and her pleasure made mine greater.

"Maybe she was the only person I ever giggled with. Giggling is precious. Nothing like a good giggle. It's so silly and carefree.

"I never wanted to tell her everything I worried about or to tell her anything that would make her worry or be unhappy."

Mae's idea was to take her mother on a shopping spree. It would be the shopping spree of her mother's dreams. While Mae's father never said a word about what Matilda spent on a dress, and even encouraged her to buy more, Matilda knew there were some limits. There didn't have to be any limits to their spending now. Because of the great success of *Sex* and *Diamond Lil*, Mae was rich, and she would give everything she had to make her mother well and happy.

Mae would take her mother in a limousine with a driver, and they would go to all of the best shops in Brooklyn and Manhattan, and buy dresses for her mother, and shoes, gloves, hats.

Mae wondered about the size of the dresses. Her mother had dieted too strenuously, Mae thought, and she weighed less than her best weight. But soon she would gain some weight. The answer would be to buy the dresses in both sizes, so her mother could wear some of them right away, and the others as she recovered.

When it came time to go on the shopping expedition, Matilda wasn't feeling well enough. Mae told her she would shop and bring home the packages. Mae visited all of her mother's dressmakers and shops until they closed. Some stayed open longer for her. Mae could hardly wait to get home and see her mother's face light up.

When Mae arrived back at home, her mother was waiting for her. Matilda seemed to be glowing. It was late, but she didn't seem tired. She had fixed her hair and put on light makeup. Mae thought again, as she always did, how beautiful her mother was.

They opened every box, tearing the wrapping paper in their haste. Matilda tried on all the dresses. Mae had known which would be her favorites. There were enough new dresses to last for years. Some of the dresses were elaborately beaded, trimmed, and embroidered for cocktails or parties. Most were afternoon dresses for promenades.

"It's just the beginning," Mae told her mother, though both of them knew it wasn't.

It was as if both of them, though neither would ever have admitted it, believed that somehow Death could be fooled and defeated, that Death would not come and take away someone who had so many new dresses yet to wear.

When Mae came home, Matilda saw to it that the kitchen was filled with every enticing delicacy Mae craved, especially sweets. Matilda even made her own warm apple strudel fresh from the oven, one of Mae's favorites.

Matilda knew how to use makeup skillfully to enhance her natural beauty and also how to conceal the ravages of her illness. She fixed her blond hair and drew on her total reserve of energy in order that Mae would not notice her rapidly diminished state. Matilda reassured Mae that all would go well, that Mae need not worry. She encouraged Mae to build her career, no matter what.

When Mae visited, Matilda spent what little energy she had left dressing up for her daughter, and then, when Mae left, she would collapse.

Mae had received a telegram from her father informing her of Matilda's worsening condition while she was performing *Diamond Lil* in San Francisco, just before the company was to leave for Los Angeles and the last stop on its West Coast tour. Mae continued with *Diamond Lil* in Los Angeles for some performances and then she moved to the Jackson Heights Shubert Theater in Queens, New York. It was during a performance of the play there that she was informed of her mother's serious downturn.

Timony encouraged her to stop the performance immediately, give the people back their money, and to rush home to her mother. Mae could not bear to face the full gravity of the situation and she felt her mother would not want her to stop the show. As the performance ended, Mae rushed home, arriving just in time.

Matilda Doelger West died of liver cancer in Brooklyn on January 26, 1930. She was fifty-six years old.

"I nearly went out of my mind when my mother left," Mae told me. "I didn't think I could bear it. I didn't know if I could live through it. I didn't feel I wanted to. What saved me was I could hear in my head what my mother would say to me. She would be thinking first of me, the way she always did. She would want me to be happy and have a wonderful life and to understand how happy our bond and my success had made her.

"I said, out loud with no one there, 'I'll never perform again.' As soon as I heard myself saying it, I knew how much that would hurt my mother. I knew I had to go back to work, for Mother's sake, if for no other reason. It had been her life and her success, too. Work saved me."

Mae continued forcing herself to go on stage for each performance after her mother's death. Then she would become hysterical afterward in her dressing room.

"When my mother died, just living was hard, but going on stage . . . I did it because I knew she would've wanted it that way. Then working made it easier.

"That was before I understood she would always be with me. She's here right now, you know. I don't mean so I can see her or hear her voice, but her presence is always with me and will be with me as long as I live.

"When my father saw how hard I took it after my mother died, he said to me. 'Mae, I don't want you to be around when I pass away. I'd never want you to go through that again.' "

Mae said she didn't say anything. She realized that her father hadn't understood the way she felt about her mother. He thought she felt the same way about him. "Just as well," Mae said. "I had feelings for my father, but I was never close to him like I was to my mother.

"I even felt angry at my father for not letting me know sooner how bad it was. Later, I understood what he was telling me I wasn't listening to, because I was sure we'd find an answer. I made excuses for him because you don't want to be angry at your own father, especially at a time like that when he was grieving.

"But no one was grieving like I was. I cried for days. I couldn't stop crying except whenever I was on stage. They thought my heart was going to give out. After a few days, I was so hysterical, I lost my voice and couldn't speak for a few days. That meant I *really* couldn't perform.

"Maybe losing my voice was a good thing, because I might have said something to my father I would've been sorry for later.

"It was like I'd died, but I had to keep walking around. I couldn't stand feeling as much pain as I was feeling.

"I don't live my life looking back with a lot of what-if's. I live in the present, and I enjoy looking forward. If you live in the past, you can't get back what you lost. You can only lose what you have in the present.

"The only time I found myself living in the past was when my mother died. I wanted to turn back time. I wanted to have a few of those days back with her.

"I felt if only my father had told me sooner just how bad it was, maybe I could have changed what happened. I guess he didn't know exactly, and maybe he shut it out, like me. I would have stopped everything and rushed back to be with my mother every minute. I didn't have long and maybe if I'd been there, maybe I could've thought of something and done something to help her, like she always did for me. I know she told him not to bring me back from performing because that's the way she was. He shouldn't've listened, but it was hard to go against my mother's wishes.

"She had been dieting and she had weakened her resistance and hurt her liver, and developed pneumonia, but it seemed she was on the mend when her heart weakened and gave out.

"I always feared burial underground when I was a child. I read a story about it, and I never got over it. I didn't want it for myself, and I didn't want it for my mother, so I bought a mausoleum in Brooklyn for all of my family.

"My mother never got to see me in pictures, but she always knew I'd be making them. She thought movies had a great future and that they were just waiting for me, and I was waiting for them to talk. It isn't that I couldn't have made a silent movie. I wouldn't've minded doing one. But words and lines are my stock-in-trade. I could have gone on the screen as titles, but they wouldn't have had my voice or delivery.

"I continued all my life to talk things over with my mother, in my head, long after she had passed from this life. I hoped her spirit would come to me. I knew she would have, if she could have. Maybe she did come and I didn't know how to see her or hear her. I tried, but I never reached the point where I saw my mother. But I shared my life with her because she was a part of me.

"My mother wanted to be an actress. She finally got that through me. She always came to see me. She had a box seat. I took her out on the stage with me for a curtain call before she died. That really made me happy, that I could give her that. On a New Year's night, I was playing with Harry Richman. Everyone came onstage, and I brought her out. She loved it. She lit up. I threw the audience a kiss, and she did, too.

"The hardest thing that happened to me in my life was when my mother left us. I never got over it.

"One thing I knew. I never wanted to love anyone that way again.

"And I never did."

The Constant Sinner was based on Mae's successful first novel, *Babe Gordon*, which was published in November 1930. When she adapted the novel to the stage, a contest was held to choose a better title, and *The Constant Sinner* was the winner. The prize was $100—in 1932, enough money to buy last year's Ford. Most of the action in both the novel and the play takes place on the fringes of Harlem, where black people and white people mix freely.

The Constant Sinner (1931)

Babe Gordon (Mae West), a white woman, is strongly attracted to prizefighters. One of them, Bearcat Delaney (Russell Hardie), becomes so obsessed with her that he throws away a promising career in the ring to marry her. When Babe tires of him, he is reduced to driving a cab for a living.

Babe's next conquest is Money Johnson (George Givot), a black drug dealer. He recruits her to sell cocaine, heroin, and morphine to addicts while working in a department store. While Johnson is serving a three-month sentence in prison, the department store owner's handsome son, Wayne Baldwin (Walter Petrie), falls in love with Babe. He puts her up in a Park Avenue apartment.

When Johnson is released from prison, he comes to see her in the apartment. Baldwin finds out and kills him. Delaney, still Babe's husband, is arrested and tried for murder. With the help of a legal defense provided by Baldwin, he is acquitted on the grounds of justifiable homicide—the unwritten law.

Although Babe goes back to her husband, she still sees Baldwin.

After tryouts in Atlantic City, *The Constant Sinner* opened on Broadway at the Royale Theatre on September 14, 1931. Reviews were unfavorable. Mae was generally praised as a performer, though unanimously ridiculed as a playwright. The language and situations were condemned as vulgar, indecent, and immoral, but the legal sanctions she feared would be imposed against her as in her earlier plays did not happen.

The play closed on November 7, after sixty-four performances. Some of the material, notably the relationship of the boxer to an irresistible woman and that woman's attraction to a rich playboy, was used again in the 1934 Mae West film, *Belle of the Nineties*.

Mae briefly worked on the idea for another play she had written, called *Frisco Kate*. In it, she would have been the only woman on a ship full of motley sailors. Mae dropped the project because it didn't hold even her own interest.

"If I admit it," Mae told me, "and it's hard speaking the words out loud so I hear 'em, I date my happiness before my mother left and after. I never had the same carefree total happiness after that. There was always a shadow over it.

"There were two kinds of happiness in my life. One was the carefree, joyful, taken-for-granted kind of happiness I had before my mother left us. It took me a few years, maybe three, not to feel numb.

"Then, there was what there was afterwards. It was a restrained pleasure. I enjoyed things, but there was always a shadow. I knew my mother wouldn't have wanted that. Last thing she'd ever want. But I never had the kind of happiness I'd known with her.

"It was like I'd lost my arm, both arms."

Chapter Four

---◆---

HOLLYWOOD

(1932–1943)

I
T'S A FACT that I saved Paramount Pictures," Mae told me. "It's an 'incontroversial' fact that in 1933, Paramount was going down the drain. If they hadn't had me then, Paramount wouldn't be here now." Mae's film *She Done Him Wrong* brought in the box office receipts Paramount needed.

"Mr. Zukor [Adolph Zukor, then head of Paramount] told me so himself. 'You saved us, Mae,' he told me. That was kind of an emotional moment. But he didn't say it in front of anyone else. It wasn't something he was going to advertise. But I didn't need a lot of people knowing it. *I* knew it.

"I noticed right away that movies were different from the stage, because they could come in so close on you, they saw stuff you'd never seen. When they blew your face up so big, you could see every little thing, audiences got to know you better than you knew yourself. It's a good thing I had a perfect complexion that doesn't go away. Even when I was a girl, I never had pimples.

"In vaudeville or on the stage, you have to think of the public in the last rows of the balconies. You don't want them to leave the theater and go straight to a hearing doctor because they thought they've gone hard of hearing. I never had any trouble with that. I could go back and forth between the stage and the screen. I love them both, but, oh, that permanence of the film!

"It was nice to have the live audience, but the films are so important. We can look at them now. All those people who weren't even born when the films were being made are my fans now. My pictures are on television just about every night. I hope you've been watching. I haven't changed, have I? [She doesn't wait for my answer.] Men were always most of my audience. They got to the box office first! But seriously, I used to wonder about it. Even when I was doing the nightclub act, there were still a lot more men in the audience. But some of the men brought wives, so I decided to ask the women why they were there. 'It's for our husbands.' "

Mae arrived in Hollywood with more than thirty years of onstage experience with audiences. Her credits were impressive.

She had performed extensively in vaudeville, with stock companies, and on Broadway. She understood audiences from firsthand experience. She had carefully observed their reactions and adjusted her performances to their tastes.

She had written most of her own material, and had created her own unique stage persona. She had starred on Broadway in her own plays and had written two novels, *Babe Gordon* in 1930 and *Diamond Lil* in 1932. "I didn't go to Hollywood humble," she told me. "And I had my carfare home.

"After what people have been paying on Broadway to see me, I'm a big bargain for the movies," she said shortly after her arrival in Hollywood. "They'll turn out in droves."

She told me, "Hollywood wanted me. I wasn't sure yet I wanted Hollywood."

Paramount Studios was in bad financial condition, and it was reported and generally believed to be on the verge of bankruptcy. The studio was considering selling its theaters to the Loew's group in order to raise money during the Depression. At that time, plates were often a greater attraction than pictures at theaters. People went to the movies each week to complete their free dishware sets.

Mae had made her decision to work for Paramount, even though she said she had received other offers. The other studio offers were vague, while Paramount's deal, which Timony had negotiated with her input, was exactly what she wanted. What she preferred was the chance "to explore," which she always liked, meaning that she would not be required to sign a long-term contract unless she chose to do so. Paramount also had a reputation for making the kind of comedies Mae could respect, like those by the Marx Brothers.

Mae remained wary, however, rather than exhilarated about making her first film, even though she was told she would have a starring part in a perfect vehicle for her talents as her second film.

It turned out to be true.

"They'd promised to show me a script as soon as I got to California. I was willing to take a chance. All my life, I'd been taking chances, and I hadn't done so bad.

"People said to me, 'You haven't got anything to lose. You can sit in the sun while you wait.' Well, it's the last thing in the world I'd ever do, expose my delicate complexion to the sun. I always keep the drapes drawn in my apartment. Outside, I like big hats that offer shade, or a nice black veil.

"When I got there, I found out right away that they hadn't given me my script before I started out because it wasn't a question of perfecting it, it was a question of writing it. They were paying me, but they didn't think anything of wasting my time.

"Every week, they promised. After something like twelve weeks, Jim [Timony] told me, 'Treat it like a paid vacation. You're getting all your expenses and you went on salary the minute you started your trip. If it doesn't work out, you've had a holiday in California. Give it a chance. The films could be great for you. The size of the audience can be tremendous. It expands your audience all over the world. You have nothing to lose.' "

Mae had the greatest respect for Timony's intelligence. "I loved his brain and I liked what he was saying about the geographic implications, and how many more people were going to see me perform. And doing something new was something I always found stimulating."

When she agreed to go to Hollywood, Mae let it be known to Paramount that she required a place to stay that was near the studio. "I said that I wanted to be walking distance from the studio, but I didn't really mean it. I wasn't planning to walk.

"They found the Ravenswood for me. It was less than a mile from Paramount. I could've walked, but I never did."

The Ravenswood, at 570 North Rossmore, became Mae's permanent residence for the rest of her life. She found a special significance in her apartment number, 611: Six plus one plus one equals eight, which her mother considered her lucky number and Mae's, too.

"When I first came out to Hollywood, a cameraman asked me, 'What's your best side, Mae?'

"I told him my right and my left. I don't have a bad side."

George Raft had listened to Mae's advice and became an actor. "Then, the next thing I know, he was on his way to being a movie star, and he was coaxing me out there, to Hollywood. Well, it didn't take too much coaxing. It sounded worth trying and I didn't mind being close to George Raft.

"The producers had Texas Guinan [a famous New York cabaret personality] on their minds for my part in *Night After Night*, and Raft told them he knew a great gal who would be even better, and she was already a Broadway star—me. He could give a good pitch about all kinds of things, which I knew from *very* personal experience. It wasn't easy to say no to him, and why would you want to? I know I preferred to say yes to him.

"He had credibility with the producers because he was their new star, and he had talent. He persuaded them, and he persuaded me to try my, umm, wings in Hollywood. He told me I'd conquer the screen, and it would change my life. And it *did* change my life.

"I thought Raft had it, in every way, on-screen and off. I'd picked him out early, in New York when I first spotted him. He was hard to miss."

Although Mae was already one of the brightest stars on Broadway, the magnitude of her New York fame did not precede her when she reached Hollywood. New York and California seemed much farther apart in 1932. Broadway's urbane, sophisticated audiences were small compared to those of the movies, yet Mae expected star treatment.

"I'd been brought out from New York to make a movie, and they left me sittin' on my reputation for a couple of months. I told them if *they* didn't get a move on, *I* was gonna wend my way back to Broadway.

"The studio reminded me that I couldn't go anywhere because I was under contract to them, and they were paying me to be there, doing nothing. I told them in a very ladylike, but no-nonsense way, that they could keep their money and even get a refund from me, but I wasn't sticking around like a prisoner. They thought I should be happy getting a little extra time off, but it wasn't the way I was built. I wanted to work, and for me, my work in life was performing.

"If they wanted to throw their money away, that was their business, but they couldn't throw away my time. Time is more valuable than money, anyway. Money is interchangeable. And you can always get more money. You can't never get more time, no matter what you do. I think you should do everything you can to preserve the quality of your life, and maybe good, clean living gives you some more days. I don't know. I guess I think it's mostly each person's destiny.

"My mother, for example, lived perfectly. She was dainty in everything she did. She ate daintily. Never too much. She was careful crossing the street, especially when she had us children with her. Even so, she was taken away early. It was her destiny.

"After my mother passed away, people told me it would get easier, with time, to face my loss. Some people said to me, it was a good idea for me to go to Hollywood and have a change of scene from Brooklyn and New York, because I couldn't stop grieving for my mother.

"How could a change of scene help me? It would have had to be a change of me.

"The reminders of my mother were constant, and I didn't want to get away from them. I wanted to hold on tightly to every memory. I wanted to keep her with me as much as possible. It was her memory that was my comfort."

Mae stopped speaking. She had to pause before going on.

"I started packing to leave Hollywood," she continued. "That took a lot of time and care because of my beautiful dresses. I had the most beautiful clothes in the world, and I am speaking with perfect objectivity. Every dress was designed to best show off my *attributes*. I still have them, in fact, the dresses—and the attributes.

"But I decided to give Paramount one more chance. I laid down the law. I said give me the script [for *Night After Night*], and I'll fix it for you. I told them I'm a fast worker, in more ways than one, but they didn't seem to understand the double entendre. I guess they were too overwrought.

"They didn't wait for me to say another word. They said they'd send the script right over, but I could only change *my* part. Well, that sounded okay to me, because I was sure I could carry the picture if I could write my own lines and write up my own part.

"When I'd made the trip to Hollywood, I thought the part in any film I made was going to be much bigger than the script they sent me. I didn't exactly envision a Mae West starrer, but I figured it would seem like it when I stepped up on the screen. The audience would be so dazzled, they wouldn't see anyone else."

Night After Night starred George Raft and Constance Cummings, not Mae. Even Wynne Gibson was higher in the credits than Mae who, in the ads, shared a low line with Alison Skipworth.

"Well, the part turned out to be a lot smaller than I thought it would be, but I knew I could still make a lot out of it.

"Working with George Raft was a real inducement, if you know what I mean. There was a thing between me and him after *Night After Night*. We stayed friends for life. We had a kind of bond.

"George Raft gave up being a gangster in real life for being a movie gangster. Good trade. I thought he'd be a big star. Well, he didn't make that, but he had a swell career. I think it was because he didn't have enough drive. He settled for what came easy, and was easily satisfied, where his career was concerned.

"There were people who called him a lowlife, and they said he wasn't good for me personally or professionally. What did they know? I had my intuition, and he had a good heart—and more.

"I had an idea for a play. In it I would be a gangster's moll.

"Gangsters always liked me. They could be very chivalrous with me, and I felt protected. They never let me see the shady side of what they did. They liked gambling and, I admit, so did I. And the ponies.

"There were a lot of masculine-type men in that category, the gangster category. Some of them were *very* good-looking. Very. I was drawn to dark-haired men who were kind of hairy. Not *too* hairy. Just on the hairy side."

She stopped, then asked me, "I hope I'm not embarrassing you, honey...?

I assured her that she wasn't.

"George Raft was one of the peripheral guys. He just drove the car and picked up cash receipts, like I told you, in the 'lower-archy.' Nothing dishonorable.

"I was crazy about him. Crazy out of my mind. I didn't usually let myself go, but I saw my emotions and passions were going haywire, running amok.

"He was as passionate as I was, and since between us we didn't have anyplace we could go, we had to rush for the nearest broom closet as soon as we set eyes on each other...

"I said to myself, 'Mae, you're lucky that guy's not the marrying kind, or you could get into trouble.'

"I could've married him. It's a good thing I couldn't because I didn't want anyone to know I already was married.

"Then he let me down. He wanted to marry me. Well, I couldn't, because I already was married, even if I hadn't seen the guy in years.

"But I couldn't tell Raft that.

"So I said, 'Let's leave things the way they are. Marriage could spoil what we feel.' I know he didn't like it, but what was I going to do? He was a real gentleman about it all. We really had something going together. He was all man, I can tell you. I can personally testify to that, very personally."

• • •

Mae had gone to Hollywood with many preconceptions. "Like I told myself, the trip was 'purely exploratory.'

"They thought I was just a little girl from a little town trying to make good in the big town. Well, they were wrong. I was a big girl from a big town making good in a little town."

Mae was neither awed nor intimidated by Hollywood. Though she saw great possibilities in making films, she had her pride. She had to believe that whatever she did was worthy of the Mae West image. She felt keenly a responsibility to the character she had created.

"I believed in being open to things and giving them a chance. You've got to have a little patience. That's important, but it's just as important *not* to have *too much* patience. I think too much patience is even worse than too little. I made a kind of deadline for getting out if I saw that things weren't going my way. It wasn't like I was stuck there.

"But it turned out good, for me and for everyone. I brought a lot of good luck and happiness to a lot of people around me. I was always lucky for people and that made me happy."

Night After Night (1932)

Ex-professional boxer Joe Anton (George Raft) wants to get out of the speakeasy business. "I'm sick of being a pal to a lot of drunks," he tells his factotum, Leo (Roscoe Karns). He changes his mind, however, when a menacing gangster, Frankie Guard (Bradley Page), makes him an offer for the club and threatens him.

Joe employs an older woman of genteel bearing, Miss Mabel Jellyman (Alison Skipworth), to teach him how to be a gentleman. He wants to impress a beautiful young socialite, Jerry Healy (Constance Cummings), who comes to the club every night, unescorted. She encourages Joe by likening him to a carefree, swashbuckling pirate. He asks her to have dinner with him at the club.

At their dinner, which includes Miss Jellyman, Joe's attempts to make a good impression are complicated by the unexpected arrival of an old girlfriend, Maudie Triplett (Mae West). She is just paying a friendly visit, but at an inopportune moment. Asked if she believes in love at first sight, she replies, "Well, it saves a lot of time." Miss Jellyman is delighted to distract Maudie so that Miss Healy won't be too shocked.

Far from being shocked, Jerry Healy is delighted by Maudie's rowdy good nature. Jerry's attraction to Joe's speakeasy, however, isn't slumming. The mansion Joe converted into a Prohibition-era nightclub belonged to Jerry's family before they lost their fortune. Now, a wealthy man, Dick Bolton (Louis Calhern), has asked her to marry him, and she can't make up her mind. The security he offers isn't what she really wants. She is looking for the excitement Joe can provide.

Despite their differences in background, Maudie and Miss Jellyman are quite compatible and get drunk together.

Later in the evening, Frankie Guard shows up, eager to close the deal for Joe's nightclub. Joe delays the transaction, which he has no intention of completing. In his bedroom, he finds Jerry. Familiar with the mansion and slightly inebriated, she is reveling in its masculine ambience.

Another old girlfriend, Iris Dawn (Wynne Gibson) breaks in, holding a gun and threatening to kill him. Joe confronts her without fear. Jerry is thrilled by his bravado.

Joe disarms the hysterical woman, and she is escorted out. Before Jerry leaves, she kisses Joe, her pirate hero.

Joe asks her to marry him, but she says no. The kiss, she explains, didn't mean she loves him, only that she admires his bold spirit. She has decided to accept Bolton's proposal. Joe is more angry than disappointed.

He turns down the gangster's offer for his nightclub and prepares for an attack by Guard's armed thugs.

Maudie and Miss Jellyman are still there, having slept off their hangovers in Joe's unused bedroom. After they leave, Jerry arrives. In a rage, she ransacks the place. When Joe finds her in what's left of the bedroom, he realizes that she *does* love him after all, and they kiss. Maudie and Miss Jellyman are witnesses to the couple's embrace, as a shootout begins downstairs.

Maudie tells Miss Jellyman, "Come on, Mabel. Get out those books. Looks like he's gonna take more lessons."

It was in *Night After Night* that Mae delivered one of her most celebrated lines. As Maudie enters Joe's nightclub, Patricia Farley, who plays the hatcheck girl, exclaims, "Goodness! What beautiful diamonds!" to which Mae replies, "Goodness had nothin' to do with it, dearie." Mae wrote this line, stipulating that afterward the camera follow her into the club on one tracking setup. Director Archie Mayo, however, wanted a fade-out just after she delivered the line. When Mae persisted, it was shot both ways, but Mayo's version was used in the film.

Mae always maintained that George Raft was a much underestimated actor and performer. "He was a greater character in life than on the screen. The character he played in that picture—he really *was* Joe Anton. It was based on him, but only *part* of him. The character had a lot to live up to. Raft was, you might say, a tough guy. That was what he played, and that was how he lived, but he never called himself that.

"I remember when the director, Mayo, got on him about some line he wasn't getting right. Well, Mayo was a fat Englishman who could get pretty abusive if he wanted to, and he did this time, but George never said one word.

"The next morning, George made it a point to get there early, when he knew Mayo would be alone. He cornered Mayo and grabbed him by his collar. 'Listen, you so-and-so,' he said, 'I'm no tough guy, but if you ever talk to me like that again, so help me, you'll find out how tough I *can* be.'

"Let me tell you, Mayo was all sweetness and light from then on.

"After we did *Night After Night* together, George used to say to me, 'You stole the show, kid.'

"I said, 'Wrong on both counts, *kid*. I didn't steal the show, you did. You were the star, and you were great and *you* stole the show.

" 'And don't call me 'kid'. You call all kinds of people that, and I'm special. I don't like your addressing me in a common-currency way. *Un*dressing, maybe, but not *a*ddressing.'

"He said, 'You're right, Mae. You *are* special. And you *did* steal every scene you were in.'

" 'Well, all right, if you want to put it *that* way.' "

Mae told me that she had insisted on wearing her own diamonds. "They only had fakes, and I couldn't have them next to my skin. They'd have given me a rash. I have a very delicate complexion—all over. And it was important to my character because she knew the truth. My character was never highfalutin', but she was true. No false airs.

"I sprinkled in a few of their costume pieces, but the real diamonds I used gave the picture a touch of class. I never told anyone because it would've scared the producers. They would've thought about insurance. Well, I told Jim Timony because he was my confidant, and I didn't like keeping secrets from him. I thought he'd try to talk me out of doing it, but he didn't because he said, 'Mae, only you would do that. Just don't tell anyone. No one will try to steal the diamonds because nobody will believe you'd do that. Only you, Mae.'

"And, I thought to myself, no one would guess I had such big ones. Diamonds, that is.

"No replicas. It gave my part a subtle shading."

Throughout the film, Mae wore only one dress, a beaded gown with matching jacket and a white fur wrap, created by leading costume designer Walter Plunkett. Even though she had been dieting for her motion picture debut, she photographed plump. "The camera adds ten or fifteen pounds," she noted. "More than I expected, so I asked Ernest Haller [the cinematographer] to use his skinny lens on me, and he thought I was kidding. I wasn't.

"*Night After Night* wasn't a picture I created, but I was able to make a contribution, adding lines to my part. It wasn't just to make my part bigger, though that was in the top of my mind because I hadn't come out to California to be a bit player. I wouldn't have done the picture if they hadn't let me make those changes in the part they had written for me. The main thing was I had to instill the Mae character, and Lil, into the character they had, not just how I looked, but how I talked and *what* I said.

"This picture got my foot in the door. It's a tiny part, and I have a tiny foot, size five, but even an icon's got to start somewhere."

When *Night After Night* premiered in Los Angeles, Mae, who wasn't usually nervous, couldn't find the right mood to face the event. She had to admit to herself that her perfect confidence wasn't so perfect after all.

She became especially apprehensive when she heard that a favorite part of her first scene had been cut. The ending of the scene, for which she had so fervently argued, her slow, sashaying walk up the stairs after saying "Goodness had nothing to do with it, dearie" was not part of the finished film.

"My reason for the walk had been to protect my line. An audience has got to have time to hear the line, absorb it, and then laugh," Mae explained.

"Everyone at the studio who saw *Night After Night* told me they loved it. They said I was 'wonderful,' 'fabulous,' 'sensational,' 'extraordinary,' 'great.' I was afraid they might be exaggerating a little.

"But what if *I* didn't love it or *I* didn't like the way I was in it? What if I wanted to stop there?"

Seeing herself up there on the screen for the first time suddenly loomed as terrifying. "I wasn't prepared to see my nostrils so big you could drive a couple of Mack trucks through them.

"I've never trusted second chances. I don't think they come along very often. It's hard enough getting the first chance. You might not get one at all, but even if you do, that second chance isn't the same as a first chance." It was terrible for Mae to think that as brilliant a career as hers, lovingly and laboriously built over three decades, could be grievously injured by a small part in an insignificant movie.

As the time for the premiere approached, Timony told Mae, who was still dressing, that they would have to hurry or they would be late for the movie. Mae told him she didn't have to hurry because she already had decided that they weren't going to see *that* movie.

That night they went to a different film.

"I'd heard so much about it, and I'd even *said* so much about it, that I have to stop and think. Have I seen it? But no, I remember. I never did.

"The real reason I didn't go was I knew I wanted to stay in Hollywood to make my next film. I was in big demand. Vaudeville and movies were having trouble during the Depression. Movies were right for me.

"What if I'd gone to see *Night After Night*, and I didn't like the way I was? I might have left Hollywood.

"So, instead of going to the premiere, we went to some other movie, I've forgotten which one. I always intended going to see *Night After Night*, but I never have."

Mae West loved the stage, but very early, with her first film, she realized "the movie medium is lasting and the stage is ephemeral." She did, however, return to the Broadway stage several times after her successful film career.

"I like things that come easy, and I like to have everything the easy way, but sometimes that ain't so easy to do. I lived at just the right time for me. A big part of luck in life is you've got to get your timing right.

"You can spend ten or twenty years making your way toward success, and then, if you strike it right—a film, a play—they write that you're an overnight success. Some overnight! It can be a pretty long night."

As Mae awaited the filming of her second picture, *She Done Him Wrong*, she was robbed of several thousand dollars in cash and what she claimed as $12,000 worth of jewelry. She said that was her cost, as a result of shrewd buying, but that replacement value would have been more than double that.

"It happened once to me that I was robbed. I was sitting in my car and an armed man asked for my jewels and my money. I turned over about a thousand dollars in cash. I wasn't giving up my life for paper money, which is interchangeable, and I knew I could always earn more.

"My diamonds, that was another story. Until that moment, I thought I knew what I'd do. I'd refuse. Even if it would have cost me my life. But what are you gonna do?

"When it actually happened, I wasn't wearing my favorite diamonds. That was important. My favorite diamonds were my biggest and most perfect ones. I did a quick inventory in my mind, and the ones I was wearing weren't worth dying for. I did have one around my neck and let it fall into my bust. The diamond felt cold, but it was warm and safe. The robber didn't notice because he was probably as nervous as I was. More nervous.

"He said something like 'your jewels or your life.' I decided it was stupid to be brave. Maybe the police could get my diamonds back, but they couldn't get my life back. So I handed them over.

"I did get them back, and the police found out it was an inside job. The driver of my car and his accomplice did it.

"The police got back all of the diamonds. The robbers only had time to spend five hundred dollars. They went to jail for a pretty paltry sum."

Despite the Depression, audiences came to theaters anxious to escape their very real fears and problems. Some people thought the bad times even helped the film business. The audiences were made up of people who had lost money in the stock market, people who didn't have jobs, people who had a bleak present, and people who feared a bleaker future. Under those circumstances, there weren't many performers who could entertain audiences and make them glad for having spent their money. But there were even some people who were willing to miss a second meal in order to see *She Done Him Wrong* and Mae West a second time.

She Done Him Wrong was filmed in only eighteen days. Mae suggested, and then insisted strongly, that the cast should rehearse for a week before they began shooting and then do the scenes in one take each. The Paramount plan had been to shoot the scenes in sequence, in the order they took place in the finished film. Mae had the idea that all of the scenes in which the same costumes were worn should be shot at the same time so as to save changing time. Her idea worked.

Mae was anxious to save Paramount's money because she would not compromise on the budget limitations for her dresses. As far as she was concerned, there should be no limitations, "because my character would be put in the position of going out there naked if I didn't have great dresses. I had to be decked out."

Mae had been promised Travis Banton, Paramount's head of costume design, but when she was told that he would be away in Europe, she wasted no time in establishing great rapport with the junior person she had been assigned. In the first minutes with the tiny designer, "one of the few people I could look down on, but not in talent, only in height, I knew I had found the perfect person for me in Edith. You know, Edith Head."

This offered Head a marvelous opportunity, of which she took full advantage. A great professional and personal friendship grew out of this collaboration, which lasted until Mae's death.

Mae found that she could communicate perfectly with Head and that Head could translate her wishes perfectly to paper and then cloth. She also felt that Head understood her figure and "how to play it up." Mae said she felt more comfortable working with a woman in this intimate relationship, and Edith Head understood what form-fitting meant.

Originally, someone from Paramount had suggested that costumes from the wardrobe department be used. Mae was appalled at the idea that anyone thought someone else's dress could be altered to fit her unique shape.

"When I was making a film, I would stand during the whole shooting—five, six, seven hours a day, so I wouldn't wrinkle my dress. I even stood to eat. They'd say to me, 'Mae, aren't you tired?' But I didn't let myself get tired. I'd say to myself, Do I want to look my best for my public that expects it of me? Or would I rather sit down? That wasn't any choice.

"I never deliberately wore a dress that was too tight or too skimpy. Sometimes someone in the press, usually a woman, had the nerve to write that I was wearing something too revealing just to attract attention.

"Well, I never *had* to do that. I never had to try to attract attention. I couldn't help doing that just by being myself.

"The reason the outfits were the way they were was because the producers were always trying to skimp wherever they could, and they wanted to save a few cents of fabric. I always insisted on the best fabric, and I knew the difference. And I knew that my audience knew the difference, too. You couldn't fool me, and you couldn't fool my public.

"The producers didn't care if I had to be poured into the dress, which was so tight I could hardly breathe, let alone move. They forgot to allow for my curves.

"First impressions are what count. I was always careful about the first dress I wore on stage or in a picture. It's like when you arrive at a party. That's the important moment. That's when people take a real look at you, size you up, and if they're impressed, that's how they think of you and remember you.

"If your makeup fades a little and you get a few creases in your dress later and you look a little tired, that isn't what they remember."

"Women wanted to have an hourglass figure and proudly show off their bosoms, those who had them," Mae told me. "They tried to copy my look, as best they could."

Mae's brief appearance in *Night After Night* had served to introduce her to movie audiences, who were then eager to see more of her. When she arrived on the screen in her first starring role, they were well prepared for her risqué brand of humor. Paramount desperately needed a moneymaking hit, and she gave it to them in *She Done Him Wrong*. She also gave them Cary Grant, in his most important role to date.

"Cary Grant. I heard him before I saw him, talking in the alley outside my dressing room at Paramount. Then I went out to take a look, and I liked what I saw. I liked his voice first, but I saw right away that the rest of him measured up. They didn't want him for my second picture, but I insisted. He got to dress up, and he got noticed."

Although *She Done Him Wrong* was based on the *Diamond Lil* stage play, the Hays Office insisted on many changes. The dancehall-brothel had to be changed to a saloon, and counterfeiting replaced white slavery. Captain Cummings, the disguised policeman, could no longer pretend to be a Salvation Army officer, but he was allowed to wear a similar uniform and run an independent Bowery mission. Some of the characters' names were changed, including that of Diamond Lil, who became Lady Lou.

She Done Him Wrong (1933)

Lady Lou (Mae West) reigns over Gus Jordan's Bowery saloon, which is a center for illegal activities. Ward boss Jordan (Noah Beery, Sr.) uses his influence to buy off the authorities, and he is strong enough to fend off all competition. A federal agent called "the Hawk" is spying on his counterfeiting operations, and a bitter rival, Dan Flynn (David Landau), is threatening his business.

Russian Rita (Rafaela Ottiano), arrives at the saloon with a fellow countryman, Serge Stanieff (Gilbert Roland), and a young girl named Sally (Rochelle Hudson). Sally, jilted and left pregnant by a lover, was contemplating suicide when Rita and her companion "rescued" her. Lou advises Sally to leave the country or she will be exploited by men. Lou understands that it's a man's world, and she knows how to play by their rules and win.

Captain Cummings (Cary Grant), a Salvation Army–type preacher, has set up a mission next door to the saloon. He interests her as no other man has because he seems impervious to her charms. In spite of this, she tells him, "Why don't you come up sometime, see me?"

Another man in her life, Chick Clark (Owen Moore), is a thief who is serving time in the penitentiary for stealing diamonds to give to her. He got caught because Flynn betrayed him.

When Captain Cummings's mission is threatened, she buys the property from Jacobson, the landlord (Lee Kohlmar), so that he isn't evicted. Then, she makes no move to stop Sally when she goes with Rita. Cummings is concerned for Sally's well-being, but Lou believes it's up to the girl to save herself. As the captain leaves, he tries to kiss Lou, but she turns away. After he has left, she smiles.

The next visitor is Clark, who has just broken out of prison. She manages to placate him, saying they will meet later. He leaves in search of Flynn.

Serge comes to see Lou, offering her diamonds in hopes of a love affair. Rita, suspecting this liaison, arrives with a drawn knife. In a fight, Rita is killed.

While Lou is performing downstairs Flynn enters the saloon, and she motions for him to meet her upstairs in her room. Waiting there is Clark, who shoots him.

When the police raid the place, Lou rushes to her room, where she is confronted by Clark. As he is about to shoot Lou, too, Captain Cummings arrives and disarms him. He is really "the Hawk," an undercover policeman.

The captain takes her past the paddy wagon, to his car, where he removes her diamonds so he can put one of his own on her ring finger. In a mockingly admonishing tone, he says, "You bad girl."

"You'll find out," she replies, smiling.

"Lady Lou," Mae said, "is really Diamond Lil, who, as I've told you, is my alter ego. I based her a lot on my own character.

"I made up my mind very early that I would never love another person as much as I loved myself. Maybe that sounds selfish to you. It is. But I saw what a mess a lot of people could make of their lives when they're smitten. Some of them go temporarily insane.

"They find a person who they think holds the key to their happiness—the only key to their happiness that exists. They don't understand they're the ones who give the other person that power. It's like a fever. The person in that condition may ruin their own life, and the lives of others, as well.

"Not long afterwards, the great passion may have run its course, and the lovestruck one can't understand why she or he—it happens to men, too—felt that way or what they ever saw in the divinity that is now nothing.

"My work has always been my greatest happiness."

Mae's signature line, "Come up and see me sometime," was introduced to film audiences in *She Done Him Wrong*, although she didn't say it quite that way in this picture. The first time she said it, she told Cary Grant, "Come up sometime. See me." Later, it was repeated as "Come up and see me sometime," and became perhaps Mae West's most readily identifiable quote.

"Marlene Dietrich was at Paramount in '33, and our dressing rooms were very close to each other, practically side by side. She was very sweet, and kinda lonely and insecure.

"We could tell each other secrets in German, though we had to be careful because there were other people around who might understand, especially with all the refugees coming from Europe. They thought things would get bad there. They were right.

"My German was what I remembered from my mother speaking with her family and friends when I was little. I learned it by accident. Marlene didn't mind my accidental German and understood it just fine. Hers was very different from the way Mother spoke it.

"When I said my first words to her in German, she laughed. I didn't mind. I sounded pretty funny to me. It *was* her first language and my second, if you could even call it that. I asked her why she laughed. I told her German was a childhood language of mine and that it was kinda rusty.

"She said, 'No, it is very good, but it is the accent. It is very strong Black Forest.' I told her my mother came from Bavaria. She said she knew. She was from Berlin.

"I tried to show her the ropes, to give her some of my insights into how to handle herself, so the producer types wouldn't try to handle *her* and take liberties. We exchanged what we knew about camera angles and lighting. She knew quite a bit from the German films she'd done. She liked my makeup tips, especially for drawing on lips.

"The biggest pointer I gave her was about her lipstick. I showed her how to make her lips seem fuller and poutier and sexier, by not bringing the lipstick all the way to the corners of her mouth.

"She was a real pretty girl, but very shy. I was always sensitive to shy people, because of my own shyness. There wasn't anyone in the world, except my mother, who would have said I had a shy side.

"Anyway, she said to me she was thinking of going back to Europe because she couldn't get rid of her accent, and she was worried she couldn't make it in America. She was more confident about what her career would be in Europe, but she didn't really want to go back there, especially to Germany.

"She gave me a pair of opera glasses. Who else would give *me* opera glasses? I loved opera and had recordings of opera, but I didn't exactly need to use opera glasses in my bedroom.

"I treasured the gift. It was one of the nicest things anyone ever gave me.

"I'll tell you something Dietrich said to me once. We used to talk a little about sex, but we never talked dirty. Most of the time, I was just giving her advice on how to rebuff the studio Lotharios. There were a lot of them with the octopus tendency.

"My technique was to try some humor, but that wasn't her style. She wasn't very funny when she was trying to be funny. I remember we were having an intimate conversation about men and about how careful a girl had to be, and she said this funny thing to me, which I didn't understand, but remembered.

"She said, 'You should only make love with a man you love or a man you hate.'

"I didn't understand. It didn't make much sense. I wouldn't've wanted to do it with someone I hated, and I was avoiding being in love. I didn't think it was polite to ask her what she meant. Maybe she was just joking and I didn't get it because she delivered it so straight, and I wasn't expecting it. Deadpan. I meant to ask her sometime, but our careers went in different directions, and we sort of drifted apart. I think of her often because she gave me a lot of gifts I still have, scarves and the opera glasses.

"One time I told Timony what she said. I asked him did he think she was being funny or serious.

"He said, 'She was being enigmatic.'

"I didn't know any more than I did before I asked the question.

"Jim explained the word to me. It's like a riddle without an answer or a joke without a tag line. So I learned another word, but it still didn't exactly answer my question.

"Marlene Dietrich was a good friend. She used to bring me food she cooked herself—soup, a beef stew—and it was good. It was substantial and full of vitamins.

"She loved to cook. She was very talented at it, like Mother. Maybe it's what girls learn in Germany. I, personally, was happy to stay out of kitchens, except as a visitor.

"Sometimes she got some bad press, and I don't think she deserved it at all. You ought to at least have the pleasure of doing something if you're going to get pilloried for it. I think she had the same problem I did, of the audience confusing her with the parts she played. She did them too well, so no one thought of her the way I did, a nice girl who cooked delicious chicken soup for her friends."

"It was called *She Done Him Wrong*," Cary Grant told me, "but speaking personally, I can only say, 'She done me right.'

"Not only did she spot me, select me for this wonderful role, but she fought to have me get it. Then she did everything off camera and on camera to coach me.

"She told me that she understood good camera angles, and would protect mine. That was an understatement. She was so generous."

Mae told me that she didn't have to do anything to make Cary look better. "He had no bad angles. It wasn't possible to find one. You might say he was perfect. I would. And that voice!"

Mae said, "I had him once, and I knew I wanted to have him again. Professionally speaking.

"Personally speaking, I wouldn't have minded, but I was—busy.

"I usually wasn't attracted to actors, but I could've made an exception for Cary Grant. Mostly they didn't seem manly enough to me. I preferred men who lit up when they saw me, not when they looked at themselves in the mirror."

In addition to doing well at the box office, *She Done Him Wrong* created quite a stir.

"After my picture about Diamond Lil, sex was more out in the open. I'm proud of that because I always believed that sex was nothing to be ashamed of. I didn't see love as a sin. Overwhelming desire is wonderful."

I asked Mae if she thought sex was better with love.

"Honey, sex with love is the greatest thing in life. But sex without love—that's not so bad, either. Sex is the best exercise for developing everything. It's very good for the complexion and the circulation. Keeps it all moving along."

In *I'm No Angel*, the film in which she tames lions and which was originally called *The Lady and the Lions*, Mae insisted on riding an elephant. "It made a much more interesting scene," she said. "Riding a horse was so routine for an entrance."

The ad for *I'm No Angel* repeated one of Mae's favorite quotes, billing her character, Tira, as "Just a sensitive girl who climbed the ladder of success, wrong-by-wrong."

I'm No Angel (1933)

Tira (Mae West) works as an exotic dancer and lion tamer in a small-time traveling circus owned by Big Bill Barton (Edward Arnold). Her companion, Slick Wiley (Ralf Harolde) is a pickpocket. While Tira distracts the "suckers" with her sinuous dancing, Wiley moves through the crowd, picking pockets. Slick is insanely jealous of her attentions to other men.

One of these men, Ernest Brown (William B. Davidson), attracts her because of his large diamond ring. She invites him up to her hotel room. While they are talking, Slick breaks in and hits Brown in the head with a bottle. They leave him for dead.

Tira calls her lawyer in New York, Benny Pinkowitz (Gregory Ratoff), asking him to advance her enough money to get to Manhattan. She promises an act worthy of Madison Square Garden, in which she puts her head into the mouth of a lion, but he can't afford it.

Tira goes to Big Bill, who accepts her proposal. In the meantime, Slick is arrested. Rajah (Nigel de Brulier), a fortune-teller, sees a dark man in Tira's future.

In New York, Tira's lion-taming act is a sensation. Among her many male admirers is Kirk Lawrence (Kent Taylor), who is just Tira's type—a handsome young millionaire. He also fits the description of a dark man. Lawrence puts her up in a luxurious apartment.

Visiting her there is Alicia Hatton (Gertrude Michael), Kirk's previous fiancée. She asks Tira to break her engagement with Kirk because she is unsuitable. Tira refuses, replying, "The only difference between you and me, we break different commandments."

Kirk's business partner, Jack Clayton (Cary Grant), approaches Tira with the same argument. He's *another* handsome dark man with money to throw around, and she can't resist him. Jack and Tira become engaged.

Big Bill, furious when Tira informs him that she's retiring from the lion-taming business, conspires with Slick, newly released from prison, to spoil her relationship with Jack.

Jack appears at Tira's apartment to find Slick there in a bathrobe. He doesn't know that Tira has been delayed, and Slick has broken in.

Jack breaks off their engagement, and Tira sues for breach of promise. In the courtroom, the judge (Walter Walker) and the all-male jury are won over by Tira. The prosecutor (Irving Pichel), presents a string of witnesses, all of whom have been involved with Tira. She cross-examines them herself, winning over everybody, even Jack. They reconcile.

A well-remembered exchange occurs near the end when Cary Grant asks her "What are you thinking about?" and Mae answers "The same thing as you."

At the end, she admits to him, "I'm no angel."

"That's very exciting for a man. When men sense a woman is ready for sex, they're ready right away. Men are simpler than women that way. It's the way they're made—very uncomplicated. When men came to see me, I had to try to calm them down a little first.

"You know that thing with the lions where I'm in the cage with them? That was as real as it looked. More real.

"But," Mae confessed, "when I put my head in the lion's mouth—I haven't really told this before, dear—that wasn't *my* head in his mouth.

"I wanted to do the stunt myself. I desperately wanted to do it, but Paramount wouldn't let me. I don't know if they were worried about me, but they were sure deeply concerned about my character, and they knew I wouldn't be able to do a good job finishing the picture without a head, *my* head.

"I always admired lions. When I was a little girl, my father took me to Coney Island to see the lions. He had to hold my hand tight because I wanted to get too close to the cage. Lions are so beautiful. When I'd go to a new city, I'd go to the zoo just to see the lions. I'd stand outside their cages and have this fantasy:

"I'd be in there with them, and they'd be doing just what I wanted them to do, surrendering to me. I would totally command them. I had this tremendous passion for it and no fear. I knew the lions would recognize me and wouldn't hurt me. I'd always wanted to be a lion-tamer. It was a kind of dream of mine.

"I'm asked all the time, would I want to put my head in a lion's mouth now? It's a simple answer: No.

"No one could induce me to do that. As for the lion's cage, I wouldn't even want to do that. At the time, I had no fear. You know why?"

"No," I answered truthfully.

"Stupid, I guess," was her response. "I thought I was invulnerable. I thought the lions would recognize that I wasn't afraid of them and how much I respected and admired them, and they would receive me appropriately and never do me any harm. I didn't understand, at that time, all there was that could go wrong. For instance, they could like me and, just playing, give me some pretty big scratches. I met a very successful lady lion-tamer who was all scar tissue, and she said the lions loved her, and they were just playing, but their claws were awfully sharp.

"Then, I heard another story about a lion-tamer, a man, who was badly clawed because a dog had been near his outfit, and the lions didn't approve of the smell of that dog.

"I think it's kind of like with those young soldiers and sailors who go to war, so brave, and they don't think anything will happen to them. And then, a lot of terrible things *do* happen to them. It's a way you feel when you're very young and you don't know any better.

"After that, when you're older, you wonder who that person was who didn't know about fear. It's a funny thing how you risk everything when you're young and have a long, wonderful life ahead you could be giving up, and then when people are old and the future isn't as bright, they fight for every day."

In 1934, Mae earned almost $400,000, making her the highest-paid female performer in the world. Marlene Dietrich was second, with considerably less. Mae suffered a loss that year, however, that could not be measured in money.

"I'd like to show you my memories," she said to me, "but I can't because most of them are only in my own head now. That means they only live as long as I do. It's my photographs I cared most about, the pictures of my family, especially my mother and me together. Some of the people, I didn't even know who they were anymore, but they were the background of my life, my early life.

"I kept wishing I'd taken one more look at the photos before the flood came and took them. But if I'm going to say I wish I'd done something different, then it's that I hadn't left the pictures in the basement here.

"I always felt so secure at the Ravenswood that I didn't feel any danger. Everything was ruined. They were the worst floods, before or since.

"Sometimes all these years later, I go and look for something and I look a while and I can't find it.

"Then I remember it was something I had in those trunks in the basement, and I'm *never* going to find it."

"In *I'm No Angel*," Mae said, "I have this line which people loved, and it became memorable, even though no one understood exactly what it meant. I'm going to tell you a little secret, but when I tell it to you, it won't be a secret anymore. I didn't know exactly what the line meant myself.

"I say, 'Beulah, peel me a grape.'

"I said it full of innuendo, and it came out right.

"The line was inspired by my pet monkey. My father gave me my first monkey when I was a child, and I liked to take him for a walk, holding his little hand. He was very human, more human than some people I've met.

"When I did *I'm No Angel*, I had two monkeys. I had two so they wouldn't get lonely. When one of them died, I gave the other one to a preserve where he would have company.

"The thing about my monkey was that he was finicky. The thing he loved best was grapes, but he wouldn't eat a grape unless it was peeled. That was my inspiration for the line."

After being robbed of her jewelry in 1932, Mae hired Mike Mazurki, before he was an actor, as a bodyguard. He was a boxer. Mae had a special preference for boxers because of what she referred to as "my affinity for boxers like Battlin' Jack, my father. My mother told me she always felt safe when she was out with my father, because she knew he would protect her."

Mazurki proved to be satisfactory in his employment with Mae. "Too satisfactory," she said. "I was so pleased that I decided to cast him in my new movie, *Belle of the Nineties*. No regrets. He was good.

"He started to get offers of parts. He asked me what he should do. I said, 'Take 'em.' They were all parts for his character, not too small and not too big. He couldn't go wrong. I sure wasn't going to stand in his way.

"He said, 'Miss West, it's been a great pleasure guarding your body.' That was nice. I was always very good at discovering male talent.

"When he left, I didn't get another bodyguard. I didn't think I could do that well again, and I never liked second-best.

"Do you know what William Randolph Hearst said about me? 'Isn't it time Congress did something about Mae West.' I was flattered. People didn't love him. They loved me. The only person who loved him was Marion Davies. She was a sweet girl. People said he kept her, but in the end, she kept him. When he was strapped for cash, she sold her real estate and jewelry to save him. Imagine selling her real estate and her jewelry. She turned out to be a *real* lady.

"I think Hearst didn't like me because I made almost as much money as he did. He said he didn't like my morals, and there he was, a married man with a mistress. Who was he to throw words at me when he lived in a glass house, even if it was San Simeon?"

For *Belle of the Nineties* Mae wanted to include blues and jazz. "I had my heart set on having Duke Ellington," she said. "I knew his music from back in New York. I'd heard him at the Cotton Club.

"The studio wanted me to have the studio orchestra and paper it with black extras all around. I persuaded them it wasn't the same thing. It wasn't just black people who would know the difference. I'd know the difference. And plenty of the audience would know the difference.

"I was sure that people would come for Duke Ellington. Black people saw all the black performers I was using and they made a good audience. A lot of people wrote to me that I helped them discover this music.

"I had a maid named Libby Taylor, and I thought she'd be good in the film. I'd hired her to take care of my apartment. After *Belle of the Nineties*, I let her go to be in movies. She'd been a wonderful maid in my personal life, but she had talent, and I would never have stood in her way." Louise Beavers, Gertrude Howard, and Hattie McDaniel were black actresses in the 1930s who were all helped by Mae West.

Belle of the Nineties (1934)

The Tiger Kid (Roger Pryor), a young boxer, is jeopardizing his promising career because of his infatuation with Ruby Carter (Mae West), a popular vaudeville performer. His manager, Kirby (James Donlan), cannot distract him from his obsession with the singer.

Kirby finally succeeds by convincing the Kid that Ruby is also seeing other men. Ruby, trying to forget the Kid, leaves St. Louis to accept a job singing at the Sensation House in New Orleans. Disembarking from the steamboat in New Orleans, Ruby and handsome Brooks Claybourne (Johnny Mack Brown) notice each other.

Ace Lamont (John Miljan), owner of the club, instantly falls for Ruby. His attention to her causes his girlfriend, Molly Brant (Katherine DeMille), to become rabidly jealous.

In the club's casino, Ruby and Brooks meet again. He is losing heavily at roulette, but not enough to ignore Ruby.

As their relationship grows, so does her collection of diamonds. He can afford to keep her in better style than Ace. When Ace sees what is happening, he becomes as jealous as Molly.

Ace is also a fight promoter. Because he needs a replacement for an upcoming championship bout, he hires the Tiger Kid, who has just come from St. Louis with Kirby and is looking for work. He hires him on one condition. He is being blackmailed by a woman, and he wants the Kid to stage a robbery so that he can get back the diamonds he has given her. Needing money, the Kid agrees.

The robbery is staged at night along the riverfront while Ace is taking Ruby for a ride. The Kid, masked, is surprised that the woman is Ruby, but he takes all her diamonds. She notices that he doesn't take Ace's diamond ring.

Back at the club, Ruby sees Ace depositing a package in his safe that the Kid has just given him. Ruby approaches the Kid, and his behavior confirms her suspicions.

Ruby gives Ace her remaining diamonds for safekeeping. As he dials the combination of the safe, she sees the numbers with her opera glasses.

Knowing that Ace has bet heavily on the Kid, she drugs the Kid's water bottle, and in the fight he is knocked out.

While Ace loses heavily, Brooks wins handsomely. Ruby gave him a tip so he could recoup his losses at the club. The Kid confronts Ruby in her room. She blames Ace for drugging him, implying that he really bet *against* him.

When the Kid corners Ace in his office, there is a fight, and Ace is accidentally killed. The Kid smells kerosene. The office has been saturated with it. Ace intended to burn down the club in order to collect the insurance, blaming the Kid.

Ruby opens the safe and retrieves her diamonds, but she drops a match, setting the club afire. She hears a voice screaming for help and releases Molly from a closet where Ace had imprisoned her.

Ruby can't reach the firehouse because their line is busy. Everyone escapes from the raging inferno, except Ace, who burns to death in the flames.

Ruby and the Kid are married.

"Leo McCarey was good [as director], but I was really always the director. Nobody could tell me how to be me. George [Cukor] was the only director I ever wanted to work with. I never worked with him. He's the biggest and the greatest. I was ready to listen to him. I know he appreciated and understood me. There's still time.

"The difference between a great director like George Cukor and an ordinary director is that the great director makes you create. It isn't that he tells you exactly what you *should* do. That would cramp my style. I feel George could help me be more *me*."

In *Belle of the Nineties*, there were several boxing scenes that Mae said were inspired by her father's career. She also re-created the scene in which she had been robbed of her jewels. Mae liked to use her own life as a reference for scenes. In this film, the character was sitting in her carriage rather than in her limousine, as Mae had been in the real-life drama.

As a hobby, Mae enjoyed backing professional boxers of promise. She never discovered a champion, inside the ring, that is. Outside the ring, she was luckier.

"The boxers had a hard time, even some of them who were pretty good. There was one I backed named Gorilla Jones. I don't know why he was called 'Gorilla.' He wasn't that kind of fighter. I saw he was getting pounded too much, and he didn't really like fighting anymore, but he didn't know what else to do. He was ready to sacrifice the glory because there wasn't any anymore, but he needed to earn a living, and I found out he had a mother to support, too. He really cared about his mother, and I could understand that.

"So I talked it over, and I asked him what else he could do besides punch people. And he laughed and said he didn't seem to be able to do that much anymore. Mostly, he said, he was a punching bag. He smiled, and he didn't have all his teeth.

"I asked him how he was at driving a car. He said he didn't count that as a skill, but, sure, he could drive a car. So I hired him as my chauffeur. He turned out to be a very good driver, and he was also protection.

"I asked about his mother. He said, 'She's a great lady. She's always done everything for me. Now I don't want to let her down.'

"I asked him if she would consider being a maid, *my* maid. I needed one at the moment. He said, 'She keeps the best house you ever saw.'

"I asked him if he thought she could take care of my dresses. He said she loved pretty dresses, and he was going to buy her a lot of them, but he never got to that stage. I didn't say anything, but I was thinking. I had a lot of stuff I wasn't using she might like. 'What's her name, Gorilla?'

" 'Daisy.'

"Daisy came to work for me for a long time. She was a person I could trust, perfectly. When I had to go on the road, I told her it would be hard and said, 'I don't suppose you'd want to do that?'

" 'Oh, Miss West!' I've never seen anyone so excited. She said it was her dream. She'd never been anywhere, and she'd always wanted to travel. I observed she'd fallen in love with show business. 'Oh, Miss West, thank you for choosing me. I'll never forget you for it.' "

Mae said, "And I'm paying you double while we're traveling."

Daisy stayed with Mae until Gorilla's eyesight began to fail so badly that he couldn't be alone. It was from getting hit in the head so much, Mae believed.

Mae had bought some small houses near the Ravenswood, and she had Daisy and Gorilla move into one. It was arranged that neither of them would ever pay rent. Each received a monthly pension from Mae, and when Daisy died, Mae found someone to move in and take care of Gorilla for the rest of his life.

At Anthony Quinn's Upper East Side New York art studio, the actor responded with a deep, mirthful laugh when I mentioned Mae West's name.

"I was a young Chicano actor, an aspiring wannabe kid. Someone who knew Mae West told me she was backing a play about John Barrymore. I didn't know if it was true, but in those days, I believed everything anyone told me, which I think is a very good way to be if you can hang onto it. Our mutual friend got me an appointment with Mae West.

"In those days, I used to do a pretty good imitation of John Barrymore. That was before Jack and I became good friends.

"I went to her apartment in Hollywood. She was tiny, very, very tiny, and she spoke in that suggestive way she had, with her hand on her hip.

"She was very cordial and tried to put me at ease, but she was a very big star, a presence, and I was terribly nervous. I kept looking down at the floor, and she noticed. She said, 'You ain't gonna see much lookin' down *there.*'

"I was surprised how petite she was, not at all the way she photographed, which was a little overweight. She wasn't plump at all and even though I was very nervous, I couldn't help noticing that she had a very good figure.

"She listened to my imitation of John Barrymore and seemed to like it. Then we talked about what I was doing, which was mostly going to auditions.

"Then, she offered to show me her apartment. Her bedroom was just like they said, with the mirrors on the ceiling, but I didn't say anything about this. I guess I was a little embarrassed to notice. Looking back, it seems more embarrassing *not* to have noticed.

"After the tour of her apartment, she looked me straight in the eye and said, 'Do you mind if I feel your biceps?'

"I was pretty flustered. I opened my mouth and nothing came out, so she took that to mean yes.

"She squeezed my arms. Then, she squeezed my calf and leg muscles. I was like a trembling statue.

"She was quite professional, very serious. She really did seem interested in my muscles.

"She didn't say much, just a 'very nice.' There were no sexual innuendos.

"She said, 'I'm glad you were able to come by.' I understood that was my cue to leave. I thanked her for seeing me and left.

"When I got to know Jack Barrymore, I told him the story. He looked at me and said, 'You mean with a come-on like that, you didn't *do* anything? That's not a very good imitation of *me!*' "

While Mae was shooting her next film, *Goin' to Town,* her father suffered a heart attack and died.

"I've never been a drinker," Mae said. "I think it's because my father drank enough for both of us.

"I never saw him drunk. Never once. He could handle his liquor. At first, it made him more gregarious, though he didn't need much in that department. He was outgoing and loved going out. He began his career in pugilism before he was eleven. He was like me. He knew what he wanted to do. He was precocious and had the talent.

"I have a theory that people drink because they're bored, bored with themselves, even more than with other people. So they drink, and after drinking, they bore everyone else.

"I remember Father always ready to put up his dukes, and he didn't need much cause to do it. Alcohol made him more aggressive. Perfectly sober, too, he was very spontaneous and never thought about consequences to himself. But he was very responsible toward my mother and me, and the other children when they came.

"When he came out to California to live in 1934, he was sick and old, and I didn't recognize his personality. The way he looked was different but not as different as the way he was. I guess my mother's going took its toll on him, more than I understood, because I was so deep in my own grief, I wasn't aware of anything else, and my father had to be strong for all of us. He was no crybaby.

"He'd mellowed. He didn't seem to have his extraordinary energy. When I didn't recognize his full-o'-fight personality, it made me sad. I guess I'd admired him more than I knew."

When Battlin' Jack West died of a stroke on January 5, 1935, his fighting stature had largely been forgotten in Brooklyn. His fame had not extended to California, so when he moved there to be where his three children were, he left his old connections and associates behind. He arrived at an age and with health problems that made it unlikely he would be able to begin a new life at all comparable to the one he had left behind.

Mae remembered when she was the proud daughter of Battlin' Jack, the toast of Brooklyn. When he arrived in Los Angeles, he would be "Mae West's father."

He moved in with his son, John Jr., who lived in a house with land that Mae had purchased. Her father was near daughter Beverly and not far from Mae, who within a few months bought him a house nearby. He didn't have long to enjoy it. In November of 1934, he had a heart attack. Then, in January, he died.

There had always been more differences between Matilda and John than similarities. The differences may have added to the glamour each had for the other, especially in the early days of the courtship. Swept away by the emotions and passions of youth, the teenage girl from Germany had married the handsome young man, the first young man she had really known, without telling her family. She told them afterward only because she knew they would not approve of her choice of a husband. They wouldn't believe that Battlin' Jack would be able to provide for her as they had hoped her husband would. They felt eighteen was too young to make a decision to last her whole life.

Mae, who was filming at the time her father died, took off only one day to attend the funeral. It was quite a different reaction from the one she had experienced after the death of her mother.

"I remembered what my father said to me when my mother left us. He said he didn't want me to be there when he died, or to feel for him what I felt for her. I didn't, but I was sad, even sadder than I had expected to be.

"In so many ways, I was more like my father than I was like my beautiful, feminine mother, for whom I had such love."

When Mae received the call notifying her about her father, she planned to stay home from the set, but when she was told that five hundred extras were awaiting her arrival and that they would be sent home without pay, she decided that there was nothing she could do any more to help her father.

"I didn't like to see all of those people who probably needed the day's salary, maybe to eat, have to go home. I didn't know if they'd even get their carfare reimbursed. I figured it was what my father would tell me I should do, to go to the set. I took off only the day of his funeral.

"Over the years, I found myself thinking of him and what a good father he'd been to a little girl. If his spirit had come back to me, smoking one of those terrible cigars he loved so much, I don't think I would have minded at all the smell of that smoke."

Although *Goin' to Town* begins as a period western with cowboys and horses, most of the action takes place in Buenos Aires and Southampton in modern times. "It starts out as a horse opera an ends up as a grand opera," Mae commented.

Beverly's two Russian wolfhounds made guest appearances in *Goin' to Town*. "They seemed to enjoy their work," Mae recalled.

"My sister liked Russian dogs and Russian husbands. Her relationships with the dogs went better."

Goin' to Town (1935)

In a small western cattle town, the queen of the Danse de Pavillion saloon, Cleo Borden (Mae West), agrees to marry suspected cattle-rustler Buck Gonzales (Fred Kohler, Sr.) if he will sign an agreement deeding all of his land to her upon their marriage. Before they marry, however, Buck is shot dead by the sheriff in a rustling raid. Cleo learns from Buck's business manager, Winslow (Gilbert Emery), that she is the new owner of Buck's land. He has left it all to her.

She immediately authorizes drilling for oil. The chief oil engineer, Edward Carrington (Paul Cavanagh), catches her eye, and she, his. He loses interest, however, upon learning that she has made a bet that Carrington will easily succumb to her charms. Carrington, an educated Englishman, rejects her, making Cleo feel socially inferior.

On Buck's land, there is a stable. Among the horses is a magnificent steed named Cactus, who everybody believes could be a champion.

Oil is discovered on Cleo's property, and she becomes fabulously wealthy, though she still can't interest Carrington. When he's transferred to Buenos Aires, she follows him. A wealthy socialite, Mrs. Crane-Brittony (Marjory Gateson), is also there with her gigolo, Ivan (Ivan Lebedeff). She has come to race her horse, Montezuma, in the Argentine sweepstakes.

Anxious to emulate Mrs. Crane-Brittony in every detail, Cleo sends for Cactus, so he can be entered in the race, too. She places a side bet with Mrs. Crane-Brittony that Cactus will beat Montezuma.

Mrs. Crane-Brittony instructs Ivan to drug Cactus on the night before the race. Taho (Tito Coral), an Indian trainer, stops him, but Cactus catches cold and is unable to run fast. Cleo solves this problem by having Taho stand at the finish line with a pistol.

As Cactus nears the finish line behind Montezuma, Taho fires the pistol into the air. Cactus, who is gun-shy, becomes so frightened he spurts ahead and wins the race.

Carrington still treats Cleo as someone socially beneath him. In a last-ditch attempt to impress Carrington, Cleo arranges a marriage-in-name-only with Mrs. Crane-Brittony's dissolute nephew, Fletcher Colton (Monroe Owsley). They leave Buenos Aires to live on his Southampton estate.

Cleo stages an opera ball in the mansion. She invites a distinguished list of guests to come and hear her sing the leading role in Saint-Saëns's *Samson and Delilah*. Among them is Carrington, now the Earl of Stratton, and Mrs. Crane-Brittony. He admits to Cleo that he has always loved her, but now it's too late.

Ivan sneaks into her room while Cleo is singing, intending to embarrass her in a supposed assignation while a private detective (Paul Harvey) is witness. Fletcher, in need of money to pay off a gambling debt, enters and opens her safe. There is a struggle, and Fletcher is killed with his own gun. When Ivan is caught, he implicates Mrs. Crane-Brittony.

Cleo finally becomes a lady, officially, when she marries the Earl of Stratton. They spend their honeymoon on the *Aquitania* bound for England.

Mae actually sang "Mon coeur s'ouvre à ta voix" (My heart at thy sweet voice) from Act 2 of Saint-Saëns's *Samson and Delilah* for the soundtrack of this film. She was not looped by another singer. Her friend and secretary, Tim Malachosky, said she was especially proud of this achievement. The famous aria is difficult, demanding—and in French.

Mae liked opera and enjoyed playing her collection of operatic recordings. She had been told as a girl that she had a lovely soprano voice and could be a successful opera singer. She was the one who decided to put the opera scene in the film, so she could sing.

Mae told me that when she met Beverly Sills, she said, "I sing opera, too."

Speaking with Beverly Sills many years later at Lincoln Center in New York City, I asked about her meeting with Mae.

"I don't think she knew who I was," Sills told me. "The person who introduced us told her I sang opera.

"I certainly knew who she was. I'd seen some of her films, though not the one she referred to [*Goin' to Town*], the one where she sang *Delilah*.

"She was a very original talent."

In April 1935, almost a month before *Goin' to Town* was released, news of Mae's 1911 marriage to Frank Wallace broke. At first, Mae denied it through Beverly and Timony. They claimed it never happened, and besides, there was more than one Mae West, they said. Then, when a record of the marriage was located in the Milwaukee City Hall, Mae admitted her early "mistake." Complicating matters, Wallace had remarried in 1915 without divorcing Mae. He divorced that wife in 1935 before he went public with his first marriage. In 1937, he sued Mae and demanded recognition as her lawful husband. The dispute would last until they were divorced in 1941.

"I knew I didn't want children," Mae told me. "When I was a little girl, I wanted a doll. But I knew that a doll wasn't a baby. You can just put your dolly away when you don't feel like playing that game anymore. Maybe if I missed something, that was having a baby. But I don't think I was meant to be a mother.

"I don't think a woman should have a baby unless she's prepared to love that baby more than she loves herself. Like my mother did. I didn't think I could do that.

"People think about what a baby is going to do for them when they should be thinking about what they are going to do for the baby. It's a tremendous responsibility to bring a new person into the world, a person who'll be changing every year. I felt about the same age all my life; a child lets you know you aren't.

"I respect those who make the sacrifice. Motherhood's a full-time career. I already had a career. I didn't think I could do both things right. And they never persuaded me that men don't have the more fun part of having babies."

Though *Goin' to Town* was nominally affected by Hollywood's newly invigorated Hays Office, the film was successful. The censors, however, would not approve Mae's next film, *Klondkike Annie*, unless certain changes were made. These changes rendered the plot difficult to follow and eliminated two striking scenes.

Mae's character, Rose, being held as a virtual slave by a Chinese man, Chan Lo, can endure no more of his sadistic cruelty and she kills him. The scene in which she stabs him to death had to be cut, and the audience only finds out what she has done well after she has fled San Francisco on a steamer.

Another important scene met with the disapproval of certain religious groups. The scene in which Rose elaborately applies makeup to the dead woman, which will make her look like her character, "Frisco Doll," and puts on the drab apparel that will transform her into Sister Annie, had to be cut. This anticipates by thirty-five years Michelangelo Antonioni's *Profession: Reporter* (also called *The Passenger*), in which Jack Nicholson almost ritually exchanges identities with a dead man. The deleted footage of *Klondike Annie* has not survived, as far as anyone knows. Mae always hoped it would be found.

"Frisco Doll," Mae told me, "is summed up in her line, 'Between two evils, I always pick the one I never tried before.' Doll is a bad girl gone good."

Klondike Annie (1936)

Frisco Doll (Mae West), the singing sensation of San Francisco's Barbary Coast, is really Rose Carlton. Once saved from a life of degradation by Chan Lo (Harold Huber), she is now treated as a virtual concubine.

When she attempts to escape aboard an Alaska-bound steamer, Chan threatens to kill her. Instead, she kills Chan in self-defense, and then she escapes on the ship.

Bull Brackett (Victor McLaglen), the captain of the ship, not knowing Rose is wanted for murder as Frisco Doll, accepts her rejection of his advances. When the ship reaches Seattle, however, he finds out, and Rose can no longer resist.

Another passenger, Annie Alden (Helen Jerome Eddy), boards in Vancouver. She is an evangelist bound for a mission in Nome. Her mission is to save souls, and she tries to save Rose's, but before she can accomplish this formidable task, she dies.

When the police board the ship in Nome searching for Rose, she changes places with Annie. Bull doesn't give her away. Instead, he offers her an alternative escape with him to the South Seas, but she declines.

In Nome, Rose, now Klondike Annie, feels obligated to carry out Annie's destiny. When she finds the mission is in a sad state of repairs, she revives interest in religion by applying her show business experience to the task of saving souls. It works, and Klondike Annie becomes the toast of Nome, just as Frisco Doll had been the toast of San Francisco.

Among her new admirers is a Canadian Mountie, Jack Forrest (Phillip Reed). He loves her even when he finds out who she really is, but Annie can't let him ruin his promising career as a policeman by marrying her. Too much of Annie Alden's goodness has rubbed off on her. Instead, she goes back to San Francisco with Bull after providing for a much bigger Annie Alden mission. They are both confident that she will prove herself innocent of the murder charge and be able to establish that she acted in self-defense.

"Victor McLaglen got the part in *Klondike Annie* because I'd been eating too much," Mae explained. "I cast him because I'd let my weight go up, and I didn't want to take it off fast and look gaunt.

"He was not only tall, but big and bulky, so he was great for the part of Bull Brackett, and he made me look petite."

In 1936, Ernst Lubitsch was made Paramount Pictures' chief of production. Mae was not pleased, even though she had admired him as a director. She feared his influence on her films might be "heavy-handed."

"Lubitsch and I got off to a bad start," Mae told me. "You might say he stubbed his tongue."

"You would think," George Cukor said, "that Mae and Ernst Lubitsch would have been compatible, both professionally and personally, but they were more combatable than compatible.

"Mae told me that while she might have liked knowing Lubitsch as a director, she could not get along with him in his job as the Paramount head of production. She appreciated Lubitsch's sense of comedy and believed he could have been an excellent director for her. Second-best only to me, of course. She told me I was her number-one preferred director.

"She always hoped to get directors she could learn from, she said, but I don't know if she was really ready to accept direction that she didn't agree perfectly with. It was probably better for our friendship that I never directed her. Mae liked to call the shots, and she had intimidated quite a few directors along the way. There was a rumor that Lubitsch wanted to step in and direct a few scenes of her upcoming picture. It was probably only a rumor, but it disturbed Mae.

"When Mae met Lubitsch, it was in his capacity as production head. He probably was wearing his executive hat and trying to mind Paramount's money. He probably cautioned Miss West about going over budget. She never took well to being given marching orders and didn't like even a wrong tone of voice. She would have found the word 'budget' a dirty word. You might say they didn't hit it off well. She said she hit him with a silver-handled hairbrush. That was very out of character for Mae. She didn't like to argue, even verbally, and I can't imagine her having a physical argument. Lubitsch was in a position of authority with power over her, and all of us have certain problems in our acceptance of people who have authority over us. I never knew exactly why Lubitsch didn't like Mae, but I did get Mae's version of her aversion.

"There was a specific incident that led to bad feelings, according to Mae's version. It happened in Mae's dressing room, and there were no witnesses, and she has always had what you might call a selective memory. You could say she wore rose-colored glasses, but not with Lubitsch. He may have stepped on her rose-colored glasses.

"Mae didn't appreciate what she called his sticking his nose into her business. They had a few words, likely more than a few, probably about the budget and production time. I believe I remember he didn't like her *Catherine Was Great* idea. He didn't want to look at it. She thought it was because he had his own idea for that story.

"Mae said he used some language 'not respectful and not appropriate to be used in front of a lady.'

"Mae could be, at times, a prude.

"She told me she asked Lubitsch to 'vacate' her dressing room in as controlled a manner as she could manage. When he didn't move fast enough, she began pummeling him with her hairbrush. 'I had no alternative,' she told me. 'That got him out.'"

Paramount executive Emanuel Cohen had formed an independent production company, Major Pictures, which would finance the last two films on Mae's contract. He would continue to use Paramount's facilities and contract players; Paramount would then distribute the finished films, splitting the profits fifty-fifty with Major.

Their first film under the new agreement was *Go West Young Man*. The screenplay was based on Lawrence Riley's stage play *Personal Appearance*, which starred Gladys George on Broadway. The "West" in the new title has an obvious double meaning. The story resembles *Bombshell*, in which Lee Tracy is Jean Harlow's frenetic publicist, as well as *The Taming of the Shrew*.

Go West Young Man (1936)

While Mavis Arden (Mae West) plays the world's most desirable woman on the screen, she's far from that for Morgan (Warren William), her manager and publicist. For him, she's an unmanageable, temperamental shrew. His job is to protect her smiling public image from the frozen pout of her private self and to keep her from getting married.

Her five-year contract with the studio is only valid as long as she is single. Being married, the producer believes, would jeopardize her image as a sex symbol. She, on the other hand, believes in marriage for every girl.

While they are attending a showing of her latest film in Washington, Mavis rekindles an old romance with Francis X. Harrigan (Lyle Talbot), a presidential candidate who knew her when she was a chorus girl in Chicago. Learning that they are planning a quiet rendezvous on a hotel roof garden, Morgan alerts the press.

Just as Mavis hopes Harrigan will propose, the media barges in to record the event for the world. Since the press is more interested in Mavis than Harrigan, she outlines a platform for him demanding that every woman who can't afford to get married be subsidized in matrimony by the government.

Harrigan thinks he's ruined. Then he realizes such a union could win votes. Harrigan sets out for the next stop on Mavis's tour, Harrisburg, Pennsylvania, determined to marry her.

On her way through rural Pennsylvania her new limousine breaks down. Morgan finds a repair shop at The Haven, an old mansion that has been turned into a boardinghouse. They stay there while the car is being repaired.

Everyone at The Haven is excited by the prospect of a Hollywood star boarding with them. Mavis is her usual unpleasant self until she notices a muscular young man, Bud Norton (Randolph Scott), a brilliant, and handsome, inventor.

His latest invention is a revolutionary motion picture sound recording process. Mavis offers to take his invention, and him, to Hollywood. Meanwhile, she tries to seduce him, and Bud's girlfriend, Joyce (Margaret Perry), becomes jealous.

One of the guests, Professor Rigby (Etienne Girodot), threatens to sell his unfavorable view of Mavis to the newspapers. Morgan talks him out of it by promising him a Hollywood career.

Harrigan thinks Mavis has been kidnapped, and he calls the police.

Since Joyce is always seen knitting an infant's sweater for a cousin who is having a baby, Morgan convinces Mavis that Bud's girlfriend is having the baby. Mavis cancels her plans to take Bud to Hollywood.

Harrigan arrives with policemen. Finding out that Morgan was lying about Joyce, Mavis socks him and then turns him over to the police as a kidnapper. As he's being led away, she changes her mind.

At fade-out, Morgan and she are seen embracing in the back of her Rolls-Royce. "Men are my life," she says.

Critical response to *Go West Young Man* was unfavorable, and theater attendance disappointing. Audiences possibly expected Mae to play a more sympathetic character than the selfish, shrewish Mavis. Earlier, Mae wrote a similar character for herself in *The Wicked Age*, and she would play another such character in *The Heat's On*. "I never wanted to be type cast," she explained.

Mae was proud of having chosen Randolph Scott, and said she had "a knack." She had to admit that she had chosen him not for his talent, because she didn't know about that yet, but because she thought he was "a great-looking guy. He was sort of an American guy next door, or one you *wish* you had next door."

She added, "I liked to call him 'Randy' because he was. We weren't intimate, but I could tell."

Just before *Go West Young Man*, Mae had allowed her weight to go up to the highest it had ever been. She said it wasn't because she indulged herself for enjoyment, but because she had felt pressure and calmed her nervousness with "instant gratification."

"It doesn't take long to put it on, the pounds, but it's tough to get it off fast. I didn't think starvation was the answer. It would have left me feeling weak and deprived me of my full resources. And I don't need any stretch marks.

"Nobody said anything to me except my mirror, which told it all, and I knew the camera wouldn't lie for me, either."

In 1937, Mae was invited to make a radio appearance with Edgar Bergen and Charlie McCarthy on the prime-time *Chase and Sanborn Hour*. Bergen was a popular ventriloquist whose dummy, Charlie Mc-Carthy, accorded him no respect. Mae accepted the invitation because she had something of her own she was interested in promoting, her new film, *Every Day's a Holiday*.

Mae was asked to submit her material. Since the program was live, the producers wanted to be certain that she didn't plan to say anything that might upset the radio audience and thus the sponsor. To her surprise, the finished script came back with no major changes. She was shocked that *they* weren't shocked. "I wondered if I was slipping," she said.

What no one "heard" on paper was Mae's delivery, her tone of voice, the way she played with her lines, and how she said them rather than the exact words. In two rehearsals, Mae did not read her lines the way she would say them on the air.

The show was broadcast on Sunday, December 12, 1937. Mae's skit with Don Ameche and Charlie McCarthy was called "What Might Have Happened in the Garden of Eden." It was written by Arch Obo-ler, who later became famous for his radio dramas.

"I was there, at the broadcast in Hollywood," Doris Stine told me as we sat years later at a New York luncheon honoring George Cukor. "I thought it was mildly funny, a little risqué perhaps, but not at all objectionable. Then I called my husband in New York, and he was outraged." Jules Stine was the head of the Music Corporation of America. "He thought people would consider it sacrilegious. He was right."

Satirizing the Bible on a Sunday just before Christmas with Mae West as a sensual Eve caused a public outcry that reached Congress, where an investigation by the Federal Communications Commission was informally proposed.

There are some relatively innocuous lines, such as "He's so naive," spoken by Charlie when Bergen accepts Charlie's explanation that he only went up to Mae's apartment to see her etchings. Mostly, Mae turns lines like "You're all wood and a yard long" into double and sometimes triple entendres. Mae's sensual Eve shocked some people, or perhaps her reputation alone was too much for America's living rooms in 1937.

"I was banned from the networks for a decade," Mae said. "I was never so insulted! I should've gotten at least two." An official ban was not probable, since the two major competing networks, NBC and CBS, were unlikely to get together and make such an agreement. It was, however, what Mae believed, and she wasn't invited to appear on many shows, as she had been before.

During the year between *Go West Young Man* and *Every Day's a Holiday*, Mae lost the extra weight she had added "and a little more for good measure."

The Parisian designer Schiaparelli had been commissioned to design the costumes for the new film. "It wasn't my idea," Mae said. "It added extra expense, and I felt less in control because of the geography involved. I was happiest with Edith [Head]. It was funny to have a designer with a name I had to learn how to pronounce, a Parisian designer with an Italian name. I was somewhat conversant with French, but I had no experience with Italian. I knew the name Schiaparelli because she'd done some wonderful hats I'd seen in a magazine.

"One thing I was adamant about, I let everyone know they weren't shipping *me* to Paris.

"I wouldn't've minded being in Paris, but it was the getting there I didn't want to go through. I don't like to fly, which is putting it mild, though I wouldn't have minded doing it with Lindbergh—fly that is. Ship travel took too long when you were anxious to get things done, and I never felt as good on water as I did on land. Maybe it was because I never learned to swim. But I don't know what difference that would've made. If anything goes wrong, the Atlantic Ocean's too far to swim anyway.

"I guess I never got the story of the *Titanic* out of my head. All those poor, poor people. You know, even the ones who got through it, it must have stayed in their heads, so they could never get over it, no matter how long they lived.

"They reassured me. Only a dress form of me and my measurements would have to travel.

"When the dress form arrived in Paris, the dressmakers there said, in French, 'Oo-la-la!' and so on. 'This is *impossible*.' Then, they looked at the measurements, which exactly matched the form. They couldn't believe their eyes.

"There is no woman living with this figure, is what I guess they thought. Well, I was sure living, and that was *my* figure.

"So they went ahead and made all the dresses—too big. Well, it was a blessing they didn't make the dresses too small. I'd chosen all the most expensive materials. Some of it was the last pieces, and you couldn't even replace it.

"When the dresses arrived, I couldn't wait to see them and try them on. I knew that my dresses were a vital part of my character. They were essential for my audience, and they were pretty important for me, too, because they got me in character and made me feel good. Beautiful dresses always dressed up my spirits, just like they did for my mother.

"It was important that my costumes were not tight, but exactly fitted to show off my hourglass figure.

"Everyone was pretty worried when they saw that one and a half of me could wear each dress. There was a lot of fretting, but not by me. I had a secret in my corner. I had dear Edith Head on the alert, waiting on pins and needles—a small joke—from the moment I knew my dresses were being made abroad. It seemed a long shot that they would come back just right. As a betting person, I thought it was a long, long shot. I liked gambling on the ponies, but not on my movie.

"There were some people who wanted to send the dresses back to Paris for refitting, again without me, and working fast.

"I put my foot down—hard. Edith and I started work while they were quibbling. The dresses looked beautiful in the film, and on me afterwards. One of the benefits of having a unique figure like no one else is they didn't have anything else to do with the dresses. I said, 'I'd like to have some of the dresses when we finish the film.' They said, 'Of course, Mae, but those dresses cost a lot, so we'd like to deduct about fifty percent, give or take a few dollars, from what we're paying you.'

" 'Give or take a few dollars,' I said, 'keep 'em.'

"I'd learned a little about bargaining from observing my father making a business deal. I knew I had 'em. They changed their tune in midstream. Lots of false smiles and plenty of dresses. They were mine for the taking, and I took."

Schiaparelli wasn't angry, but impressed. Later, she introduced a perfume bottle in the shape of Mae West that looked like the dress form, which had stayed in Paris.

"It was a very expensive perfume called 'Shocking.' " She sent some bottles of the perfume to Mae, who liked the scent, the name, and the shape of the bottle.

"Schiaparelli couldn't link my name to it, which was just as well because I wouldn't give endorsements, but the word got out on a small scale, anyway. I guess my shape got recognized."

Production on *Every Day's a Holiday*, Mae's last Paramount film, began at about the same time as her appearance on *The Chase and Sanborn Hour*, and the film was released widely in early 1938. It was greeted with unfavorable critical response and unenthusiastic audience attendance.

Stricter Hays Office censorship was said to be making it impossible for Mae West to be funny anymore. Mae disagreed.

"I *believe* in censorship. If a picture of mine didn't get an 'X' rating, I'd be insulted. Don't forget, dear, I *invented* censorship. Imagine censors that wouldn't let you sit in a man's lap! I've been in more laps than a napkin. They'd get all bothered by a harmless little line like 'Is that a gun in your pocket or are you just glad to see me?'

"I had my tricks for handling the censors. I'd write some lines I knew they would take out so the others could stay in. You had to let them earn their money. You might say I created the Hays Office. They had to do it because of me. I'm a kind of godmother to the Motion Picture Code. Now they use nudity and talking dirty to take the place of a good story and believable characters. I didn't have to take off my clothes. Men imagined what was under them. I had this line, 'I wouldn't let him touch me with a ten-foot pole,' which the Hays Office wouldn't let me use. Forty years later, I ask an athlete in [the film] *Sextette* what he did, and he says, 'I'm a pole vaulter.' And I say, 'Aren't we all,' and nobody even noticed it."

In the 1930s, however, it seemed that everything about her films, not just sexual innuendos, was being questioned. She was becoming a victim of censorship. Mae, however, disagreed.

"They said censorship was my enemy, but I'm not so sure about that. Maybe censorship was my best *friend*. You can't get famous for breaking the rules unless you've got some rules to break.

"Where would censorship have been without me? Like I always say, I made censorship necessary.

"I made a fortune out of censorship. I never used four-letter words. Never. I don't even think them. Well, I don't think them very often.

"I don't think a lady should ever use those words. It doesn't mean she isn't a lady if she uses them. It just means she shouldn't have used them, and it leaves the way open for men to treat her like she's not a lady. Then, men are free to use those words in front of her, a sign of disrespect.

"I never tolerated disrespect from a man. No man could use four-letter words or obscenities in front of me.

"I'm sure my father knew all those words, and he used them with his men friends, especially around the fighters in the ring and at the track. But I never heard him use bad words or dirty language in front of my mother or me. Those words were not used in our house.

"As for me, I was never vulgar. The word for me was 'suggestive.' "

Mae described her character in *Every Day's a Holiday*, Peaches O'Day, as "a girl who believed if you kept a diary, some day it would keep you."

Every Day's a Holiday (1937)

At the turn of the twentieth century, Peaches O'Day (Mae West), earns a very good living by selling the Brooklyn Bridge to gullible tourists. She is protected by the two police officers who have been ordered to arrest her: Captain "Honest John" Quade (Lloyd Nolan), who has a romantic interest in her, and Lieutenant Jim McCarey (Edmund Lowe) doesn't want to send her to jail.

Just before New Year's Eve, Peaches meets a butler, Larmadon Graves (Charles Butterworth), whose employer is Van Reighle van Pelter van Doon (Charles Winninger), an eccentric millionaire who has been leading moral reform movements. Van Doon invites Peaches to Rector's for the New Year's Eve celebration.

While she's celebrating with them, Nifty Bailey (Walter Catlett) appears, hoping to get van Doon to back a show he is producing. It is not what the millionaire wants to do, but Peaches is able to charm him into it, hoping for a good part for herself in the show.

On the brink of legitimate theatrical success in Nifty's show, Peaches has to leave town in order to avoid arrest. She is replaced by a French singer, Mademoiselle Fifi, and the show is a big success. No one except McCarey notices that Fifi is really Peaches with a black wig and a French accent.

When she rejects Captain Quade, he orders McCarey to close the theater. McCarey refuses, and Quade fires him. Meanwhile, Peaches, as Fifi, manages to get all of the files that could incriminate her.

Quade puts himself up as a candidate for mayor in the next election. Peaches uses her charm to convince van Doon that he should back McCarey's candidacy.

Before the election Quade has McCarey kidnapped. Unable to lead his election parade, McCarey is replaced by Fifi, who wins even more votes for him.

McCarey escapes and is elected mayor on the reform ticket. Peaches, now a successful performer, can lead the honest life McCarey envisioned for her.

This was Mae's most expensive film. It cost one million 1938 dollars. The screenplay was by Mae, and was based on an original story by Mae and Jo Sterling.

"*Every Day's a Holiday* came to me in fifty-six seconds," Mae told me. "It was one of my best pictures. I told it to the producers in about fifteen minutes. One hour to dictate it.

"I know it was The Forces. They whispered in my ear. How else?

"I believe The Forces have a lot to do with what we call inspiration. Intuition is related, too."

"I'd have every thing in my mind before I'd start to write, so I wouldn't have to stop. I'd imagine it all first, then I'd just write it down. I'd be living it while I was writing it. And I was always thinking. I had a very active brain.

"My brain was so active, I didn't know how to turn it off so I could go to sleep. I had to wait a while till I got so tired, my thoughts ran down. I always kept a pad of paper and plenty of pencils by my bed, so I could write down some of the thoughts I had then.

"At night, before I went to bed, my imagination frequently became unleashed. I was writing notes as long as I was awake, and who knows? Maybe I wrote in my sleep. Sometimes when I woke up, I found notes in my handwriting I didn't even remember writing.

"I do my best writing in bed. A lot of what I do best, I do in bed.

"I tried writing in the bath, but that didn't work well. The bubble bath kept getting my notes wet, and I had trouble drying them out. And when I'm in the tub, I prefer to concentrate on luxuriating."

Though Beverly West appeared only in Mae's stage productions and not in her films, a member of Beverly's household did have a part in *Every Day's a Holiday*, her beloved black Great Dane, following in the paw prints of her Russian wolfhounds. He was extremely large, even for a Great Dane, and thus was a commanding presence and scene-stealer. Mae had an idea for visually enhancing his part. She had a dazzling diamond collar made for him. He wore it proudly. Mae said that was because he didn't know the diamonds were really rhine-stones.

In 1939, Universal Pictures approached Mae and Timony with a proposition. Would Mae consider working with their star W. C. Fields? Mae liked Bill Fields, and he was very respectful toward her. There was only one thing about him she didn't like—his drinking.

Groucho Marx remembered visiting Fields in the late 1930s and being taken on a grand tour of the house. Near the end of the tour, Fields asked Groucho to follow him up to the attic.

It was filled with case after case of liquor.

Groucho didn't understand. Prohibition had ended in 1933.

Fields looked around to make sure he wasn't being overheard, and said, "It might come back."

Mae said, "I knew Bill Fields in vaudeville, and I heard his drinking hadn't diminished. To the contrary. So, I got it in my contract that if he came to the set drunk, they would remove him from the premises. It looked okay for a while, and then he turned up drunk. It was pretty easy to see and easier to smell.

"I didn't hesitate. I said, 'Okay, boys—throw him out!' They looked at me to see if I meant it. I meant it. He wasn't so drunk he didn't know what was happening. He looked at me, I guess, to see if I really meant it. He saw his answer, right away. 'Aw, Mae . . .' he said.

" 'Don't "Aw, Mae" me,' I answered him, and he was gone.

"There were a lot of extras around that day, and they were all watching. There were probably some Paramount accountants watching, too. I don't know if they blamed him the way they should have for costing them the extra money, or if they blamed me. Nobody said anything to me about it. I don't know what they said to Bill. Maybe they didn't have to say anything to him because he got the message.

"After that, he was a marshmallow. He was so sweet and easy to work with, and no sign of any liquor."

My Little Chickadee (1940)

A stagecoach bound for a western frontier town is held up by a masked bandit. One of the passengers, Flower Belle Lee (Mae West), is kidnapped and then returned unhurt. She evidently has been treated very well by the masked bandit.

Word of this event reaches the respectable ladies of the town. They are not certain Flower Belle is the kind of person they want in their midst, especially when she says things like, "I generally avoid temptation. Unless I can't resist it." One of the ladies, Mrs. Gideon (Margaret Hamilton), sees her meeting secretly with the masked bandit and reports it to the other ladies. Flower Belle is advised to leave town and not come back until she is respectably married. Miss Gideon sends a telegram warning the ladies of Greasewood City of Flower Belle's imminent arrival.

On the train, Flower Belle meets Cuthbert J. Twillie (W. C. Fields), a patent medicine salesman. Mistaking his satchel of discount coupons for paper money, she has an idea that will give her legitimacy and money. She charms Twillie into marrying her in a ceremony with a cardsharp (Donald Meek) who is disguised as a cleric.

In Greasewood City, Flower Belle initiates an affair with the saloon keeper (Joseph Calleia) while holding off the advances of Twillie. Twillie even tries unsuccessfully to disguises himself as the masked bandit, whom he has heard was one of Flower Belle's lovers. Dressed as the masked bandit, Twillie is captured by the sheriff and sentenced to be hanged.

Flower Belle saves Twillie from the noose at the last moment by producing the stolen loot of the masked bandit, who, it turns out, is the saloon keeper. She and Twillie, not really married, wistfully go their separate ways after he invites her to "come up and see me some-time," and she answers, "I'll do that, my little chickadee."

Mae got to sing one of her risqué songs, "Willie of the Valley," after some of the lyrics were toned down.

"It didn't matter," she said. "I could make 'Twinkle, Twinkle, Little Star' sound racy. There *was* one line, though, that I would've liked to use, but they wouldn't let me: 'Snow White was a good gal till she drifted.' "

In her contract for *My Little Chickadee*, Mae insisted that residual payments be made to her for future showings of the film on television. Very likely working with Jim Timony, she anticipated the future of films on television.

Timony and the William Morris Agency were able to work this provision into the contract. As Timony reported to Mae, it wasn't even difficult, because the value of future showings on television, which was to become so major, was unappreciated. At that time, very few people anticipated the future for classic films. Later, a negotiation like this would have involved a considerable struggle or even been impossible.

Mae said W. C. Fields later heard about what she had in her contract, but it was much too late for him to have his people make any such arrangement for him. "It made him so angry, he must have gone out and gotten drunk.

"I had another chance to work with Bill, but I said, 'No, thank you. Don't even show me the script.' I don't know how Bill would have felt about working with me again, but I know how I felt."

In 1940, the British Royal Air Force pilots named their very bulky life jackets "Mae Wests," thus putting Mae into the dictionary. She replied that she was tickled and said the dictionary was her favorite book.

• • •

Ever since he surfaced in the mid-1930s, Frank Wallace had been forcing Mae into court to fight nuisance suits that were quickly settled in her favor or thrown out altogether. Besides suing Mae for separate maintenance, he alleged that Timony had threatened his life, implying that the Las Vegas mob would carry out this threat. The least he deserved, Wallace claimed, was compensation for having kept Mae's marriage to him a secret for so many years. This behavior had been going on for seven years when Mae decided to put a stop to it.

On July 21, 1942, she sued Wallace for divorce on the grounds of mental cruelty.

Before Mae went to court "to get rid of Wallace once and for all," she was advised by her lawyers to wear her plainest clothes.

"I don't *have* any plain clothes," Mae retorted.

She was also strongly advised not to wear her diamonds, since her husband was trying to part her from half her fortune, including her diamonds. She was only anxious to part *herself* from Wallace.

She didn't wear any diamonds to court, but not out of deference to her lawyer's advice. It was because she had chosen to wear her best suite of sapphires, which were even more flamboyant. "I didn't feel I needed to misrepresent myself.

"The marriage wasn't a secret anymore," Mae said, "so I had nothing to lose but Wallace. And that was the good part of his having brought everything out into the open. When my lawyers said not to wear my diamonds, I never liked very much being given my marching orders, but I figured since I was paying 'em so much for their advice, maybe I ought to listen a little to them.

"So I only wore my sapphires, and my lawyers couldn't say anything."

The divorce was granted, effective May 7, 1943. Wallace's second marriage, entered into without first verifying whether he was still married to Mae or not, was enough for the judge to dismiss any maintenance or alimony claims he might have had.

"I gave him a little something for old times' sake," Mae said.

During the divorce proceedings, Mae had told the court that, by Hollywood standards, she was not wealthy. From the standpoint of her annual earnings, this was true. She hadn't worked since 1939, having become very selective in her choice of scripts. More than three years had passed since she had made a film, and she was ready to work again.

Thus, when Gregory Ratoff approached her with a film project he was developing, she listened, at least politely. He was not only a friend from her early days in Hollywood, but a relative, "a sort of cousin-in-law." He was a cousin of one of Beverly's Russian husbands. Mae was receptive to anyone who could claim to be part of her family, especially if the connection could be linked, however remotely, to her mother.

"Doing *The Heat's On* was a mistake," Mae confessed. "I didn't make many mistakes in my career. *The Heat's On* was one. I can't deny this error because the evidence is there on film for audiences to see. I never liked to admit to a mistake, but if I can't deny it, it's tantamount to admitting it.

"The picture I agreed to make was called *Tropicana. The Heat's On* is the one that got made, and I got hooked like a fish.

"Gregory Ratoff was the fisherman. He came to see me, and I took the bait. He pitched the movie he wanted to do. His Russian accent had a Russian accent. It sounded like he was speaking Russian when he was speaking English.

"I understood less than half of what he said, and I didn't want to be rude by saying, 'What? What?' I should have. But what would've been the use? I don't think I'd've understood what he was trying to say no matter how many times he said it.

"But he sure had a lot of confidence, and when I started to say something, he always stopped me with a well-placed 'dollink.' Russian men are charming. I never cared for caviar, but, oh, those blintzes with sour cream! I was promised a script.

"By the time he came back again, I knew the picture was in trouble. Ratoff, who was not exactly a *rat*, but certainly *off*, told me that he had already spent a lot of the money he'd raised, all on my name, and that if I pulled out, he would be bankrupt, lose his house, and probably never work again. I did not want to see that happen to him, and I didn't think it would be good for my own reputation to have it get around that I did that. I had this idea that I could doll up the script, but there wasn't time. All I was able to do was to try and fix my part.

"The title was no good and it probably turned a lot of people off. It sure turned me off. Not that *Tropicana* was any good. I made an Old Year's resolution. Never to do a picture on a verbal pitch and always make sure I had an escape clause.

"That picture was enough to make me feel I wanted to have a little vacation time from Hollywood. I decided I wanted to go back to New York and do a play. I was craving a live audience."

The Heat's On (1943)

Producer Tony Ferris (William Gaxton), trying to publicize *Indiscretion*, his failing Broadway musical, enlists the aid of Hubert Bainbridge (Victor Moore), whose foundation polices public morals. In return for advancing the musical comedy career of his niece Janie (Mary

Roche), Hubert agrees to use the influence of his family's foundation to shut down *Indiscretion* as morally offensive.

When a police raid closes the show Tony explains to star Fay Lawrence (Mae West) that it was just a publicity stunt to keep the show open, but instead it is permanently closed.

A rival producer, Forrest Stanton (Alan Dinehart), offers Fay another starring role in *Tropicana*, a new show, and she accepts.

To get her back, Tony starts a rumor that Fay has been blacklisted. After hearing the rumor, Stanton offers Tony the show for a bargain price, and he accepts. He then tells Hubert that he will replace Fay with Janie, if Hubert agrees to back *Tropicana*.

Fay finds out and informs Hannah Bainbridge (Almira Sessions), Hubert's sister and the real head of the foundation. Hannah withdraws the foundation's backing from the show and from Janie.

With Fay again as the lead, Tony easily gets new backing. Everything goes smoothly until Janie appears unexpectedly on opening night. She informs Tony that her boyfriend (Lloyd Bridges) has packed the house with his military buddies. Unless she gets to play the lead, the troops will boo Fay off the stage.

Janie has her night, and becomes a star. Fay returns to the show, and it has a long run. Tony, to get Fay's sympathy, pretends to have a mental breakdown. He does not fool Fay, who leaves him in the insane asylum.

"When I came out to Hollywood in '32, I didn't know if I'd like it or not, but I took Jim Timony's advice and gave it a try. I liked it a lot, but I understood it was like having a passionate affair with a very attractive man. It couldn't last forever. So, I always treated it that way.

"One thing I knew was, when the magic wore off, I was gonna be the one who ended the affair, not the other way around. It was how I lived my personal life, and also how I lived my professional career.

"Hollywood and I needed some time apart. I knew I could always come back whenever I wanted. So I decided to go back to my first love, the stage, the Broadway melieu, for a while, anyway."

Mae had a number of theatrical projects in mind, including *Catherine Was Great*, which she had been trying for years to make into a film. In 1943, she returned to Broadway to make *Catherine* into a theatrical reality.

Chapter Five

ON THE ROAD

(1944–1964)

I'M GLAD YOU liked my Catherine," Mae said in a curtain speech to the audience at the end of each *Catherine Was Great* performance. "She ruled thirty million people and had three thousand lovers. I do the best I can in two hours."

Mae repeated that speech for me in 1980, saying, "I remember it perfectly. I'll never forget it. You know, it got the biggest laugh of the show, every performance. It was really outside of the play proper, or maybe I should say outside of the play *im*proper."

The Broadway premiere was at the Shubert Theatre on August 2, 1944. Opening night tickets were so sought after that standing room was considered. The decision was made that standing room would not be proper for opening night. The second night, the theater was filled, and so was standing room.

It was predicted that the play would recoup its extremely high production costs, but it didn't live up to that early optimism. The bad reviews did not seem to diminish audience turnout. People really came to see Mae West, and her costumes were among the most dazzling and expensive ever seen on a stage.

There were costumes that weighed as much as fifty pounds, and one of Mae's costumes not only weighed fifty pounds, but also had a headdress that weighed twenty-five pounds. All of these dresses and headdresses were planned by Mae, and she relished wearing them. She never complained about any discomfort.

The cost of production, as well as the payments to Mae and others, precluded any possibility of eventual profit, but the show was regarded as entertaining and memorable by all who saw it. Mae's only regret was that it was never made into a film, so that future generations could enjoy it.

From the first moment she learned about the existence of the Russian empress, Mae longed to be *Catherine* on the stage. If Mae had believed in reincarnation, she said she would have thought *she* was the empress, reincarnated. "Catherine the Great was the Mae West of her day."

In Hollywood, Mae had envisioned *Catherine Was Great* as a Technicolor spectacular, but nothing ever came of it. When J. J. Shubert and Mike Todd offered her the opportunity to do the play in a lavish production on Broadway, she accepted.

Producer Mike Todd brought in a professor who was an authority on Russian history. Todd asked the professor if all of the facts had been perfectly adhered to. The historian informed the producer that *none* of the facts had been adhered to. Chronology, facts, the authentic roles of characters, had all been ignored.

Todd confronted Mae, after the rehearsal, in the presence of the professor. He repeated what the professor had said. The professor was chagrined in the presence of the star, but he had to nod his head, affirming that this was, indeed, the conclusion at which he had arrived.

Both Todd and the professor were certain that Mae would be terribly upset by this opinion. They expected her to try to defend herself. They were prepared for a terrible scene.

Far from it. Mae smiled, addressing the Russian historian.

"Were you entertained?"

He hadn't been prepared for that simple, direct question.

He answered simply, directly, and spontaneously, "Yes."

Mae was relieved and pleased. "See?" she said to Todd.

Todd was not reassured. "How will we explain this to the critics?"

Without a second's hesitation, Mae said, "Well, I'm sure the prologue will be understood by them. Don't you think the prologue makes it clear?"

Todd looked bewildered.

Mae, a bit shocked, said, "Didn't you read the prologue?"

Todd immediately sent an assistant to find the prologue in his office. A general search failed to produce it.

Mae seemed a little hurt, but she said, "It's not a problem. I'll bring a copy in tomorrow." Nonchalantly, Mae departed.

When she reached her car, she told the driver, "Drive fast."

She called her secretary to tell him to meet her and be prepared to work all night.

"The next day, without pomp or circumstance, I casually dropped the prologue on Mr. Todd's desk. 'You don't have to look for it no more,' I said. 'Here it is.' "

A grateful and subdued Mike Todd accepted the explanation that the prologue provided.

The prologue shows two World War II soldiers talking about Catherine the Great, based on a dream one of them had had about her. This allowed for some fanciful historical license.

Todd was ready to grasp at the straw the prologue offered. He hoped it would be his life preserver.

In July 1944, the Philadelphia tryouts were enormously successful.

The play opened on Broadway in August and, in spite of universal critical disapproval, ran until January 13, 1945, a total of 191 performances.

Mae wanted the sets to be as authentic as possible, so she purchased Russian furniture and hangings. The greatest attention was paid by Mae to her costumes. Tiaras and jewelry, furs, all were custom-designed. Mae's later personal assistant, Tim Malachosky, remembered the dozens of bolts of the finest material filling closets at the Santa Monica beach house. Mae sometimes had a dress she liked made in different colors. She insisted that none be too bright or gaudy.

The play was not profitable because of the tremendous expense of mounting it, but it was extremely profitable for Mae, and not a major loss for the Shuberts, who backed her strongly.

Come on Up was Mae's adaptation of a play called *Ring Twice Tonight*, a spy comedy by three other writers. Mae called herself "a Mae Hari sort of character." Male spies, anxious to win her approval, exaggerate their secret information. It played intermittently during a fifty-three-city tour from 1946 until early 1947. By then, Timony had arranged an English tour of *Diamond Lil*.

"In September [1947], Jim and I headed for England on the *Queen Mary*. We were taking *Lil* there for a visit."

They took two actors with them, and planned to cast all the others from among British actors and Europeans. There was also a maid who could assist Mae with hair, makeup, and as a dresser.

Timony and Mae took eight trunks with them. Only one of them belonged to Timony.

"I traveled light," Mae said, "except for my diamond ring, which weighed twenty-two karats, not counting its platinum setting. I took my favorite diamond bracelet and a tiara for special occasions.

"In London, we stayed at the Savoy Hotel, and it was a great experience, and comfortable. I could live there anytime. I love that hotel. My bed was wonderful, even if it didn't have a mirror over it." She told the British press, "I came to England because of your men. I love the way they talk." She was reported to be getting £2,000 a week, which was more than most people in England earned in a year.

The fame of her films had preceded her. As early as 1935, in Alfred Hitchcock's *The 39 Steps*, someone in a music hall persists in asking the performer on stage, Mr. Memory, "How old is Mae West?" Mr. Memory's answer, "I know, but I never tell a lady's age," isn't satisfactory, and the man continues asking the question as a theater-emptying riot develops. In Hitchcock's 1936 *Sabotage*, Mae appears as Jenny Wren in a Disney cartoon of the period, just before the climax of the film. When Mae reached England, she was as well known, perhaps better known, than she was at the time in America. Her last successful film had been *My Little Chickadee* in 1940.

Diamond Lil was a triumphant success everywhere in England. Mae described her reception as "simply glorious." The tour ended in Glasgow, where the performances, as everywhere, were sold out. Then, in January 1948, *Lil* opened at the Prince of Wales Theatre in London, where it was the biggest success of all.

In London, she had to give two shows a night so that all the people who wanted to see *Diamond Lil* would be able to buy tickets. Mae found it exhausting to do two shows a night, but she didn't want to disappoint anyone, even though it meant that she was doing a three-act play twice a night for more than three months.

Mae loved not only the warmth of the people in England and Scotland, but she felt that "once you've won the audiences there, you've won them forever." Mae told the British, "I'll be back," and she meant it, but she never did get back.

"In England," Mae told me, "the reviewers wrote a couple of times that I was 'cheeky.' It sounded pretty funny. I always wanted to find out what it meant."

I told her that it meant "full of nerve and spirit."

Mae looked pleased. "You know, I learned education and intelligence aren't the same thing. Then, I wasn't embarrassed about meetin' anybody. I was happy meetin' the Royals in London when I took *Lil* there, and they seemed happy meetin' me. They were royal people, but they were real people."

Diamond Lil closed the first week of May 1948. One week later, she and Timony took the *Queen Mary* back to New York, thrilled with the success of their English reception. "I received a tremendous amount of fan mail there, and it continued coming in for a long time after I got back to California."

The success of *Diamond Lil* convinced Mae and Timony that the play had strong potential for a successful Broadway revival. In November 1948, *Lil* opened in New Jersey in preparation for a Philadelphia run in December and January. Then, in February 1949, the play's New York opening was greeted by the press with the highest praise for Mae and grudging tolerance for her vehicle. The revival ran sporadically until September 1949, at the Coronet and Plymouth Theatres, for a total of 182 performances. There were further revivals of *Lil*, most notably at the Biltmore Theatre in Los Angeles in March 1951, and at the Broadway Theatre in New York in September 1951. In 1952, Mae toured theaters with *Come on Up*.

When Mae returned from England, she was greeted by a lawsuit for $1 million by two writers who accused her of stealing their idea for a play about Catherine the Great. Mae had to establish that her idea and script went back to 1933, when she was unable to persuade Paramount to make the film because of the costly sets and costumes. At that time, she had been unwilling to sacrifice even one of Catherine's great dresses.

"Baby May," before she changed the "y" in her name to an "e," in one of the few photos to survive a flood at her Ravenswood apartment building in Hollywood. Mae never got over the loss of so many irreplaceable pictures of her with her mother.

Battered and retouched after the disastrous flood, this is the only surviving photograph of Mae's mother, Matilda West, the most important person in her daughter's life.

Mae with her brother, John, and sister, Beverly, in 1927 during the *Sex* trial. Mae was a famous personality on Broadway and would soon become one of the highest paid women in the world—and an ex-convict.

George Raft was the big star in *Night After Night*, and Mae only a supporting player in her first film, identified in ads as "Diamond Lil." It was Mae who had suggested to Raft that he become an actor.

Patricia Farley didn't expect to be immortalized as the coatroom attendant who exclaims, "Goodness! What beautiful diamonds!", to which Mae replies, "Goodness had nothin' to do with it, dearie," in *Night After Night*.

Cary Grant with Mae in 1933, while they were working together on *I'm No Angel*. Thirty years later, when they met again, Mae commented, "If he'd dye his hair he could still play those young parts."

Studio head Adolph Zukor with Mae on the *I'm No Angel* set. Zukor told Mae she saved Paramount during the Depression, and she was very proud of this. "They should've erected a statue of me," Mae said. "At least a bust."

Ever since Mae was a little girl, she had wanted to be a lion-tamer. In *I'm No Angel*, she got her chance, but once was enough. She never went near a lion again.

Mae's Paramount dressing room was built to her own specifications by the studio craftsmen.

Mae standing in front of her Paramount bungalow in the mid-1930s. She didn't need a nameplate, only her doormat.

A typical 1930s studio publicity still of Mae. She personally signed every photo that was sent out to a fan. In later years, she always kept a stack of photos in her car so she would never disappoint anyone.

Mae made it her business to learn as much she could about the technical side of movie-making from experts such as cinematographer Karl Struss, who photographed many of her Paramount films.

Mae liked lots of mirrors in her bedrooms, some on tables, others on the ceiling, "so I can see how I'm doin'."

Mae in the mid-1930s with the most important man in her life at the time, attorney Jim Timony. For thirty-seven years, Mae rarely appeared in public with anyone else, and if they didn't live together, they always lived close to each other.

Mae, seated between Emanuel Cohen and Gary Cooper. Paramount producer Cohen was an important behind-the-screen person in Mae's film career.

For *Every Day's a Holiday*, Parisian designer Schiaparelli couldn't believe Mae's small waist measurement and made all her gowns too large. Edith Head then had to alter everything to fit Mae.

Gathered together at the August 29, 1934, *Belle of the Nineties* première are Mae's bother, John West, Jr.; Jim Timony; her father, John "Battlin' Jack" West; Mae; her sister, Beverly; Beverly's husband, Bobby Baikoff; and Mae's longtime friend Boris Petroff. Petroff had given Mae a gold compact with diamonds, which she treasured all of her life.

Mae and Marlene Dietrich. Good friends at Paramount, they were reunited at Universal. Mae was filming *My Little Chickadee* and Marlene *Destry Rides Again*.

While Mae respected W. C. Fields's talent, she could not tolerate his drinking on the *My Little Chickadee* set. Only once did he slip, and she shut down production until he came back sober.

Mae was delighted to discover that in England there were diamonds she hadn't yet bought. "I'd studied up at Cartier," she said.

After a Hollywood court appearance, Mae signed photographs for a local Cub Scout troop. She wrote on their photos, "When you turn twenty-one, come up and see me." One of the Cubs asked, "Why can't I come up now?"

Mae with *Myra Breckinridge* co-stars Raquel Welch, Rex Reed, and John Huston. Director Michael Sarne described the set as a "hate-fest." Mae, however, loved Sarne, who returned her feelings.

Groucho Marx with Mae as Paul Novak looks on, in 1974. Mae respected Groucho as a performer and writer who created his own character, as she did hers.

Mae with her constant companion, Paul Novak. A prize-winning bodybuilder, Novak believed that his mission in life was "to protect and serve Miss West."

Mae with her *Sextette* musclemen in 1978.

By supporting Mae with names such as Ringo Starr, Alice Cooper, and Keith Moon, the producers of *Sextette* hoped to appeal to a contemporary audience. The film was not successful, but the stars who played cameos in it loved working with Mae West.

Mae won the case, but she minded that the trial had cost her more than seven weeks. "But you couldn't buy publicity like that," she said.

"Timony was crazy about the possibilities in Las Vegas," Mae told me. "He said, 'The sky's the limit.' He thought it would be my kind of place. I wasn't so sure about it, but Timony had planted the idea of Las Vegas in my mind where it was working in my subconscious.

"He was excited about this venture where I'd get a royalty just for being me. That didn't sound too bad. I'd make an appearance once in a while at the Mae West Hotel, but I wouldn't have to perform. That sounded pretty plush, but I still wasn't sold on it. It was something different. Maybe if Jim had lived, the hotel would've happened. Anyway, Las Vegas turned out playing a good part in my life.

"He would've wanted someone strong and gentle, like he'd always been, to take care of me. Timony was a very strong man, but he was very careful about everything. He'd never have done anything strong-arm himself. He would've hired someone to get the job done.

"Paul [Novak] was the person I needed at a different time in my life. Jim was the brain and Paul is the brawn. I needed brainpower for my career, to build it and to invest the money and keep it coming in. Paul watches my weight and exercise regime, and keeps me in good shape, which is what he knows and what I need now.

"I hope Timony went to the heaven he was so sure of, and maybe he met my mother there. She would be in a wonderful place in heaven. She was the one who selected Jim to take care of me. And my father and Jim got along, so they would've all gotten together and be waiting for me.

"I know Jim would've stayed with me, if he could've, but he couldn't help getting called away. He just keeled over. He'd been weakening for a while, and when he had the final attack, it was too much for him, and he couldn't fight back. He was taken all at once, and he didn't have a chance to say goodbye to me.

"I think Timony stirred up a lot of interest in me in Las Vegas for one thing or another, so even though he wasn't directly involved in the Sahara Hotel wanting my musclemen show, Jim was very connected in Las Vegas, and that might have had something to do with it. You know someone says something to someone, and the next thing you know, two plus two equals twenty-two.

"Maybe it was his spirit watching over me like a guardian angel. Not everyone would have described him as an angel. I would. I didn't try to summon his spirit back for a long time, and I never saw him or exactly felt his presence, but maybe he put out the word for me up there in heaven. He was never as interested in the spiritual life, involving The Forces, like I was, but we both believed there was more to life than any of us could know or see. He was Catholic and very religious, and always had his rosary. Whenever we went to another city, he'd visit a Catholic church, and I'd go with him.

"I guess Timony would have approved of Paul, not when he was alive, of course, but after Jim didn't have a body anymore. He loved me so much he wouldn't have wanted me to be alone."

Toward the end of his life, James Timony saw Las Vegas as a place that held great possibilities for Mae, but before he could act, he became ill, and for several months, he lived at Mae's Santa Monica beach house with people to care for him. She was frequently there.

Timony died in April 1954.

Mae was anxious to work and be distracted from her loneliness without Timony. She had come to take him for granted and sometimes even resented what she regarded as "his ever-present overprotectiveness of me."

When he was gone, she missed him so painfully that she didn't want to see anyone and retreated to the seclusion of her Ravenswood apartment.

The musclemen act idea came to Mae when a very young Mr. America came to visit her. He was a fan who wanted to meet her. She was mightily impressed by his muscles, and the idea came to her of a musclemen act starring her that would attract women. "*I* could take care of the attracting the men," she said.

He wished to have an autographed picture, which he received. He also received employment.

Early in her career, she had had the idea of wearing beautiful dresses so that women would be attracted to the show in order to look at them. Now she thought a woman could come "to see a bevy of fantastic-looking men without admitting it was why she was there."

The musclemen act, she thought, would begin with nine muscle-men, ideally, most of them title-holders, carrying her in on a chaise longue. "That's my idea of an entrance," she said. At the close of the show, she would give out keys to her suite, "one to each beautiful young man."

In July of 1954, Mae was offered a contract to appear with her musclemen act at the Sahara Hotel in Las Vegas. "Good money, good muscles, great audiences," Mae said. There were many offers for her to tour, and she did so through the 1950s.

The act was a spectacular success in San Francisco, and it played at clubs around the country, including the Latin Quarter, the Chez Paree, and Ciro's. She recorded an album featuring songs from her act, and it was a great success. Her costumes were a part of the fascination of the act for women, as she had thought. "Anyway, women could see the show and rave about the dresses when they were really ogling the men in the show.

"When the musclemen came to try out, you could always get precise answers. No wishy-washy stuff. None of this, 'I don't know exactly,' 'I'm not sure about . . .'

"You say, What's the size of your waist, the answer comes back, '29.' Or someone else answers, '29¼.'

" 'You?'

" '30½.'

"You could ask them the size of anything they had.

"They were used to telling it because they were professionals. No false modesty there. And those boys had nothing to be modest about."

Mae wanted to hire as the next muscleman Mr. Universe, Miklós Hargitay, known as Mickey. Hargitay had driven a hard bargain and Mae had relented. Mae said it was because she wanted him for the act, and some speculated that it was because she wanted him for herself, at least on occasion. For those who knew her best, it was clear that she had already chosen a favorite, Chester Ribonsky, who had changed his name to Chuck Krauser. He was quiet and reserved, much less obtrusive than Hargitay.

When Hargitay met a twenty-two-year-old Jayne Mansfield, who was acting on Broadway in *Will Success Spoil Rock Hunter?*, he retired from the musclemen act, or was retired by Mae, who delivered an ultimatum. Whatever her private feelings were, she felt that the publicity Mansfield and Hargitay were getting was reflecting badly on her image. The idea that a man could leave her for someone else was unspeakable. She had repeated throughout her life and career, "No man ever left me. *I* was the one who did the leavin'."

On June 7, 1958 the tour was playing in Washington, D.C., when Hargitay arrived, ready to tell his story to the press. Krauser, who was there with Mae, hit Hargitay before he could say a word. Krauser claimed self-defense, that Hargitay made a wrong move, and he thought he was going to hit him.

Hargitay was taken to a hospital emergency room. He filed a complaint. The court decision went against Krauser, and he was fined.

Mae was pleased by the tone of the reporting. "Two young, handsome, muscular men engaged in fisticuffs over me. It was a flashback to my father, Battlin' Jack. He believed in hitting first.

"Paul showed what he was made of and what he would do for me," Mae said, calling Chuck Krauser by his newer name, Paul Novak. The reason Chester Ribonsky became Chuck Krauser and then Paul Novak has never been clarified. Novak simply said, "I prefer the name," adding sometimes, "Miss West also prefers the name." There were whispers that the real reason was that Mae wanted to sweep the event in Washington, D.C., during which time the name of Chuck Krauser appeared on television and in the newspapers, under her white carpet.

Not long after the death of Timony, Paul Novak moved into the second bedroom of Mae's apartment. "That could never have happened while Jim was alive," Mae said. Their relationship had remained one of great affection.

"Jim had always been in love with me, love at first sight, which lasted for him until it was love at last sight. I'd never exactly been in love with him, but when he was gone, I missed him more than I expected I would. You know, he knew my mother, and my father, too.

"He was a great friend to my father. Father came out here to live in California where his three children were, and Jim spent time with him, especially near the end. Battlin' Jack was a pale shadow of himself during the last few years of his life, but he was battlin' until he died.

"I'd never have hurt Jim if I could help it, but his jealousy and possessiveness where I was concerned had made life full of complications.

"You know, Timony had been a little domineering. He was the strong type, which always appealed to me. But he was *too* protective. He wanted to protect his place in my life, which by his definition was to be the *only* man in my life. That didn't coincide exactly with my own perspective. I was very fond of him, very, but it's like with your favorite dish of food. No matter how much you like it, no matter how good it tastes, you get bored if you only have that one dinner every meal.

"Timony didn't understand that. He didn't want to understand. He was a jealous man where I was concerned. That was natural, but it *was* inconvenient.

"He was Irish like my father, and he reminded me of my father. He was devoted to helping me, and he did, but his watching me so close made me feel squirmy. So when I saw someone who filled me with desire, we had to operate on the hit-and-run principle.

"I never wanted to lie to Timony, but I couldn't tell him the truth. He would say to me, 'Mae, there's only one of you. You're the only woman in the world for me. I don't want any other woman, but you. I'll always be faithful to you in my heart, and every other inch of me, too.'

"Well, I know what he wanted me to say. He wanted me to say, 'I feel the same way,' and he wanted me to say, 'I'll *always* feel that way,' the significant word being 'always.' How can anyone promise anything for always? It sounds good in a song, but things in life are more transitory. How can I know how I'll feel tomorrow? Feelings are fragile and can't be promised for the future, only felt at the moment.

"Sometimes I wished Timony would take a trip, a *long* trip. But when he took the longest trip anyone can, I missed him more than I'd known I would.

"I thought his spirit might try to get back to me. He was a very deep-feeling Catholic, so maybe he didn't believe my séances were proper religion. Or maybe it took him a while to learn how to make the trip back.

"Then, it happened. One night, he came, all alone, not accompanied by any other spirits. He never did want to share me. He hadn't changed a day. He looked exactly like he did the last time I saw him. He hadn't lost any weight. I was glad to see him looking so well. I was glad to see him, period.

"We didn't have any conversation. The spirits don't seem to communicate that way. But we didn't need any words between us. I guess we never had a lot of words. It was always the words that got us into trouble. The best was when we exchanged feelings.

"After that, I didn't miss him anymore because I knew he was always there with me, watching over me, and I was glad. I didn't mind, because he was a guardian angel, and he wasn't jealous anymore because he wasn't corporeal."

"Something I've always enjoyed is having a nice car," Mae said. "I never learned to drive, but that didn't matter. I always had someone to drive me. The car I always got was a Cadillac limo, and I liked keeping it a while and in perfect condition.

"Every few years, I got my sister, Beverly, a new Cadillac. She enjoyed it, and I was glad to get it for her.

"When I finished with my limos, I always gave them to the nuns. It just doesn't seem right for them to have to take the bus. I never heard one of them complain, but I like seeing them have a little luxury in their lives, so they won't be all tired out for doing their good works. I liked to see them help unwed mothers who kept their babies and who didn't have families to help them. I keep my cars a long time, but when I finish with them, they're in as good condition as when I got them.

"I just can't stand seeing a nun waiting for a bus."

Dale Olson, a highly respected Hollywood publicist and writer, began his Hollywood career auspiciously, with a Mae West interview.

"I'd been writing a column when I was in high school for a chain of newspapers in Oregon," Olson said, "and I'd been able to interview many famous people when they came through Portland.

"Before I went to Los Angeles, in 1951, where I was hoping to find work, I wrote to all of the movie studios, but the only person who answered me was Teet Carle, a key publicist on the staff at Paramount.

"When I arrived, I went to see him, and he took me on a tour of Paramount. They were filming one of the *Road* pictures, and he introduced me to Bob Hope and Bing Crosby and Dorothy Lamour, and Bob Hope talked with me and was very nice. Then I went back to Oregon.

"I returned to Los Angeles in 1953. I told Teet Carle that I was hoping to do some interviews for the papers in Oregon, and he suggested Mae West. He thought she would do it with me, and he said I could use his name. He told me that she lived at the Ravenswood.

"I left a note for her at the Ravenswood, and I called her, and she said, 'How old are you?'

"I said, 'Nineteen,' and she said, 'That's a very nice age.' We made an appointment for the next week.

"When I arrived, I was announced and a very well-built man opened the door and let me in. He said Miss West was waiting for me in her bedroom. I wasn't a very sophisticated young man, I suppose, and I came from a background where a man would never just go into the bedroom of a lady he didn't know.

"There she was, wearing a white satin peignoir and nightgown, and she was in bed. It was a very fancy peignoir and nightgown.

"Each of the times I saw her after that, when she received me, she was always wearing an elegant peignoir and gown, and she was always in her bed.

"She was very charming. She asked me all about myself, and she gave me the interview.

"She told me about all of her plans for the future, and she really had a lot of projects she was hoping to do. Her major project, she said, was making another film. She told me that the reason she felt she had to make another film was because of all the letters she received from fans, asking her to do it.

"All the while we were talking, we were being interrupted by a monkey. The monkey was just walking around and wanted our attention, especially hers." The monkey was only visiting. He lived at Mae's San Fernando Valley ranch with Beverly.

"The monkey reminded me of the one in *Sunset Boulevard,* and I made the mistake of saying that. She told me that Billy Wilder had written *Sunset Boulevard* for her and had offered it to her first. 'That movie was developed for me, but I didn't want to do it. They stole the idea of my monkey from me.'

"That was our first meeting. I left and did some research and wrote the story. I sent it to Portland, and when they published the story, I called her. I told her that I would send it to her, and she said, 'Oh, no. Please come over and bring it.' I did, and she read it with me there. When she finished reading it, she told me, 'You are a very handsome man, and very talented.' Of course I was very happy.

"I didn't see her for a few years. By that time, I'd been writing for *Variety,* and I was president of the Hollywood Press Club. We decided to honor Kevin Thomas, writer for the *Los Angeles Times.* We told him, and he was pleased. I told him that we would like to invite a few people he'd written about to speak about him, and I asked whom he would suggest. Immediately, he suggested Mae West. The other person was Rock Hudson. He asked me if I'd like him to call Miss West for me. I said, 'No, it's not necessary for you to call her. I know her.' I called, and when I told her, she purred, 'Ohhh, I love Kevin Thomas.' It was a very successful evening. She glowed over him. That night, they took pictures, and she posed with everyone.

"When I got the photographs, I called her and asked if she would like to have the photographs from that evening. She said she would very much like to have them. I brought them over, and again she asked about what I was doing. She congratulated me on my success, and we talked.

"One subject I mentioned was that I'd seen Jayne Mansfield, who was a friend of mine, and Mickey Hargitay, but I saw from the look on her face that wasn't a good subject to mention.

"I asked her about a story, gossip that was going around, and I wondered if it was true.

"The story was that one evening she had invited a gentleman of color to visit her, and when he came, he had been turned away. She never cared what color people were. Color didn't matter to her. She was very upset when her friend called her to tell her what had happened. She told him to call her back in fifteen minutes. Then, she went to the phone and called the owners of the Ravenswood and bought the building. When her friend called back, she said to come over, that she'd just bought the Ravenswood.

"I said, 'Miss West, may I ask you, is that story true?'

"And she said, 'It's not altogether true, but there's *enough* truth in it.'

"So, she didn't deny it. She didn't confirm it.

"She said, 'There's a great deal of truth in it, so you can use it.'

"I thought about it. I feel Mae West knew what she was doing at all times, who she was, and the image she projected."

After Mae had lived for a few years at the Ravenswood and she showed no interest in moving even as her fortunes and fortune had increased, people began to believe that she owned the building. After the rumor had persisted for sometime, it was regarded as a fact, but it was not.

One evening, Mae had invited a friend to drop by. Every friend of Mae's knew that she considered it a sign of disrespect if anyone came late. Mae waited five minutes, ten minutes, fifteen minutes. Then, the phone rang.

It was Mae's friend. He said he had been turned away because of his color. He had appeared on time in the lobby, but the man at the desk had not believed that Miss West was expecting him and had refused to call up. The clerk apparently did not believe that Mae West would be entertaining "a man of color" in her apartment. It had taken her visitor fifteen minutes to find a phone he could use.

Mae was extremely upset. She asked her friend to come back. She said there wouldn't be any problem. The switchboard operator always called up to announce visitors, and it never occurred to Mae to make any special arrangements. Then, she made two calls. The first was to the telephone operator at the desk of the Ravenswood. This time, there would be no problem, and she gave clear instructions to send her friend right up, as soon as he returned.

Her second call was to the owners of the Ravenswood. The owners had called earlier to talk with her about a serious cash flow problem that was putting the Ravenswood in jeopardy. Unless money could be raised quickly, the Ravenswood was in great trouble and could be lost.

It was impossible to do anything with banks about mortgages. The Great Depression had made it very difficult to raise cash for anything, especially for houses and apartment buildings. All of the banks already owned far more properties than they had ever contemplated owning. Mae was one of the few people with extra cash on hand. Her earnings had soared during her phenomenal success in Hollywood.

Mae said, "I'll do it. I'll let you have the money." She agreed to make them a loan. That saved the Ravenswood.

When her friend arrived, she told him, "I was so disgusted by what happened to you that I bought the Ravenswood, so you won't have any trouble again."

The story spread quickly that Mae had bought the Ravenswood. She was besieged by phone calls from people who knew her and from people who knew people who knew her. They all had the same idea. It seemed everyone wanted to live at the Ravenswood, and they hoped for a low rent. Then, worse, it turned out that almost everyone who lived at the Ravenswood had at least one complaint, and some had several. They began calling to petition her to fix a window with a cracked frame or to do something about a closet door that would stick or to get a plumber.

Her maid took the calls and did her best to redirect them. Paul had to park the car out in front, and Mae had to rush into her car whenever she left the building in order to avoid residents with complaints and requests, and then rush in when she returned.

Mae didn't like the idea of owning the building in which she lived, especially when she *didn't* own it.

Eventually, the loan was paid back and though Mae, indeed, had never owned the Ravenswood, the story lingered that she did.

Mae loved to discover new talent, and when she went to see "a kid named Elvis Presley," she said, "I knew he was going to the top, and I told him so, and we stayed friends.

"He was a fan of mine, you know, and he wanted me to be in his movies when there were parts for me, and when there wasn't a part for me, he said a part could be written in.

"I first met him when I was touring in the fifties with my nightclub act, and I was told there was a kid in town I should see who was something special, worth seeing. He was doing this show in a tent. I liked him. I knew right away he was going places. He had a sex personality.

"It reminded me of my own sex personality. I went back after the show. He knew who I was and told me he was a fan. I told him he had great things in store, that he was going to make it big, that he wasn't going to stay in a tent. He was going to the big time, and he was going to be the biggest in the big time. I told him I was the one who selected Cary Grant, and he was going to be *that* famous—in a different way.

"He smiled and was very pleased to have the encouragement. He knew I was sincere. He felt I'd never say things to him I didn't mean. He was right. I'd never do that. I didn't like to hurt people's feelings, but I never heaped praise on anyone unless I meant it. That would have been unethical.

"His looks were the greatest. His singing was the greatest. His dancing was the greatest. He had it all and something more. It was so much sex appeal you could hardly believe it. I told him I called it 'a *low* sex quality.'

"He had them offer me a part in *Roustabout* and another one in *Frankie and Johnny*. They were both his idea, to give me a part in his films. He wanted to work with me, and it would have been fun. The thing he couldn't get me was control over my character and my lines. They had rules like that. I *had* to be able to write my own lines so they were right for my character, and the producers considered that unacceptable. I thought maybe their reason was because they were doing 'Elvis Presley pictures,' and they thought I would take something away from him by being too showy and dominant and diminish their picture. I know Elvis Presley didn't feel that way, and I didn't. My being great would only make him look greater. He really wanted me, but he couldn't get the control of himself as a property the way I always did for myself.

"Every time I did something, he was one of the first to send a telegram and congratulate me. He understood how insecure most performers are. He just didn't understand that I wasn't one of the insecure ones.

"I saw that deep down he didn't have the perfect confidence he should have had. Sometimes he acted like it, but it was an act. The whole world had told him how great he was, but that wasn't enough. When you need as much reassurance as he did, that's too much reassurance, and you're in trouble.

"He was in trouble, but not when I first met him. He was a happy kid then. He was trying for something, and his goals weren't too big for him.

"You used a phrase, dear," Mae said to me, "which I kinda like. 'When there isn't there.' I think he got 'there' and it didn't feel as good as he thought it was gonna feel, so he was too disappointed and couldn't handle it.

" 'There' was there for me. From the time I was a little girl, I loved every minute of the success, and it felt more wonderful than I could have imagined.

"There was something he was missing and searching for, and he couldn't find it. I guess he couldn't find it because he didn't know what it was, so even if he found it, he wouldn't have known. He had the greatest fame, but it wasn't enough. Or maybe it was too much. I know what that's like when you can't ever be incognito. But I enjoyed it, and when I wasn't in the mood for fan-love, I stayed home.

"He sent me all his new recordings as gifts, and I never missed one of his movies. I always enjoyed them. He had even more potential, so

I hoped he'd get a part that would really let him show what he could do and develop his acting more.

"Toward the end, I saw he wasn't taking care of himself. He was looking haggard and out of shape. He was kind of running down. And the worst part of it was he didn't seem to care. It was like he'd given up, like he wasn't going to find what he was looking for, like he wasn't even going to find out what it was.

"He told me once that he had a twin who didn't live, and that sometimes that made him feel guilty, like why was he the one chosen to live, and in some way, maybe he had something to do with the other one not living. I suggested that he try a séance I would organize and maybe he could make contact with his twin and find out more about what had gone on. I thought that might give him peace.

"I told him how it had worked for me—and had not worked. I'd really begun all my interest in the spirit world because there was only one spirit I really wanted to contact, my mother. I was never successful in that, but I did get to meet a lot of hooded figures and others. And that gave me some reassurance, because it meant that my mother was somewhere and watching over me, even if neither one of us knew how to make direct contact. Elvis Presley listened with interest, but he didn't accept my séance offer. I think he felt he was too busy. He was pretty busy. He was in overdemand.

"When I heard he died, I couldn't believe it. I thought they were going to say it was a mistake. Well, they never did, but it sure *was* a mistake. So young, so very young. Terrible. It was a mistake for everyone, and especially for him.

"Elvis wanted to accommodate me, but he didn't have the power, if you can believe that. He let the powers that be own him in his professional life. They told him what to do, and he had to follow the script. You know why? Because he didn't have the confidence. He was afraid it could all go away. And because he was afraid, he was his own worst enemy, and he did everything to make it go away. So it did. I just couldn't believe it when I heard that dear, beautiful, talented boy had died so young. He looked older than he was because he didn't take care of himself.

"He told me once, 'Sometimes I feel kind of empty, if you know what I mean.'

"I said, 'Sure,' because I didn't know what else to say. I didn't want to make him feel bad, and he seemed to feel bad enough.

"He wasn't enjoying his success. That's terrible. I always enjoyed every minute of my success."

In 1959, Mae appeared on a Dean Martin TV special. It was her TV debut. "He was a handsome guy, and he had a good line, speaking of sex personalities. He said to me, 'Call me Dino.'

"People said he performed drunk. I don't think so. I never saw him drunk. He was naturally a high guy, so he didn't need anything, though I'm sure he knew how to drink if he wanted to.

"I found him very professional, and he cared too much about the show to do anything to jeopardize it. Playing like he'd been drinking was part of his public personality for his act. He made everybody feel good because he shared his good mood with the other performers and with the audience. He saved any bad mood he ever had for in private. He was a professional, and he had an image to safeguard. I know what that's like."

Nineteen fifty-nine found Mae involved in a number of different projects, each highlighting a different aspect of her personality and talent.

She did a return engagement with her musclemen troupe at the Sahara Hotel, and it was as successful as the first had been.

That year the Academy of Motion Picture Arts and Sciences invited Mae to appear on the Oscar show, singing "Baby, It's Cold Outside" with Rock Hudson. Mae's gown was designed by Edith Head, who also had done the gowns for her musclemen act. She wore a black-sequined dress with a long train and a headdress. In the fall, *Goodness Had Nothing to Do with It*, Mae's autobiography, was published. She traveled around America to promote it, and because of the book, she agreed to appear on the television program *Person to Person* with Charles Collingwood.

She wanted her interview to be filmed entirely at her Santa Monica beach house. She didn't mind "going public" there, but she didn't like the idea that they wanted to go into her Ravenswood home. Finally, Mae agreed to be interviewed in her apartment, as well as at her beach house.

While she was in San Francisco signing books after doing the interview, Mae learned that CBS had decided not to broadcast it.

The press asked her why she believed her show had been canceled. She said she couldn't imagine why. There was one question that sometimes bothered a few people, and Mae said she'd seen someone flinch when she gave her answer.

The question was one she was frequently asked, but this time it was as part of a national interview going into people's homes.

" 'Why do you have mirrors on your bedroom ceiling over your bed?' was the question, and all I said was, 'I like to see how I'm doin'.' Is that so bad?

"When I was asked, do I have any advice for teenagers, I said, 'Grow up.' I think with that one, it wasn't so much what I said, but how I said it. I was a little on the sultry side, if you know what I mean. I could have said it a little less sultry, but that was the way it came out.

"It was all pretty innocent, I thought, but they pulled the plug on me. I was really disappointed. Then, I gave it a good think, and I wasn't so disappointed. I think I got more publicity for being canceled than I would've had if the show had gone on.

"So it wasn't just a waste of time, it was a waste of entertainment. I put a lot of heart into it. Maybe someday it'll turn up, and people will be more broadminded, and I'll be the broad on their minds."

Over the years, Mae was offered innumerable television opportunities, but she accepted very few. These lucrative offers were always for her to star in her own series or to appear in specials built around her. She declined all of these, and it was generally thought that she wanted too much money, and no one could meet her demands.

"There is no truth in that," Mae said. "If all I'd wanted was just more money, I'd've asked for more money. I wouldn't've been coy. There's a time for being coy and a time for not being coy, and believe me, I know the difference.

"The truth is, no amount of money would've bought my signature on a contract without a clause that gave me control over my character and let me write all my lines. No one was willing to give me enough control."

Mae appeared a few times as a guest on a situation comedy series, a very special guest, and even as an interview subject. These appearances, however, were rare.

She believed that the television audience would not appreciate what they got free in the same way they would a film or a stage play for which they paid admission. She didn't feel the performance would receive the proper respect in a living room. "I was concerned about Mae West being seen too much.

"I've stayed in demand because I never gave 'em too much. I've always left 'em wanting more. Today television is the fastest way to finish yourself off. Now you don't see great people like there used to be in the world. It's like you said, dear, 'Giants are in short supply.'

"Too many people see you for nothing. They're always wanting me to be on those talk shows, but I don't go. Television's okay for people who've got something to sell. I don't need to."

Among her television appearances was a *Mister Ed* show, which featured a talking horse, and an interview with Dick Cavett, which was intelligent, witty, and serious.

Mae was tempted by the suggestion of a program on which she would give "advice to the lovelorn."

"But that idea didn't get very far. The sponsors were afraid of what I would say."

Mae liked the comedian Red Skelton and agreed to appear on one of his shows. She was asked to submit a script for her appearance. Knowingly, she went too far.

"I went overboard," she said, "so they could use up their energy censoring it. Then, when they were all worn down, I submitted the script I really wanted, and they just accepted it with no problem."

After this, Mae temporarily retired. She said she didn't feel like traveling anymore because she'd had enough.

In 1961, Mae appeared at the Edgewater Beach Playhouse in Chicago with her last stage play, *Sextette*. She was in her late 60s at the time. When her leading man, Alan Marshall, died suddenly of a heart attack, his son, Kit Marshall, who had been playing a smaller part in the production and was familiar with his father's role, stepped in and replaced him. Paul Novak had a small part.

"I'll tell you something interesting," Mae said to me. "Have you ever heard about my relationship with the Spirits? That's Spirits with a capital 'S', not a small 's'. I hardly ever drink at all."

"I've heard vaguely about it," I said, "but please tell me more."

"You can say that again about the Spirits," she said. "The ones I knew specially, at first, were pretty *vague*. I could hardly see them, myself, in the beginning.

"Later, they clarified themselves. I don't know if the process was slow because they were out of practice or because they had to find out if they could trust me.

"It was in 1941. I was right on top of the world. Had it all, my career going great guns, but I felt like something was missing, like life was incomplete.

"I was rich, and I understood what rich meant. It was never having to think about money. My money could think about me.

"I never liked too much paper money. I didn't really understand stocks. They weren't any fun to look at, and I never liked things that went down. That's why I changed my name from May to Mae when I was about six or seven 'cause 'y' went down. What I liked was good California real estate. There wouldn't ever be any more of that, and you know how I feel about diamonds.

"The best thing was I knew I could always work and earn money. The best is knowing the powers within you. But some land and some diamonds don't hurt none, either. I could always look at my diamonds and feel good. I liked to spread them out and sort of play with them. I liked riding around in a car and looking at my properties. I preferred land that had a house or something on it.

"I'd reached the point with my career where everyone in the world knew me, and I could stop for a few months without feeling I'd be forgotten if I took a little adjournment.

"I wanted to clear my mind, to see what more there was of a spiritual nature. What I found out was, there *is* something more. When I knew that, I was satisfied.

"I made up my mind to take six months to explore the world of the spiritual, not just religion, but the whole of There-Is-More-Than-We-Know. It was always my hope I could make contact with my mother. The first thing was to find out *how* to find out."

Mae had, in fact, been thinking about it since 1928, when she met the Indian mystic Sri Deva Ram Sukul. Through him, she became interested in Eastern mysticism. Then, after her mother died, she hoped to make contact with her "on the other side," but séances and spiritualism proved unsuccessful. "I couldn't bear the thought of never seeing my mother again," Mae said.

Since there was a spiritualists convention in Los Angeles in the fall of 1941, Mae sent Timony to investigate, hoping to find someone there who could help her make contact with her mother. Timony was impressed with the Reverend Thomas Jack Kelly of the Spiritualist Church of Life in Buffalo, New York. Kelly said that he had been tested by Duke University and found to possess parapsychological powers. He claimed that he had been able to help the police through his powers of extrasensory perception. Timony arranged a meeting with Mae.

Kelly told Mae that later that year the Japanese would launch a surprise attack on America. The impression Kelly made on her personally and the subsequent attack on Pearl Harbor made her a firm believer. "When I met the Reverend Kelly, I felt he could steer me right.

"I didn't want tarot cards or fortune-telling or Ouija boards. I did try that stuff, but it wasn't fulfilling. Meditation looked like a good thing to try, but I had to learn it. The woman who taught me how to meditate said I was a quick study. I think I learned in about a week how to get my mind blank so it was receptive for the spirit world.

"For anyone who wants to try it, you have to do it in the dark for the best results. I never got to where I could get my mind blank in bright light, but once I made contact with the Spirits, I found they stuck around, even in the light."

Kelly maintained that one could stimulate one's sensitivity to the metaphysical, but that some people were more gifted than others in this respect. He told Mae that she was one of those with "the gift."

"The Reverend Kelly taught me that the human mind is much more powerful than we realize. It can connect with the force of life that's all around us, but we can't see it. It's like radio waves.

"The Forces are always hanging around. Sometimes they do very important things, and sometimes they are very passive and not in the mood to work and just sit around yawning when you could use a little lift here and there. When they aren't in the mood, you can't get them to budge, and you have to accept their pace, because you can't afford to make them angry.

"To make contact, you've got to make your mind blank so this force can get in, like I was telling you. That's what I did for weeks. Nothing.

"Then, one morning just as I woke up, a little girl's voice said, 'Good morning, dear.' I looked and there wasn't anyone there. She sounded like an angel. The Reverend Kelly told me she was Juliet, and she comes to beginners through their inner ear. Later, a man came to me, but he didn't say anything.

"I started seeing other men, all dressed in clothes from some earlier time. They spoke in 'thees' and 'thous,' and I couldn't understand why they came to me. Some kind of mistake in traffic signals, maybe.

"After that, my mind got overcrowded with a lot of people I wouldn't have cared that much about knowing personally if they were alive, and their being dead didn't help the case. Another thing was, there were a lot of them, I think all men, and they weren't interested in me, so that didn't make any sense. They must have been *really* dead. They sort of just talked with each other.

"And I never did like crowds.

"The Reverend Kelly told me my gift was strong, but undisciplined. If I wanted to make contact with my mother, I would have to be patient.

"I didn't make any special relationships among the Spirits. They continued to seem more interested in themselves and each other than in me. Not very flattering. I felt like they were just using me. Deplorable. Maybe they didn't even see me. I decided I'd rather have my privacy. Spirits are like mice. One is cute.

"I was never afraid of the voices and the people I saw. I was fascinated by them, at first. Or I was fascinated with my own newfound ability to invite them over.

"I'm not sure they ever noticed I was there. If they did, my presence didn't seem to bother them any. They seemed to have their own lives, except they were living them in my bedroom.

"More of them arrived, and I wasn't the one doing the inviting. They were getting a little rowdy. So I said, 'Scram.'

"That got their attention. They got real quiet. And I saw they looked sad.

"I felt a little sorry, but I couldn't live like that. I needed my bedroom back. I did some of my best work in my bedroom.

"They began to fade. As they faded away, I said, 'I'll be seeing you.' As they were fading, I started to *really* feel sorry for them. They looked *so* sad. I didn't know where they were fading to. Maybe they didn't know, either. Maybe they weren't going anywhere.

"But I had to shut them out of my mind. I didn't have room. And as the atmosphere was more harmonious, more seemed to get the word and show up. I couldn't afford to be overpopulated by Spirits.

"I genuinely thought maybe I'd bring them back sometime. But I never did."

"After that group faded away," Mae said, "there were new arrivals, a different community of Spirits." She began waking up in the morning surrounded by black-hooded figures.

"They gathered around the bed and chanted. It was a little startling when they first came. It was exciting at first, but it turned out to be disappointing. I had hopes of learning something, but I wasn't able to establish any communication with this group. They would chant in some language I couldn't understand, and they would rudely ignore me when I spoke to them. I cannot tolerate rude people, even if they aren't alive.

"I didn't know if their chanting had anything to do with me, or if they were just using my place and me. And on top of it, they were coming too early in the morning and waking me up. I've always considered getting the right amount of beauty sleep very important, not just for looks, but for health. I try never to let anything interfere with my getting enough sleep and the right hours, if possible, the same hours every night. I like to get up at ten in the morning.

"So, I said, 'Okay, fellas. Enough is enough, and I've had enough. You're not what I wanted. Go away.' It was an interesting thing. They paid attention to me when I was provoked and let them know it. I didn't have to speak twice to them. They left. And they never came back."

Mae told me that she had been asked many times who could play her in a film story of her life. She considered that a very foolish question, and she said she always answered the same way:

She was the only one who could play Mae West.

There was *one* actress, however, who "with a lot of coaching— the voice, the walk, the style"—she thought *might* have been able to play her.

"Marilyn Monroe could've played me.

"She was a real sex symbol, but different from me, of course.

"She was pretty, too, but I didn't like the idea of the dumb blonde. She didn't have to do that. Maybe she played it so well, she convinced herself she really *was* one and then acted like one.

"She was a helpless performer. She had the looks to attract and be a star, but she didn't have much variety in her performance. She was limited because she became dependent on the writers and her directors. "I always wrote my own dialogue, and I pretty much directed myself, though nobody could ever say I was uncooperative.

"Posing for a nude calendar wasn't smart. I would never have done that. If you take off all your clothes, there's nothing left for anyone to wonder about.

"I've thought about why so many blond sex symbols died young. Harlow, Mansfield, Monroe. I have a theory. They needed help they didn't get. They didn't have a mother like mine. But nobody did.

"One thing I know about Marilyn Monroe is that she didn't commit suicide. That I'm sure of. Even though we aren't the same type, I can empathize with her. She had dreams and plans, and I can tell you, a woman who's got dreams and plans doesn't end it all by taking too many pills, even if things aren't going right. Things might change.

"She was a romantic. Vulnerable. She was also a grown-up woman who played a little girl. I'm sure she had her share of experience, but she wasn't worldly. I think she stayed a pretty innocent kid.

"She let herself become a victim of men she thought were her betters, and she let men break her heart and define who she was and what she thought of herself. She gave men that power over her. They didn't love her, but she let them use her. She let men break her heart, but she didn't die of a broken heart. Nobody dies of a broken heart. She was vulnerable, maybe, but I'm convinced she never committed suicide.

"I have intuition about those things, ESP with The Forces. I felt this through intuition. But I also had some hints from The Forces.

"She was a fool to keep taking all those pills. I'd never put stuff like that into *my* body when I didn't know what was in them.

"I'm convinced there was foul play. Something nefarious happened to her. She wouldn't have given up all hope.

"I'll let you in on a little confidence. I've kind of kept it a secret, but now, I wouldn't care if you divulged it. I got this inside information from The Forces when Marilyn Monroe died. It wasn't direct. I never made contact with her directly, and I never tried because I didn't want to get involved.

"It was too late to help her, and I don't like gossip. I also don't like filling my mind with unpleasantries.

"But my intuition was so strong I wanted some confirmation of what I felt I knew. I got it from some of the Spirits who knew other Spirits who were closely involved. They communicated to me that she didn't commit suicide, but they were playing it kind of close to the chest, and that's all I got.

"I've had this gift of intuition for a long time. There's a difference between intuition and ESP. Intuition is based on experience and on thinking, but ESP comes out of the air. 'It's a gift,' as Bill Fields said. I think a lot of people don't know they have it or could have it, but you've got to put some time into developing it, and you've got to have a great guide to facilitate it.

"Who knows," Mae said to me, "you might even have it yourself, honey."

Film historian Dan Price talked with me about Mae's psychic gatherings.

"Miss West used a small community room at the Ravenswood, downstairs, right off the lobby, where she had get-togethers with psychics. She was partial to those psychics who took their work on the stage, that sort of thing. Miss West would invite her friends to these events.

"I remember this one psychic who was elaborately blindfolded. When the guests entered the room, you wrote down on a piece of paper what was really on your mind, a question you wanted answered. You folded up the paper and put it in a fishbowl.

"The psychic would pick up these pieces of paper and he'd rub them between his hands. He would read the questions, and he would answer them. He seemed fantastic.

"Miss West sat in the back of the room. She looked like she was really enjoying herself. My guess is that the reason she liked this so much was because she was simply a fly on the wall, in the back of the room, and she got to find out what was on the minds of her friends.

"I told a magician friend of mine at the Magic Club, and he said he knew how it was done. He offered to explain it, but when I told Miss West, she didn't want to know how it could have been done. She changed the subject and moved away. As far as she was concerned, it was *not* a magic trick, and that was that."

Mae's brother, John West, Jr., died of a heart attack in October 1964. He was sixty-four years old.

"When my little brother was born, how I loved him!" Mae remembered. "He wanted a career in Hollywood. I got him some jobs, but he didn't have the passion for it. He loved horses, so we tried a ranch and racing some.

"He never had to want for anything. I had plenty, and I was happy to make life easy and secure for my family, but I think he would have liked to have done something very successful on his own, especially before my father died. I just wanted him to be happy. He never disappointed me, but maybe he disappointed himself.

"When it happened, I said to Beverly, 'Now there's just you and me.'"

• • •

"In 1964," Tim Malachosky told me, "Miss West went to the hospital and the doctors found that she had diabetes. This became the biggest secret in Miss West's life, because she thought it was a very unglamorous disease and that she could not be a sex goddess if people knew. She was totally dedicated to protecting her image like she was the guardian of it, and it didn't even belong to her. She never said the word, the name of the disease, out loud. She understood it was something serious, very serious. Except for the doctors and Paul [Novak] and me, and Miss West, no one knew. We never said the word out loud, either. Paul dedicated himself to her diet and to her exercise program.

"It was an interesting thing the way Miss West never had any self-pity. She never wanted any pity from anyone. Pity was the last thing she wanted, not even her own, from herself. She went about her life, not letting it change things. She believed in enjoying every day of her life.

"She loved her life and knew how to enjoy it.

"Once in a while, she would get a little annoyed with Paul when he hid the box of chocolates, or wouldn't let her have a second portion of dessert. She used the opportunities when we had dinner with other people, especially at their homes, to get a second portion of dessert. They would offer her and everyone a second helping, and she would be ready. It was harder for Paul to stop her in front of other people. He never wanted to embarrass her. He'd try to give her a look, but she wouldn't glance in his direction, and if she did, she would ignore it.

"He'd try to make up for it the next day by not letting her have any dessert at all, and I think the doctors had told him to give her a little extra insulin before she went out to a dinner party. Paul took total responsibility for her problem, and that allowed her not to think about it, or not to think about it much.

"When people would offer her chocolates, and she'd have two and she'd want more, Paul would do whatever he could to get the dish away from her. He'd get criticized for that. People would say, 'Oh, how can you be so heartless? Why don't you let her have another chocolate or two?' And he would smile and try to make something light out of it. He would say that it was *his* responsibility to watch Miss West's figure, and it was what she had instructed him to do. So they would say, 'What difference can one or two chocolates make?' He would repeat that Miss West had instructed him to do it.

"Paul had to bear the brunt of a lot of criticism for it, but he never minded what anybody said because he was always only thinking of Miss West's health and happiness and best interests.

"I think she had mixed feelings about Paul telling her what to do, even though he always did it in the most respectful tone. On one hand, she was used to being totally in control of everything and not having to do what anyone told her to do. On the other hand, she knew Paul was only doing it for her and that meant a lot to her.

"It wasn't as if Miss West hadn't always had a lot of willpower. She ate in a healthy way because she wanted to be healthy and she knew she had to be careful about her figure, so other people would keep on watching it. But she'd never had to be *so* careful."

Chapter Six

---◆---

HOLLYWOOD ENCORE

(1965–1980)

IN THE 1960S, Mae had only a few close friends, because that was the way she had always preferred it. She knew relatively few people beyond her family, the bond of family being precious to her. Jim Timony had become her extended family. Later Paul Novak became her constant companion, living in the second bedroom of her Hollywood apartment. In 1969, Tim Malachosky entered Mae's world as her personal secretary.

Occasional visitors whom she welcomed were Edith Head, Dolly Dempsey, a fan who had become a friend, and Kevin Thomas, who had come from the *Los Angeles Times* to interview her and became a frequent guest. Director George Cukor occupied a special place in her heart, though they communicated largely on the phone.

Mae always regarded her Ravenswood apartment as totally private, and only a few people were invited there. It was where she kept many of her diamonds. She had been willing to entertain more people when she had her Santa Monica beach house. After she sold it, she used the

public room downstairs at the Ravenswood even more for her entertaining of larger groups.

It was in the mid-1960s that Kevin Thomas was assigned to interview
Mae West.

When the young writer arrived at her Ravenswood apartment, he
found her waiting for him in a form-fitting silk-satin nightgown, over
which she wore an open peignoir. It showed off her flat stomach and
curvaceous figure, of which she was obviously proud. The outfit was
a design by Jeul Park, the primary designer of lingerie for the films, as
well as for the private lives of Mae, Marlene Dietrich, and other glam-
orous Hollywood stars. The long peignoir and gown covered most of
Mae's platform shoes.

Thomas confessed he might have found it a little uncomfortable
because of her unconventional dress for the interview, but she was so
comfortable, it put him at ease.

Mae was impressed by the intelligence of the tall, good-looking
young man who treated her with so much respect. Then she found
him to be a fine writer. Mae said she loved what he wrote about her,
and over the years he became one of her small circle of friends, one of
the people who knew her best. Their friendship lasted until the end
of her life.

In February of 1968, George Cukor arranged for Mae to be honored
by the University of Southern California. On the program were
Mervyn LeRoy, Robert Wise, James Stewart, and Cukor.

Mae reclined on a chaise longue in a setting which was supposed
to give the illusion of being a bedroom. The curtain went up on three
USC All-American football players gathered in a huddle around
something, their huge shoulder pads hiding the center of their huddle.
Then the huddle broke up, and Mae West was revealed reclining on a

chaise longue. One of the players was O. J. Simpson. There was a lengthy standing ovation and tremendous applause, and Mae thanked the audience for their "heavy breathing."

"The idea for my dinner party with Greta Garbo and Mae West was Roddy McDowall's," George Cukor told me. "He said to me, 'George, you're the only person who could get both Greta Garbo and Mae West to your house for dinner together, and I want to be invited.'

"I took the dare, even though it wasn't much of a dare, because Garbo was around my house all the time, not for me, but for my swimming pool. My pool was quite private, and she always swam in the nude.

"She invited me to join her, but I never did. She was prouder of her body than I was of mine, for good reason in both cases.

"When I introduced Mae and Garbo, I was rather surprised when Mae kissed Garbo. Mae was not a kissy person, which was the reason I was a bit taken aback. Garbo hadn't seemed to mind. When, on another occasion, I spoke with Mae, I asked her how it happened that she'd kissed Garbo. And Mae said, 'I wanted her to feel at home. And I felt like we knew each other because we were the biggest stars in the world.'

"At dinner, Miss Garbo didn't say much, and Miss West didn't say much, either. The reason was each one was really quite shy. After dinner they got together, and the two girls really hit it off. They were over in one corner, away from everyone else, and when I glanced over, I saw Garbo on the floor. So I took another look and Garbo was taking off one of Mae's shoes. Garbo was always curious about things, and obviously she was curious about Mae's unique shoes, which were so heavy, nobody else could have walked in them.

"I saw the startled look on Miss Garbo's face as she studied the shoe. She put the shoe back on Mae's foot and got up, not holding on to anything as she got up. That impressed me. Garbo was so trim and athletic. I was filled with envy.

"They both spoke softly as they always did, and my hearing wasn't all that it had once been. I moved along the wall like a spy in my own house, hoping to catch a few words of the conversation in which they were both so engrossed. As I drew close, I realized they were speaking in German, for that moment at least. My own Hungarian background did not extend well to eavesdropping in German.

"Mae's German had a funny Brooklyn accent and was especially hard to understand. I did catch something Garbo said: '*Eine Frau kann nicht alles haben*,' a woman can't have it all. They were having rather a deep conversation!

"The next day, I called Mae and asked her if she enjoyed her meeting with Greta Garbo.

"Mae summed it up in terms of what was important to her, physical attributes and working in show business.

" 'She has a beautiful complexion,' Mae said. 'I always notice a woman's complexion first. I think it's the most important feature. You can't be beautiful without beautiful skin. There's no way to look young if your skin gets old.

" 'She carries herself well, and she's a pretty girl, a very pretty girl, though she does have kind of a boyish shape.

" 'She could get work.' "

Mae volunteered to do a Christmas broadcast on Armed Forces Radio in 1971. She was given a list of questions and invited to take out anything she didn't like and put in anything she preferred. That pleased her because it was just the way she liked to work, rewriting the script, as she said, "to suit my personality." She rehearsed over and over with her secretary as she tried out different lines, different intonations.

Malachosky remembered, "She was as anxious to please and intent on doing a good show as if it were a major film or a Broadway opening.

"We worked many hours on it. Miss West wanted to do anything she could for our troops in Vietnam and around the world. The response to Miss West was tremendous. They loved her. And she loved doing it. She asked if she could do the Armed Forces Christmas show the next year, in 1972. They were thrilled to have her do it again, and she did it."

The only aspect of it that made Mae unhappy was that she opposed the war in Vietnam. She did not speak out about it publicly because it didn't suit her Diamond Lil image, she believed, and she didn't feel she could do anything about the war.

"I would do anything I could for our wonderful soldiers and sailors," she told me. "It's so sad. They won't all come back, and some of them won't come back the same as when they went, handsome and whole. I hate all war, and I love those boys. And this is no joke. I'm dead serious."

"Do you know how they always refer to the Myra Breckenridge movie?" Mae asked me. " 'The Mae West movie.' People go to see it because *I'm* in it.

"My spiritual adviser advised me to do it. Michael Sarne, the British director, wanted me. I never could resist an English accent, especially if a good-lookin' Englishman was speakin' it.

"But I never liked the idea much of ending a movie by it all having been a dream. Once I have my character in my mind, I like to think of how it ends first. Then, I make everything work toward a satisfying end. It's the only way you can be in control, or else your characters will run away with you."

Mae told me that when she decided to do the part of Leticia in

Myra, she insisted on spelling her character's name Letitia. "It was subtle, but it was too choice an opportunity to let it get away."

I talked with director Michael Sarne in London, while he was working on *Life at Any Price,* a mystery film with a Holocaust setting. He told me why *Myra Breckinridge* had to be a dream.

"I got the idea while I was in New York, looking for another project after my picture *Joanna.* I thought I was going to do a film with Leslie Caron. Then, I happened to see in *The Hollywood Reporter* that Fox didn't know what to do with Gore Vidal's script for his best-selling novel *Myra Breckinridge.* I remembered having read the graphic rape scene in *Myra* and being disgusted by it. I chucked the book I had found somewhere into the waste basket.

"When I saw that Fox was having trouble with it, I remembered something the hero, if you can call him that, said. He awakens from a dream, feeling his beard stubble and saying, 'Where are my tits? Where are my tits?' So, that was how you do it. It's all a fantasy, the wish-fulfillment of a man who wants to be a woman.

"I walked across Manhattan, with about twenty cents in my pocket, to David Brown's Fox office. He was very enthusiastic. When I told him about the dream, he said, 'So it's all a dream?' Then he called Richard Zanuck in Hollywood, and he liked the idea, too. 'Fly him right out here,' he said, which was a good thing, since I didn't have the fare to get back to my Manhattan hotel.

"When I met with Zanuck on the West Coast, he wanted me to do the screenplay. Then he said, 'Of course you'll direct, too.' I hadn't wanted to do that. My good friend Brigitte Bardot had told me, 'Don't do it! Don't do it! In Hollywood, they eat up people like us for breakfast,' and I believed her. I said I'd like a 'mutual option,' which is really no option at all. If I didn't like the project I could back out, and if they didn't like me, they could fire me. They didn't want that.

"I got $75,000 for the screenplay and $25,000 for each rewrite.

There were two rewrites. That was a lot of dollars in those days. It bought quite a lot."

Sarne wanted Mae to be in the film, and he wrote her a letter. Mae later told him that she showed the letter to her spiritual adviser at the time, and he became very excited, saying, " 'This man is very determined. You *must* do it. It's fate.' " Sarne continued:

"I met Mae for the first time at her apartment. I went there with the producer, Bobby Fryer. Mae looked fabulous.

"She had all of this beautiful cream-colored furniture, with a pinkish hue. She suggested we sit on her sofa. I sat down and I realized that she had towels on the sofa. The towels were dyed the exact same color as the sofa, but they were washable.

"Paul [Novak] was there. He was a very nice guy, and you could see he loved her to pieces.

"I understood Mae was very hurt when she told me later that they wouldn't give her her price, which she told me was $350,000. They offered her $275,000. She said, 'You know, dear, I saved Paramount Pictures.' Her pride was hurt.

"So I said, 'Mae, if they don't give you your price, I'm out the door.'

"She said, rather diffidently, 'May I quote you?'

"I said, 'Absolutely.' I had the money for writing the script, and I figured that way I could get out of directing it.

"They gave it to her.

"I thought Mae was a black-and-white character because that was how audiences had always seen her in her films, and that she would look great in black and white.

"She liked that, but she said, 'Dear, that little girl won't wear any black and white, will she?' I assured her she wouldn't. She always referred to Raquel [Welch] as 'that little girl,' and she couldn't remember her name. Mae couldn't remember the names of people she didn't like.

"She wasn't aware of how Raquel Welch, Rex Reed, and Bobby Fryer felt. They simply did not want her on the film, and they let it be known. But Mae was protected against the negative and didn't seem to feel it, but she did say once about Raquel, 'Why is that little girl so nasty to me?'

"I planned for Raquel to wear red, white, and blue, which was as striking as the black and white, and very becoming. Theodora Van Runkle, a wonderful designer, did Raquel's costumes. Edith Head did Mae's. They were both great.

"Then, the first time Raquel's character and Mae had a scene together, Raquel wanted to appear in black and white.

"When I told Raquel that Mae would be the star of the picture, from then on, it was a hate-fest against me.

"I must say that Raquel took direction very well, and she's perfectly believable as a woman who's really a man playing a woman. She's a good dancer, too. Rex Reed is not a professional actor, but he was perfect in his part.

"I didn't direct Mae at all. She wrote most of her own lines, and they got laughs. I tried to write a few Mae West lines, but mine fell flat.

"Mae wrote some more scenes for herself. She would have liked to have made it more of a Mae West picture. She wanted to have a scene or two with John Huston, but I wasn't allowed to expand her part. I felt that Mae was funny in the way the film should have been. It was a comedy, after all.

"I did everything I could to protect her material. She wanted to sing, and she was very good. It was important, but there were people who didn't even want that. David and Dick were the only ones who appreciated the picture."

David Brown remembered one of her lines. "Mae played a casting director, and a man comes in who's very tall. She said, 'Come in here, cowboy. How tall are you?'

" 'Six feet, seven inches, ma'am.'

"She says something like, 'Forget about the six feet. Let's talk about the seven inches.' "

Myra Breckinridge (1970)

Film critic Myron Breckinridge (Rex Reed) casually undergoes a sex change operation without anesthesia, so he can experience life as a woman.

As Myra Breckinridge (Raquel Welch), he/she dedicates herself to avenging all of the wrongs ever inflicted on women by men. Although Myra has replaced Myron, he remains at her side, visible only to viewers.

Myra begins with Myron's uncle, Buck Loner (John Huston), who owns and operates an acting school for students who never graduate. Representing herself as Myron's widow, Myra claims his share of the school.

Among the students are Mary Ann (Farrah Fawcett) and her boyfriend, Rusty (Roger Herren). Myra is sexually aroused by both of them. When Rusty violates his parole and is about to be sent back to prison, Myra turns to Letitia Van Allen (Mae West) for help.

Letitia is an actors' agent who specializes in oversexed leading men. In return for the new students she provides the school, she gets to represent and seduce the school's better prospects. Letitia knows the sentencing judge (William Hopper) intimately, and Rusty is saved from prison. Later, Rusty is ritually raped with a strap-on dildo by Myra, who then almost succeeds in seducing Mary Ann.

Loner, having discovered that Myron never married, confronts Myra. She shows him that she *is,* indeed, Myron by climbing up on his desk and lifting her dress. Myra and Myron dance triumphantly out into the street, where she is hit by a car.

Myron awakens in black and white. Now in a charity ward, he is feeling for the woman's breasts he no longer possesses. The nightmarish fantasy was brought on by his automobile accident.

Back in color, Myron dances onto the street where he encounters Myra, and together they take a cab into the sunset.

Clips from old Hollywood films figure prominently in *Myra Breckinridge*. Since Myron is a film critic, he sees the real world in terms of the fantasy world he inhabits in his work, especially in his dream.

"The film clips were the only way I could figure out to do the rape scene," Sarne told me. "To justify the clips during the rape scene and make it acceptable, I had to use them all the way through or they wouldn't have worked when I needed them. I wanted some clips from M-G-M and it would have been nice to have some of Mae from Paramount, but everything from other studios cost too much, so I was told to select from Fox's clips.

"I thought it would be a great idea to preview in San Francisco, and David and Dick agreed with me. There were a lot of men in women's dresses, and it was a terribly enthusiastic crowd.

"In San Francisco, the biggest laugh was during the dildo-rape when there is a Shirley Temple clip. I didn't expect how big the reaction would be to the milking of the goat, when the milk squirts out in Shirley Temple's face. I went to the preview with Dick and David. We were impressed with that big laugh and the reaction.

"So I was surprised when I was called into Dick's office, and he said that scene with the squirting milk had to go. I couldn't believe it. 'You saw what happened in San Francisco,' I said.

"Zanuck said, 'Yes, but I got a call from my father [Darryl F. Zanuck]. He got a call from President Nixon, who feels Shirley Temple, who is a dedicated Republican and has worked hard for the Republican party, would be embarrassed by the scene.'

"Somebody must have told him. So the scene went. I replaced it with a Laurel and Hardy clip that wasn't nearly so funny.

"*Myra* could have been much more awful. I was sabotaged every day. Even so, I *nearly* made the film I *wanted* to make.

"My original intention with the script," Sarne said, "was to drift in and out of reality. My model was Federico Fellini's short film *Toby Dammit*, which, like most of Fellini, is kind of dream-like."

Toby Dammit is a part of *Spirits of the Dead*, released in 1968. The Fellini segment was based on "Never Bet the Devil Your Head," an Edgar Allan Poe story.

The devil in Fellini's segment is a little girl with big eyes, bouncing a ball and looking impassively at the camera, which represents the victim's point of view, and winking. In *Myra*, a nurse who looks just like that little girl chews gum while looking impassively at the camera, which represents Myron, and winks. The wink is mirthless, almost a tick. Later, she reappears as a cigarette girl listlessly selling bananas in a glittery nightclub. "She's very important to the film," Sarne said. "I wanted to show that the devil was always lurking behind everything."

Fellini is mentioned in *Myra* when an Italian actor appears at Letitia's agency with a letter of recommendation from the director. Mae says, "He's a fan of mine," which was an understatement.

Sarne met Fellini in 1972 at Mr. Chow's, the London branch of the popular restaurant. "I wanted to talk with him about his films, but all he wanted to talk about was what was it like for me directing Mae West. He said it was his dream to direct Mae, and he'd wanted to write a picture for her. He was in London trying to raise money for his next film. Imagine! Someone like Fellini having to look for money.

"John Huston was a great friend of mine," Sarne told me, "and I loved him, but I must confess I had some misgivings about casting him in *Myra*. It was like directing Fellini or Billy Wilder. He never did a thing to undermine my authority, but I always had the feeling that everyone was looking toward him for his reactions. But now whenever I re-see *Myra*, I can't imagine a better Buck Loner.

"I went to one of Mae's spiritual evenings at her beach house in Santa Monica. She had her two monkeys there. They were wearing diapers. That was pretty great stuff.

"My daughter was born while we were in Los Angeles. She received a diamond bracelet and a diamond ring and a lovely note from Mae. Mae was a thoughtful lady, kindly, sweet. I loved her to bits."

David Brown and his wife, Helen Gurley Brown, were good friends of Mae. He remembered their times together.

"We used to have dinner with Mae West, in a restaurant no longer in existence, called La Seine, here in New York. We'd just had a lovely dinner with her, and what I remember was, during the dinner, several sort of mash notes came over from businessmen at nearby tables, and finally, when we got up to leave, the entire restaurant gave her a standing ovation.

"I remember her advice to Helen was, 'Always have two almonds a day to keep cancer away.' Helen has observed that ever since."

Brown recalled his first encounter with Mae.

"Believe it or not, it was in 1933, when I was on my way to Stanford University by ship. I was coming from New York, and my ship had docked in Costa Rica. It was a banana boat. We went up into the jungle, and I saw a movie there. It was in an open-air movie theater, where you had tables and everything, and it was the first time I heard Mae say, 'Come up and see me sometime,' which she said to Cary Grant.

"I loved her. She was very smart. I don't think very many people knew how intelligent she was. I saw her on the screen in her early life, and in person in her later life."

Charles William Bush was the photographer chosen by *Playboy* to take photographs of Mae when she was interviewed by the magazine in January 1971. He was selected for his youth, good looks, and polite manner, which pleased the leading models he regularly photographed and the actresses who were considered potentially difficult. In order to have the greatest rapport possible, Bush didn't bring an assistant when he photographed Mae.

He was struck by Mae's saucy personality and her effort to play her public character. He sensed that she was nervous, though trying not to show it. She was especially nervous about the close-ups. Bush found that not so unusual because it was also true for young models. "I had the feeling," he said, "that the camera really worried her, that it made her feel vulnerable.

"Age does that with actresses. In fact, it does it with actors, too.

"Her very fit bodyguard [Paul Novak] stayed in the room with us, as if to protect her." Usually Bush was able to encourage his subjects, but Mae was more responsive to Paul, the person she obviously knew well and trusted.

"He was constantly encouraging her. She kept looking at him as the pictures were being taken. 'You look beautiful, Miss West. Beautiful. You look beautiful,' a lot of nice words, and she was very responsive to him. He always called her 'Miss West,' never Mae.

"She was wearing a lot of makeup. Really a lot of makeup." Bush observed how soft and fair her skin was where it showed on her neck, where the makeup ended. "She would have photographed better with softer, more natural makeup that allowed her youthful skin to show."

• • •

Mae was a celebrities' celebrity. Bette Davis was one of those anxious to meet her.

"I met Mae West a few times," Bette told me, "but there was only one time when we had much conversation. It was at a dinner party.

"We talked about female impersonators because we were two big favorites with them. Many more liked to do me, but she also had her following among 'impressionists,' as they often called themselves. Mine were often rather good, even great, but she didn't think any of them really caught her.

"We both considered it a form of flattery and acknowledgment of our being unique and easily recognized. She said she didn't like it if a woman did it, and she thought that was stealing her stuff without paying for it. I never noticed any women impersonators, but I don't think it would have made any difference to me. I suppose I felt differently, because I was an actress wanting, hopefully, to play as many different characters as possible, and Miss West was a personality who had created her character and who was a writer who had written her own material in which she had rights and saw all that being stolen from her.

"Mae West told me that her mother never said a cross or sharp word to her. Never in all her life. Neither did Ruthie [Bette Davis's mother], though she may have said a few firm ones, but only to encourage me and pull me through. Anyway, I never needed any firmness, because I was firm with myself. I wanted only to do my best. Miss West struck me as that kind of performer, and person, too, who only wanted to do her best.

"I remember Mae West was not the way I thought she would be. She was rather retiring and quiet. I have to admit I was a little disappointed. She may have seemed that way because, as she said, 'I don't play my character when I go out socially. You invited Mae to dinner, not Lil. Lil doesn't accept invitations to go anywhere free. If she's gonna work, she expects more than just an honorarium for it.'

"I asked her about the secret of her youthful appearance, especially her beautiful skin. I wished mine looked like that. I thought it might have something to do with her having been a night animal, while I had been a sun-worshipper. But I did so love the outdoors. We were both blond types, but she was more of an indoors blonde.

"She answered without a second's hesitation, 'Five enemas a day.' Well, maybe it was six or four. I don't remember exactly. One doesn't keep score. Besides, I was eating dinner at the time.

"I certainly remember our conversation, but I'd rather forget the last part."

"I found Mae West a very shy person," Henry Fonda told me. "It's always easy for me to recognize *another* shy person. I wanted to be an actor so I could hide behind all of those characters and play a lot of different people who *weren't* shy. Mae West hid behind that one character she'd created for herself, which she played any time she was in public. What a great cover!

"On the other hand, in between playing characters, *I* had to go out, naked Fonda."

Mae told me that when Paul took the call inviting her to Groucho's home for dinner, and asked her about it, Mae told him to find out, "Will Groucho be smoking a cigar?"

"We were promised that no one would be smoking," Mae said, "but when we arrived, the first thing I said to Groucho was, 'No cigars!,' and then I said, 'Hello.' "

At dinner with a few of his friends, Groucho talked with Mae about his mother. "He said she was German, and I told him my mother was German, too. He said his mother came to New York when she was a teenager. I told him my mother came when she was about fifteen, and he said his mother was the same age, maybe sixteen. We had quite a few things in common, it seems.

"He said his father was a bad tailor, but a great cook. I told him my mother was a great cook, too. Nobody ever made better pig's knuckles and sauerkraut. Groucho knew what I was talking about. My father never really appreciated pig's knuckles and sauerkraut. He liked his food without a foreign accent. So when my mother cooked for her German relatives, she made my father a nice piece of beef.

"It was clear Groucho really loved his mother. He said she gathered them up like flowers, him and his brothers, and without her, they wouldn't have been anything. And I said, 'Without *my* mother, I wouldn't have been *me.*'

"Mother Nature was good to me, but without my mother, it wouldn't have mattered. And my mother had something to do with Mother Nature, too. I look a lot like her. I told Groucho she was a model, a corset model. Groucho gave me one of those looks. You know, he raised his eyebrows and looked down my dress.

"He said his father baked pies for his mother to give to agents and producers to get their boys bookings. I told him my father was called Battlin' Jack, and he was a champion boxer. He took good care of my mother, so she could take care of us children. Groucho was impressed that he was a professional boxing champion.

"He said his mother lost a baby boy, just like my mother lost my sister Katie. He figured the Marx Brothers would've had another brother in show business. I don't know what Katie would've been, maybe a performer, too.

"He said he admired the way I created my own character, and that the Marx Brothers did the same thing. He asked me if there was a moment when I created my character, and I said, no. It just gestated.

"Then he told me the story of how the Marx Brothers found their characters in a place in Texas with a funny name I can't remember, except it rhymed with 'roaches.'"

"Nacogdoches," I said.

"Yeah. They were kids singing there, singing and dancing and not making much of an impression. Then, a mule ran away, and the audience cleared out of the theater to chase him. The mule was more entertaining than their act. That was the message Groucho got. When the audience came back, the Marx Brothers insulted them, but they didn't get mad. They just laughed, and that's how the Marx Brothers got their act. I got my act the first time I stepped on a stage.

"Groucho told me his mother loved show business, too, and that he had an uncle, Al Sheen, who was famous. Of course, I knew about him, Gallagher and Sheen.

"I told him my mother was more beautiful than Lillian Russell and wanted to be an actress, but 'nice' girls didn't do that sort of thing then. He was one of the few people around anymore who knew who Lillian Russell was. I told him if my father caught a man giving my mother the eye, he'd knock his block off.

"Groucho seemed to enjoy just talking about himself. I could understand that, because I was the same. I was my favorite subject.

"Did Groucho ever insult you?" Mae asked me.

"No, he never did," I answered.

"He must've liked you. He didn't insult me, either."

"Did you enjoy the evening?" I asked.

"Yeah," she answered, "it was nice. The only thing was the dessert was kind of plain. And it was kind of a skimpy portion."

"I'm certain Groucho would have been pleased if you'd asked for a second portion."

"I couldn't because Paul would've given me one of those looks."

Elliott Gould remembered the evening:

255

"At the end of the meal, following the dessert, there was a plate of chocolate truffles, creams and bonbons. Mae carefully selected two truffles. As she reached for a third, Mae's companion [Paul] took the platter and passed it on. Groucho took two and said, 'I'm allowed two chocolates a day. When I've finished these, there's nothing to do but wait until tomorrow.' You know how he'd say that.

"But Mae was not prepared to surrender that easily. She waited for her companion to look away. He never did, until we were all leaving the dining room to take our places in the living room for the evening's entertainment. That's when I saw Mae snatch another chocolate from the plate and pop it into her mouth.

"We sank into the comfortable chairs, except for Marvin [Hamlisch], who took his position at the piano. Mae offered to let me sing with her, but I didn't know the words. Before we all left, she autographed my driver's license."

Mae said, "After I finished performing, Groucho got up and sang and told some stories, but he didn't know what a hard act I was to follow."

When I mentioned to Mae that Elliott Gould had told me about that evening, she said, "Elliott's a bear of a man. I've always loved bears.

"Say, you know what I just thought of? I remember my first sex dream. It was with a bear. I guess I was about ten, maybe younger. He came through the door standing up, a giant male bear. I never had the dream again. It worried me for a long time. I really haven't thought about this for years. I never told anyone. I learned later that the bear is a symbol of sex."

While I was talking with Groucho for my first book, *Hello, I Must Be Going*, which was about him and his brothers, I sometimes stayed at his Hillcrest home near Beverly Hills. Bud Cort was a frequent guest there, and we shared the same bedroom, though not at the same time and only when Groucho's brother Zeppo wasn't there, which was nearly all of the time. Bud was at the house when Mae came to dinner. He described the evening from his viewpoint.

"One morning, Groucho knocked on the bedroom door and came in," Bud said. Groucho asked, 'Who would you like to meet while you're here? I'm going to invite someone to dinner on Saturday night,' and he asked me what my choice was. He said, 'You name it. I know everyone.'

"I said, 'Mae West. Or Fred Astaire.'

"Groucho said, 'One at a time.'

"He came back later, and he said, 'Fred's out of town, so Mae will be here Saturday night.'

"Mae West arrived with her muscular bodyguard, and we all had dinner. Elliott [Gould], Marvin [Hamlisch], and Erin [Fleming, Groucho's secretary-companion] were there.

"After dinner, we went into the living room, and the show began.

"I sat down, and Mae rose with the assistance of her strong companion and tottered on those high heels to the piano.

"She said, 'I'm going to sing "Frankie and Johnnie." '

"Singing and swaying, she was really great.

"Then Erin did a little dance, which Groucho really enjoyed. He enjoyed just about anything Erin did. He asked me to sing 'Peasy Weasy,' a favorite of his, and he knew I knew all the words. But it was different singing for Mae West.

"After 'Peasy Weasy,' I sang 'I Left My Heart in San Francisco' for Miss West. I had my eyes on the floor, and I never looked up until the very end, when I said the line 'I left my heart in San Francisco' to Mae.

"When I finished the line, she sighed, 'Ohhhh.'

"Groucho did his repertory, the songs he loved to sing, 'Father's

Day,' 'Lydia, the Tattooed Lady,' and of course Captain Spaulding's song, which he did with Erin singing Margaret Dumont's part and Marvin playing the piano. Our little audience was very appreciative.

"The next morning, I kind of missed breakfast, so I came to lunch, and I said to Groucho, 'What a wonderful night! Wasn't Mae West great?' Groucho looked sort of livid, but was trying to conceal how he felt.

"Groucho had been measuring applause, comparing reactions.

"He said, 'She'll never have dinner at this house again.'"

Bud and I agreed that Groucho was joking, at least partly joking, but actually, she never did have dinner again at Groucho's.

Director Paul Morrissey told me about meeting Mae West in Hollywood.

"She was very reserved—except when she was talking about herself, obviously her favorite subject. Then she really came to life, all animated, filled with enthusiasm. It seemed to be her favorite subject, maybe the only one she really enjoyed.

"I remember one night some female impersonators who did Mae were invited to her apartment, and they had a film to show her, them doing her.

"We were supposed to be watching the film, but they were all watching Mae to see her reactions. Everyone kept looking at her all through the film.

"She was obviously enjoying it, but whenever there was something pornographic, she cast her eyes down."

Mae's last film was based on her 1961 stage play, *Sextette*. Among the stars playing cameo roles in the film was Tony Curtis.

"I thought it would be interesting to know Mae West, but I didn't really get to know her during *Sextette*," Tony Curtis told me. "She was very concentrated on the film and I guess she was saving all her energy for it. She'd sit very composed, waiting, and then when they were going to shoot her, she had all this energy stored up. I know all about energy. I've always had enough for a few people.

"As soon as I spoke to her, the first thing she said was she liked my accent. My accent is the east side of New York. My parents were from Hungary and that was the only language I spoke until I was five or six, which is why I started school late.

"Maybe it reminded her of people she knew when she was a child in Brooklyn. Her mother came from Germany. But her mother married someone here, so she didn't have the problem of speaking a language as a child that would have come in handy if I'd been in Budapest.

"She told me she liked the way I talked, so I told her I liked the way she talked. And she said she liked my style. You know how she said it, in that sexy way of hers. It was like the most suggestive thing anyone ever said to me. I let it go at that.

"I'm a good mimic, but I can't do such a great Mae West. She could mimic herself better than anyone else could.

"I only did the picture because of Mae West, and I can't say I was glad I did it. No, I can't say that. I don't think too many people saw it. Just as well. I didn't get to be friends with Mae West, but maybe it's better that way. You know, sometimes you meet people you've idolized and they turn out to be greater as people than you'd imagined they'd be, like Cary [Grant]. And Burt [Lancaster]. Then, sometimes, it's better you only know the parts the person plays."

Archivist and film historian Marvin Paige was the casting director on *Sextette*.

"We thought it would be a good idea to have George Raft in *Sextette* because he'd been the star of her first film, *Night After Night*, and this was pretty certain to be Mae's last picture.

"After we met with Raft, we figured it was going to be *his* last one, too. He said he didn't think he should do it. He wasn't well. He said he didn't want to hold us up. But we assured him we'd work around any health problems he had, because we really wanted him.

"He never liked to wear his hairpiece. He had a gray hairpiece, and he didn't like to wear it at all. He sent it down to the set to have it cleaned. We were shooting at Paramount, even though it wasn't a Paramount film.

"At one point, Mae called me into the dressing room he was using, which was one of the portables they have on the sets. There was this poor thing on the table, and she said, 'What's *that*?'

"I said, 'It's one of George's hairpieces.'

"She looked surprised, sort of shocked, and she said, 'God! It looks like one of my old wigs. That isn't like *his* hair *was*. I want him to look like he *used* to look.'

"I said, 'But, Mae, that was kind of a long time ago. It was right after the Valentino period, that kind of greasy look . . . '

"She said, 'I like him greasy.'

"We finally found the way to avoid the hairpiece. He wore a hat instead."

George Raft's appearance with Mae in *Sextette* was quite poignant. He had been largely responsible for her trip to Hollywood and her first film, which led to her Hollywood career. They had remained friends over the years, and she had insisted on having him in *Sextette*, which, as it turned out, was the last film either would make.

The ailing Raft was certain it was his last film because of his rapidly declining health. Unlike the time when Mae felt her part was too small in their first film together, he believed his part was too large. He knew he was dying. Mae, on the other hand, was filled with exuberance, energy, and excitement, glad to be back at work. She was pleased she still had her boundless good health and that her looks hadn't changed. She looked forward to the years, even the decades ahead. She had no idea that Raft would live longer than he expected, and that she herself had only a short time remaining. The old friends would die only a few days apart.

Sextette (1978)

During the Cold War, a London world peace conference competes for press attention with the wedding of Marlo Manners (Mae West) to Sir Michael Barrington (Timothy Dalton). He will be her sixth husband. Her second husband, Alexei (Tony Curtis), is a member of the Russian delegation to the peace conference. Before the wedding, Marlo hopes to meet secretly with "Sexy Alexei" for a brief peace conference of her own. Among other things she hopes to persuade him to stop voting against peace.

Other ex-husbands arrive in London, intent on keeping her from marrying someone else. Husband number five, gangster Vance Norton (George Hamilton), arrives at the same time as husband number four, film director Laslo Karolny (Ringo Starr).

Marlo has been keeping a taped record of her recent assignations, some of them with important peace delegates. Somehow, this tape is misplaced. It turns up in a cake for the delegates, being transported there innocently via the bakery, by the U.S. Olympic team.

When U.S. delegate Chambers (Walter Pidgeon) hears what is on the cassette, he confronts the delegates who have been voting against peace.

Marlo becomes the heroine who saves the peace, and her new husband turns out to be a secret agent. This makes him seem even more attractive in her eyes.

Ringo Starr spoke with me about his appearance in *Sextette*.

"I only agreed to the thing in *Sextette* because I thought it would be interesting not just to meet Mae West, but to work with her. I can't claim it as a career highlight, but I can say Mae West was not a disappointment.

"I don't think she was pleased by some of what was happening to her script. I heard her say to this big, muscular guy who came with her, 'They're flushin' my play down the terlet.'"

There were days during the shooting of *Sextette* when Mae West would sit patiently on the set, talking with Tim Malachosky while she waited for her scene.

"She never got annoyed with the waiting," Malachosky said, "which I guess she'd learned was a waste of energy. I could ask her any question and she would love to talk about her career. She was perfectly prepared for her part in the film, so she wasn't at all nervous.

"She was so confident in the way she looked, knowing she looked wonderful. After her hair and makeup were done, and she was in a great dress, then she didn't need to keep looking in the mirror at all. She sat very carefully and arranged it so the dress wouldn't wrinkle. They would come by from time to time and tuck in a wisp of hair or freshen her powder.

"When I could see the time was getting close for her part, I would be very quiet and fade back into my chair, so she could save all her energy for her performance.

"But it wasn't really necessary. When she got out of her chair for her call, she was the Miss West I knew, the one I ate breakfast with before she did her makeup. I was one of the few people who saw her without her wig. Her own blond hair was much prettier.

"As she rose, something came over her, and she had a glow, and this wonderful energy, and she was the Mae West from all of the movies of hers I'd seen."

Events planner and writer Barry Landau was with photographer Francesco Scavullo on the *Sextette* set. "As Scavullo was about to shoot some stills of Mae West, she said to him, 'Shoot me from above, not from the belly button. She knew all about photography, and even Scavullo's fame didn't intimidate her at all," Landau told me. "The lady knew just what she wanted."

When I first wrote to Federico Fellini in the hope of doing an interview with him for a chapter in a book I was writing, I told him that I had written a book, my first, *Hello, I Must Be Going*, about Groucho Marx and the Marx Brothers. I said that I was also writing about Mae West. I wrote a great deal more, but I didn't know that I already had said the magic words.

When I met Fellini at our first lunch in a restaurant just outside Rome, he began my interview by saying, "Tell me about them. What were Groucho and Mae West really like?" When Fellini first fell in love with American films, it was in their Italian dubbed versions. Only much later did Fellini hear the Marx Brothers and Mae speaking for themselves in English.

"I would have liked to meet Mae West," Fellini told me. "I admired her enormously. She was wonderful. She was so anti-erotic.

"She always seemed to be anti-sex because she made a joke of sex and made you laugh, and that is anti-erotic. I think work was really her sex. It seems to me that her career was everything, and that she cared so much about it she probably had no time for sex. A person cannot do everything in life.

"If a woman chooses to have sex in her life, she must spend her time in that, with *la toilette*, making herself attractive. If she chooses the career, the investment of time and energy is there. Personally, I have always been attracted by women who didn't seem to spend a great deal of time and effort on their looks.

"I wrote Mae West a letter once when I was going to be in the United States, telling her I wanted to meet her. I rewrote the letter several times, but then I never mailed it. So, it was no surprise when she didn't answer.

"It's difficult to know what to say to someone who has been a part of your life, but who doesn't know you exist. Writing to her, I felt like I was still the little boy in the movie theater in Rimini. She looked so big on the screen, but I heard that she was really very tiny, wearing extremely high-heeled platform shoes. It would have been strange for me to be standing with her, looking down at her. So much of life is illusion. I wonder if she really had a mirror on the ceiling over her bed . . .

"I wanted to offer her a part in one of my films. I would have written a part especially for her. I would have written a film especially for her. But it was not our destiny. She belonged to America, and I belonged to Italy.

"She was one of the persons I would most like to have known. Maybe it is frivolous to choose her instead of Einstein or Churchill or a nuclear scientist. I cannot imagine talking about nuclear science. But Mae West, I feel we would have been kindred spirits.

"Do you think she would have liked me?" he asked.

I told him I was certain of it. "She would have loved the drawings you have done of her." Fellini had a set of sketch books with many cartoon-like pictures he had drawn of her.

"Mae West had a genius for entertaining people," Fellini explained. "She was able to bring out the humor of the situation between the sexes so brilliantly, perhaps more brilliantly than anyone else. She was the supreme mistress of the humorous relations between the sexes in life as shown on the screen.

"She had the experience of vaudeville in America, which I liked very much in Italy. Italian vaudeville was very good. I made *Variety Lights* about it. Mae West loved the circus, which I loved so. She wanted to be a lion-tamer. She was fearless. I could understand the desire to do it, but I was never brave like she. I would not have been able to go into a lion's cage, with a lion in it.

"We could have talked about the circus. Circus people are different from other people. They have a bond, and people who love the circus have a bond.

"There was that wonderful film with Mae West in which she tamed lions. I would like to have directed that film.

"I like to think that Mae was inspirational for me. She came to me in my dreams, those waking dreams, you know; the ones I have when I'm no longer really asleep, but haven't quite wakened. I have dreamed many times about her. Once she was a nurse leaning over me in the hospital. That woke me up. Once she was an angel in heaven with big wings. One time, she was in the street directing traffic, only all of the traffic had stopped to stare at her, so she was causing a lot of confusion. Each time I dream about her, I draw her pictures that morning, the way I saw her in my dream."

In Beverly Hills, Gore Vidal talked with me about his friendship with Federico Fellini, and about Fellini's interests, especially his fascination with Mae West.

" 'Fred' could never hear enough about Mae West, although he did almost all of the talking on the subject. I always called him Fred, and he called me 'Gorino.'

"We would sit at cafés with lots of wonderful food and talk about subjects of importance, like *Myra Breckinridge*. Movies are the lingua franca of our culture. Fred wanted to know about Mae West. He never tired of hearing about her.

"I told him I thought the fun of writing books instead of making films was serendipitous. I liked writing books because it was something I could do alone. Fred said that for him making films was serendipitous.

"Because I was an American, I suppose that he felt I must be a Mae West specialist. Actually, I wasn't that much of an authority on the lady, but Fred waited hopefully for any words of wisdom I might have to offer. I think he just enjoyed so much having anyone to chat with about his favorite.

"I asked him once if he saw a resemblance between Anita Ekberg and Mae West. I saw a resemblance. He answered, 'No.' I didn't pursue the subject because I didn't want to do anything to spoil our appetite with all of that wonderful food there, and I understood that Mae was sacred like a goddess, and Anita Ekberg was very much on land, someone he knew."

Fellini's dream would have been to make a film with Mae West, but maybe that would have brought her to the level of reality. Who knows . . . ?

In Paris I spoke with Roman Polanski:

"My film *Knife in the Water*, was nominated for an Oscar in the Best Foreign Film category, and in 1964, I was invited to go to California. A treat was planned for us—Disneyland. In our little tour group was Federico Fellini, whose *8½* was competing against my film. I knew I didn't have a chance, but I was happy. I met Snow White and Giulietta Masina.

"I remember Fellini liked Disneyland, or I think he did. But what he *really* wanted most to do in Los Angeles was to meet Mae West.

"That day at Disneyland with Federico Fellini talking about Mae West is one of my earliest and happiest memories of America. It stands apart from the life I was later to live there."

"There was a private screening of *Sextette* at the De Mille Theater on the Paramount lot," Tim Malachosky told me. "All of the stars were there, and Elton John came. My mother, Eva Malachosky, received a very special personal invitation from Miss West. Miss West was in the center of the theater, surrounded by the famous people.

"Miss West was pleased by her performance, but the movie hadn't turned out as she had imagined it would. She looked wonderful in her own great dresses. The spectacular wedding dress was from the play, and she had saved it. She liked to save everything, believing it would have a future use.

"Then, there was a sneak preview at the Mann Bruin Theater in Westwood, near UCLA. There was no announcement that Miss West would be there. She chose to appear as a surprise, and the audience was so thrilled. It wasn't easy to get her through the crowd. At the end of the film, as Miss West left, the audience gave her a standing ovation. Being there was something they would never forget.

"The gala premiere was on March 2, 1978, at the Cinerama Dome in Hollywood. There was a huge crowd waiting for Miss West, who arrived wearing a white satin gown with a diamond tiara. She said a few words after the film, and then all of us who were invited to the party went to the ballroom of the Beverly Hilton Hotel. There was a sculpted figure in ice of Miss West, similar to the more permanent one at the Ravenswood.

"Miss West had agreed to go to the San Francisco premiere. She would not fly, so Paul drove the limousine while I sat in the backseat with Miss West. We started late in the afternoon, and by nine P.M., we were starving when we saw a Holiday Inn in Pleasanton.

"Everyone in the restaurant recognized Miss West and wanted an autograph. She signed before and after the meal, but no one was allowed to disturb her during the meal, especially during dessert. The chef received one of her larger, more elaborate autographs.

"We all went to the Mark Hopkins Hotel in San Francisco, arriving about midnight. Miss West had the Garden Suite.

"In the morning, I had breakfast with her and Paul in the suite, and her hairdresser, Mr. Thaddeus, arrived from Los Angeles, to do her hair.

"Miss West gave interviews, and we had dinner before going to the premiere. Miss West liked to keep her regular schedule. The traffic was jammed for blocks, and it was really a major event. There were mounted policemen, but they had trouble keeping the people back.

"We had to sneak Miss West in through the side. Inside, Miss West and Paul sat in a roped-off section with bodyguards. I was planted in the audience because she wanted me to be able to tell her about the audience reaction. Any time she appeared on the screen, the audience screamed and hollered so much, it wasn't possible to hear any of the dialogue.

"A group of musclemen were waiting on the stage afterwards, and Miss West appeared holding Paul's arm.

" 'I hope you enjoyed my demonstration of progressive education, *Sextette*.' That was what she said.

"She'd been rehearsing that line all the way from Los Angeles in the car. Paul and I knew it pretty well. She had said it every possible way it could be said, every tone, every syllable. She placed tremendous importance on her delivery. Then, she would ask Paul and me which way we liked it best. At the end, we all agreed on the same way, and she said it just that way.

"In the car afterwards, what she wanted to know from me was what the people in the audience were saying. I had written some of it down, especially later that night before I might forget, because I knew exactly what she would want. I knew she'd want the exact words, not just the general idea, and a description of who said what. She was happy with what I had to tell her.

"Later, she was disappointed that the film didn't have better distribution. We got so many letters from people who wanted to see the film, asking Miss West where they could see it.

"Mae thought *The Drag*, her 1927 play, might be revived. She asked me if I would go on the road to keep an eye on it. I was very flattered. I'd never done anything like that, but she knew I would always have her best interests at heart."

In April of 1969, Mae received a fan letter from a high school student in Santa Monica. His name was Tim Malachosky. After reading a feature article about her in a magazine and seeing *Belle of the Nineties*, he had written a class paper about her. In the letter, he said that he worked in the research department of the school library.

"I guess by accident, I put in my phone number in the hope I'd hear something," Tim told me. "I sent it to the beach house, and I thought that would be the end of it. About two weeks later, I got home from school and the phone rang. A voice said, 'Is Tim there? This is Miss Mae West.' And I said, "Who *is* this?' I thought someone was playing a joke on me. And she said, 'No, it really is,' and I could tell it was true by her voice.

"She thanked me for the letter. She said she enjoyed it. She was having some friends over for a gathering at the beach house for an ESP demonstration, and she wanted me to join her and she wanted to meet me. She was just about finishing up *Myra Breckinridge*. She told me where, and I went.

"I was kind of nervous and waited until everybody else talked to her, or whatever, and then I went up and introduced myself. She said it was very nice to meet me, that she enjoyed my letter, and we just kind of talked for a few minutes about *Myra* and whatever she was doing. She said to give her a call sometime, that she was in the telephone book.

"So, I waited about two weeks and I called, hoping she would remember me. A woman answered the phone, but it wasn't Miss West. She said, 'Ravenswood.' The number that was in the telephone book was actually for the apartment building. I said I'd like to speak with

Mae West. She said, 'Who's calling?' I said who it was, and she said, 'Just a moment.' And then the person came back on and said, 'Go ahead.'

"We talked, Miss West invited me up to the apartment. Afterwards, we saw each other a few times.

"One day she called and said, 'I'm in a jam.' A secretary and assistant had left, and would I be interested in helping her out? I said yes. I was happy to take the job.

"I met her and Paul at the beach house, and she said, 'Where would you like to go for dinner?' I was happy to have dinner with her anywhere she wanted. I wasn't really thinking about the food at all. We went to Knoll's Black Forest German restaurant in Santa Monica. After that, I started working for her. She gave me three huge boxes of fan mail that needed to be answered.

"I'd just finished high school, just graduated. I was free. They would come to Santa Monica and pick me up with the limousine, and we'd go to the beach house, where she was having appointments, having her nails done, her hair. Or I'd go to the apartment. It was fun.

"A lot of times, I would sit there and just kind of be in awe, thinking people would give anything to have just one second with her, and I'm spending all this time with her. She considered me part of her family, of which I was very proud. I was privileged, because she didn't have that many people around her, just a few.

"A lot of people thought I signed some of the autographs, but I never did. She never allowed anyone to sign her autograph. She had such a unique way of signing things, you could never copy it, unless you were a real pro. She would go out of her way to sign an autograph for somebody. There were several instances, like one time we were in Marina del Rey, and Paul went into the grocery store.

"She and I were sitting in the back of the car, going through mail, and she was autographing. A lady came out to the car, and I got out to talk to her.

"She said she had written a script for Miss West, and she wanted to talk to her about it. I said, 'Well, you need to send the script to the William Morris Agency. Everything has to go through channels.'

"When I got into the car, she went back into the store and told everybody that Mae West was out there. So, they all came out, and they were just lined up outside the car.

"Miss West always carried a portfolio of photos in the car. So, we rolled the window down a little bit and they'd talk, and she'd sign a photo, and I'd stick it out the window. There were probably sixty people, but she wanted everybody to get their signed photos. It was always important that no one go away disappointed.

"Wherever Miss West went, everyone knew her, but she didn't know them. She suffered from mild claustrophobia. Frequently Paul had to make an aisle for her, an escape route.

"Every day when she wasn't working outside her home and didn't have a full schedule of commitments, she would go out with Paul and me to her favorite food markets. She enjoyed riding around in the car, and she enjoyed the food shopping.

"Paul would drive, and I would sit in the backseat with Miss West, to keep her company and work on the fan mail with her. She enjoyed doing the mail that way, and she would get ideas for stories and lines and characters while we were riding in the car, and she would tell them to me, and she would write them down, or I would.

"Sometimes she liked to see real estate that was for sale, even though she wasn't buying any anymore. She said her father had been interested in real estate. She'd say, 'Look Tim, that's a nice piece of land,' but she wasn't so interested in just land because she said you had to keep the land and pay taxes, but if it had a good building, you could rent it and make money."

Tim recalled going with Mae and Paul to see one of her properties. It was a Saturday night, and she owned a car wash.

"What Miss West actually owned was the land under the car wash, but she had allowed the people who leased it to build-to-suit. Now the car wash was going out of business.

"She waited in the office while Paul and I took a look about. When we returned to the office, Miss West was ready to go.

"She hesitated for a moment and then she said, 'Tim, just one thing: Don't tell anyone that this was what Mae West did on a Saturday night.'

"Miss West never wanted meat and fish that had been refrigerated overnight in the apartment. She talked about her mother shopping daily so everything she put on the table was fresh.

"Much as she enjoyed going out, the ride in the car and the shopping, she couldn't just look about in the market. She would soon be overwhelmed by fans who wanted autographs or just wanted to stand near her, or who followed her and watched what she was buying. Sometimes they blocked her way while telling her how much they enjoyed her work and how much they loved her. They liked to get very close and touch her. Mae didn't want to offend anyone, but she didn't like being handled by all those strangers. So she had to stay in the car while Paul did the shopping.

"But I quickly learned Miss West didn't like to be left alone for a minute. If she thought of something else for the shopping list, she would tell Paul when he got back to the car, and he would go back into the market. She didn't tell me to go in and tell him.

"It was amazing the way Miss West couldn't leave the car and just stand outside, even for a few minutes, without drawing a crowd. The word would go through the supermarket that 'Mae West is outside,' and they would empty the market. Everyone would pour out to see her, and get that autograph. I guess some of those people who wanted that autograph so much hadn't ever seen one her films. They were getting the autograph of an icon.

"As long as Mae stayed in the back of the car, she felt safe, even when the crowd got pretty big. You could see how relieved she was when she saw Paul coming back. He always seemed to know when he was needed. She knew we could always drive out of there if it got out of hand, but it never did.

"One of the strangest times was when we were driving on the highway from Marina del Rey, and there was a fan in the car next to us. He was waving and yelling at us, 'I'm such a big fan of yours,' he was screaming out of the car. Miss West autographed a picture, and here we were, side by side, going about sixty miles an hour with me waiting to pass it out the window to the person riding with him. There was a stoplight, and Paul finally managed to get close enough for me to pass the autographed picture over to the other car. Miss West had quickly signed another picture for the other person in the car.

"The amount of mail Miss West got was unbelievable. It wasn't just fan mail. There were hundreds of requests for appearances, to do commercials, hundreds of letters asking for interviews for TV or major newspapers and magazines, for books, for school newspapers. If Miss West had given all of those interviews, she wouldn't have had time to do anything in life, not even to sleep. I was put in charge of the day-to-day social activities. In the beginning, the office was at the beach house.

"Miss West would sit with me for hours, working on the fan mail, always good-humored about it. She enjoyed reading what the fans wrote, and she signed absolutely every autograph herself. That was really astounding. It took hours, just about every day. Many of the fans asked for autographed pictures which Miss West provided at her own expense. Some of them sent pictures, which we mailed back signed. In the years we did this, she always got great pleasure from this connection with her fans.

"Usually she would get through about one hundred before she'd take a break. She was very disciplined. Then she'd come back and start again.

"There were people who sent Miss West a pile of pictures for autographing. When she found out that one of them was selling them, she was irritated, but she didn't quite know just how to handle that situation. She said she'd rather make the mistake of sending too many pictures to someone who would turn around and sell them than to disappoint a genuine fan. I found it easier to return pictures to someone who sent a big pile, and maybe just have Miss West sign one or two for the person, and I wrote a note of regret about the others. Then the sender could blame it on me.

"Something Miss West enjoyed after I went to work for her was having me read her fan mail to her, and it wasn't because I was such a great reader. After I would read each letter, we would talk about it. She especially liked getting letters which were weird, but not *too* weird.

"If I came across anything obscene, pornographic, or just in bad taste, I learned very quickly not to show the letter or enclosed photos. Miss West wasn't a puritan, but she was a little modest.

"Once in a while, there was a nude photo of some extraordinarily well-built man. The first time that happened, I wasn't going to show the photograph to Miss West, but I dropped it. It fell face upward, naturally. Miss West said, 'What's that?'

"I picked it up and held it back. 'Let me see it, dear,' she said.

"I handed it to her with some hesitancy. I thought she might lower her eyes or look away. But far from it. She took a good hard look. She turned to me and said, 'This isn't pornography. This is art.'

"Sometimes, the pictures were embarrassing. Miss West never wished to see pornography. Pornography offended her. She said the pictures had to be in good taste. Usually that meant the men were good-looking, and exceptionally well built. She could understand that. Otherwise, it was in pretty bad taste.

"She liked it when the people wrote letters telling about themselves and their lives. She never got bored. Sometimes people sent her pictures of themselves, and wanted her to keep them. She did. She felt that they had sent them in the right spirit, and it was up to her to respect their pictures in the right spirit. She said, 'I can't betray them.'

"Miss West received a lot of love letters, some of them from very young men. That pleased her.

"It was interesting that Miss West got as many fan letters from women as from men. Maybe more. Women wrote that they felt she was liberated and they admired that.

"One letter Miss West liked a lot, I always remember, was from a stripper, a stripper who was seventy-five years old! And she was still working. She'd enclosed a picture of herself. She was *very* busty. She was blond and in great shape and didn't look her age, even in a revealing outfit. She was a very admiring fan, and she thanked Miss West for her ideas on health, which she'd read about and followed. Miss West was quite touched by the letter she'd written.

" 'We have to send her a picture right away, with a good autograph.'

"Though Miss West signed every autograph herself, there was some difference in the autographs, whether she was signing it with a scrawl, quickly or fancy when there was enough time. When she wanted to do an elaborate one, she did it bigger.

"She told me that she'd been practicing her autograph since she was seven years old because she *knew* when she was that young that she was going to be a star, a really big star. She'd had her confidence that young. She felt that she had some ESP even back then, but she didn't realize it then.

"I remember she wrote this huge autograph on one photograph for someone who had written a long letter about herself and her life, which Miss West had found particularly interesting, and then, she looked back at the autograph she'd just signed. 'That's a good one, isn't it, dear?'

"People sent her all kinds of gifts, including paintings and drawings. Some of them were really awful, but she couldn't bear to throw away what they had sent, especially if they had done it themselves. She felt that would be 'disrespectful,' and so she got stuck with it.

"There was this one very big picture, huge, I found in her garage. It was terribly ugly. It was a naked woman supposed to be Miss West who was sort of walking on water. It was really big. I asked her what I should do with it. What I really meant was, 'Could I get rid of it?'

"Miss West said, 'I better keep it, 'cause I don't want to throw out someone's work.'

"I didn't know what happened to the picture, but a few years after she was gone, I saw it listed in an auction house estate sale as 'a possession of Mae West's.' It didn't sell.

"One day in the limo, I opened an envelope which contained another nude photograph a man had sent of himself. I told Miss West what it was, in case she didn't want to see it. She asked me how he looked. I said, 'Pretty good. Awesome.'

"Miss West modestly averted her eyes. Then she said, 'Put it into my purse, dear.' "

"One day, weeks later, she was using the same purse she had that day, and she reached into her purse for something, and she found that letter. She looked at the envelope, which she had obviously forgotten. 'Oh, yes,' she said, remembering the envelope, and she put it back into her purse.

"Women would come up to Miss West a lot and they'd say words to the effect of, 'You changed my life.' Miss West was always very polite and gracious, and she would act like it was the first time she had ever heard those words and that they pleased her. The woman would leave happy. Miss West understood that she had that gift—to be able to make people happy, and it made her happy doing it.

"Then, another woman would come up and say almost the same thing and Miss West would be just as gracious, and she would listen to the woman, and she didn't look bored.

"But after a while, it took a lot of energy, to keep doing that, so she stayed in the backseat of the limousine and she started to spend more of her time at home."

"Of all the properties that she owned, even the beach house," Tim said, "she preferred living at the apartment. She said it reminded her of when she lived in Brooklyn in a brownstone. She liked the security of it. She liked to go down to the beach house for just a day, and Paul loved it. After she sold it, she said, 'I'm kind of sorry I sold it.'

"At that particular time, the taxes were going sky-high. She just figured she wasn't there enough to warrant it.

"The beach house was beautiful. It was in Santa Monica. It had twenty-two rooms, and it faced the ocean. It was right on the ocean, The living room was curved, and it had all-glass windows. She had a custom-made sofa, to fit the curve of the house.

"She had two bedrooms upstairs that faced the ocean that were hers. She would alternate between them. One of the rooms was called the white room, and it had a round bed. The other room had a queen-sized bed with a canopy, and that was the pink room. There was a room for Beverly that was decorated in blue, Beverly's favorite color.

"There was an office, and there were three other bedrooms upstairs. There were two kitchens, one upstairs, one downstairs, a large formal dining room, a den, and then servant quarters. There were dressing rooms and shower areas for coming from the beach. It was quite a big house and beautiful.

"Miss West sold it in 1978. She still had the ranch in the San Fernando Valley, where Beverly lived. Usually, every week we would go over there. I remember it had a small kitchen, formal dining room, servants quarters, large living room, and Beverly's room.

"Miss West did own other properties. She had rental houses. She owned an office building. She owned a lot of properties, and she got them in the thirties, when things were reasonable. She told me she would just be out in the limousine driving, having the driver drive her around, and she would see property for sale, and she would say, 'I want to buy that,' and she bought it. She was a very decisive person.

"For a time, Beverly would come over to Miss West's apartment, but near the end of Miss West's life, Beverly was getting to the point where she couldn't really get out.

"Beverly had a good sense of humor before she started drinking too much. You could see that they were definitely related. Beverly was heavier and a little bit shorter than Miss West. She was, I think, about five and a half years younger, but she appeared older. Beverly liked to smoke, and she did drink a lot. Toward the end, she would drink and get a little belligerent, and we didn't like to have Miss West alone with her. But Miss West wasn't ever uncomfortable with her sister. She was just sad, and she didn't know how to help her.

"Beverly was starting to hallucinate. Finally we had to go paint the mirrors in her bedroom black, because she was seeing things in the mirrors.

"Miss West always said what a beautiful singing voice Beverly had, that she was a good blues singer and could have had a wonderful career if she'd had the ambition and drive to pursue her singing. Beverly also wrote some of her own songs.

"Miss West got an idea to help her sister. She was feeling a little desperate about it because her sister's drinking was increasing and was hard to control. She'd hired a caretaker to look after the property, but he was really supposed to find the bottles and separate Beverly from her source of supply, which wasn't easy. He was never more than partially successful.

"There were some songs which Beverly had written in the forties and some tests had been recorded. Miss West decided to make a 45 single. The photo she chose to put on the sleeve was one of Beverly that was about forty years old. The record was good, and Miss West wanted Beverly to give away the records to all of her friends.

"The first problem was Beverly didn't have many friends to give the records to. The second problem was the worse one. Beverly was drinking so much she thought the record had been released and was making a fortune, and that people were lining up to buy her record. So it didn't bring Beverly closer to reality, but took her farther away from it. And so, we ended up moving a lot of boxes of records out to Miss West's beach house.

"Back in the thirties, Beverly was getting a check from Miss West every week for two hundred dollars. I know because I've seen the canceled checks. That was a lot of money then.

"Her brother was partly supported by her, and sometimes wholly when a project of his failed. Miss West never minded about the money. She was glad she could help, because she really had this incredibly strong feeling toward family. She said once it was what her mother would have wanted. He would try doing things, and they wouldn't last. I think Miss West tried to get him jobs at the studio, but they didn't last. He tried raising horses at the ranch. Miss West and her brother and sister loved horses."

Being so close to Mae for so long, Tim saw a side of her that few others had the opportunity to observe.

"I found that Miss West, in person, could drop her public character and be herself, which was still closely related to the public character, but not exactly the same. She was a very human person, but she was absolutely dedicated to preserving her public character, which she had worked so hard to create. She never wanted to disappoint anyone. I thought it was a sign she liked you if she dropped the character, and didn't have to be performing.

"She would kind of go in and out of the character. She was a down-to-earth person and totally normal, and very kind. She had a soft way. She did it like it was a secret she had to hide. She was always ready to help people, but she didn't see it as exactly in keeping with Diamond Lil. The real Mae West was a gentle soul.

"A lot of times people she had worked with in vaudeville or on the stage, when they had bad times or whatever, they came to her. She would always find work for them in a movie or whatever she was doing. If she couldn't do that, or they weren't able to work, she gave them some money. She tried to give it in an easy, matter-of-fact way, not making a big thing out of it, so they wouldn't feel embarrassed. She told me she felt very lucky that she had all the money she could ever need, and what she earned had been so well invested. She always talked about getting the breaks and how some people who deserved to, didn't.

"Do you know about Eva Tanguay? Miss West had known her from vaudeville when they both worked on the circuits. It was important to her that Miss Tanguay had known her mother. Anyone with a good link to her mother was always special for Miss West. And that's why Miss West was happy to help her out at the end of her life, when she was in need.

"Paul Novak was a very gentle, caring person, and he thought the world of Miss West. He would do anything that was in her best interests.

"Paul had a gun which he always carried when he went out with

Miss West. He rarely left the apartment without her. He had a license for the gun, and he knew how to use it. Miss West knew he wouldn't hesitate to use it, if it came to protecting her. She found Paul's gun very reassuring.

"The gun was in the desk drawer when we were the only ones there. If strangers came to the apartment, he moved the gun somewhere, or wore it, so he would have it ready. Besides protecting Miss West, there were her diamonds. She kept some in the bank vault, but she liked to keep a lot in the safe in her bedroom so she could look at them when she wanted to. She figured there wasn't any danger as long as no one knew but the three of us, and no one did.

"She had a lot of faith in the Ravenswood, too, that they wouldn't let anybody come up without being announced. I think even the insurance company didn't really know how much she had at home, or they would have raised the cost of the policy. Miss West said if she never got to see her diamonds, it made her sad. It wasn't fun just looking at them in the bank. She was able to adjust to not wearing them as much out in the world. Paul persuaded her to get some good-quality fakes. He said, 'Nobody will know the difference, Miss West.'

"With a slight pout she said, '*I'll* know the difference.' Miss West always had the last word. She did make some compromises, because she knew Paul was right. Gradually, she wore more of the fakes and fewer of the real diamonds. Finally, she was wearing all the fakes, but not mentioning it, but she *always* wore at least one real one. I guess it made her feel more comfortable and happier, and not completely deprived because she really knew the difference. The diamonds made her feel cheerful, and she always enjoyed putting on the real ones in the apartment. I think they made her feel more like herself.

"Once, I remember Miss West noticed a different pattern with Paul and the way he was acting. He was staying out longer when he went out. He didn't always say exactly where he was going, or come back and say where he'd been. It was a little different from the way he'd always been. Miss West thought he seemed to have a secret, and I think she felt uneasy. She felt she had to be able to trust him perfectly. She always had. I don't think Miss West would have tolerated unfaithfulness in any man—even Paul.

"It turned out that Miss West's competitor was a sailboat. Paul loved boats and the water. Someone had offered him a small boat in bad condition for hardly any money, and Paul had been fixing it up.

"After Miss West passed on, I know Paul was living in the marina for a while. He'd wanted to see the world, but he hadn't been able to because Miss West didn't want to travel anymore. She told me that when she was a girl, she'd wanted to see Bavaria, where her mother came from, and maybe where her father's family had come from in Ireland and in England, but she'd lost interest in traveling that far. Then, Paul went around the world on a cruise ship.

"I saw Paul infrequently for about six months after Miss West's death, and then Paul disappeared. I think he wanted to be away from everybody and everything that reminded him of Miss West.

"I was disappointed that when he was so sick, Paul didn't let me know until pretty close to the end. That was about 1999. I talked to him in the hospital, and we talked for, like, two hours. I said, 'I want to come and see you.'

" 'Well, I'm going to be leaving tomorrow.' But he never did.

"If he liked you, you meant the world. If he didn't, don't cross him! He was soft-spoken and very kind, but he was very strong."

"It was very sad for me to see Miss West in the hospital, but when she was gone, it was hard for me to believe and hard to accept. She was larger than life. There was never anyone like her. It seemed she would always be there. It all happened pretty fast. Maybe if you have someone like that in your life, and you lose that person, you never quite get over it. Anyway, I want to do everything for her memory that I can. I'd like to see her things kept together as much as possible.

"I would describe her as one of the wittiest, most humorous actresses, or human beings, who ever lived. She could walk into a dark room and have this aura about her that would light up the room.

"I was there when she passed away, and more important, I was there with her during the last ten years of her life. I have such great memories.

"It's kind of funny, over the years, how I looked around the apartment, Miss West's home, everything she loved, just the way she wanted it. And I said to myself, Who knows when it will be the last time I'm going to see all of this? So, I took it all in."

Chapter Seven

———◆———

THE LAST ACT

(1980)

P
AUL NOVAK WAS thirty-three when he met Mae. He had been in the Navy and the Merchant Marine. He had run a gym and was a famous bodybuilder before he joined Mae's Las Vegas muscle-men troupe. As Mae spoke with me, he was passing through with glasses of mineral water and the chocolates I had brought.

Mae told me, "I hope to have every one of my teeth outlive me—and not because I'm planning a short life. I'm very lucky to have inherited wonderful teeth. My smile is a great part of me that people remember, but the most important thing to remember is that when you're smiling on the outside, you're smiling on the inside, too. It's more important for you than for the people you're smiling at."

On his way back to the kitchen, Mae's gaze followed him. She said to me, "That's a nice pair of shoulders, isn't it?"

For a moment, he could be heard puttering around. Then, there was a loud crashing sound of glass from the kitchen.

"I hope he didn't break anything . . . important," Mae said.

"Paul's the great man in my life. It's pretty well-known that every man, well, just about every man I ever met fell in love with me. I suppose it's possible *someone* might not have fallen in love with me . . .

"So, it doesn't raise any eyebrows that Paul is madly in love with me, though we try to be discreet. I like some privacy. What we don't want people to know is that ours is a genuine love story. It's both sides of the street, not a one-way relationship. You can say this, but don't push it too hard, if you know what I mean.

"I don't like to have the word get out *too* much, because it isn't my image for my audience, but, honey, I love Paul as much as he loves me, and that's a whole lot.

"Love grows. That's the best kind. And when love grows, passion doesn't diminish."

Mae didn't believe in love at first sight, at least not for herself. She told me it was fine for others, but that she didn't believe the feeling should be called "love" at first sight. "It's that something else that we've got to watch out for, dear.

"Personally, I don't think it should be called 'love' at first sight. I call it 'the pleasure.' "

Paul, she said, had told her that he had fallen in love with her at first sight. While Paul was still arranging things in the kitchen, she said to me, "I'll tell you one thing I was wrong about.

"In the beginning, I figured passion fades. A pretty good assumption, since it always does, and not only the sex goes, but the whole relationship loses its luster. I figured that even with Paul it would have to fade, eventually, but I was wrong, dead wrong.

"With Paul, it's different. Everything only got better. And better. And better."

Well into her eighties, Mae shared her private feelings for Paul with Kevin Thomas.

"At this point in my life, one man is enough for me, especially when that man is Paul, who's got it all."

Mae smiled and gave Thomas a nudge with her elbow.

"But I can still look.

"You know, I still look at other men besides Paul. He understands that. He knows I'm not dead yet, and I'll be looking as long as I'm alive. But I'd never want another man. Paul's the only man for me now, and he knows that.

"If he looked at another woman, I'd understand, as long as he didn't do any more than look. But he tells me he doesn't want to even look at anyone else, because he only has eyes for me.

"There are two things I require in a man—chivalry and a good sex drive. Paul's sure got those two things.

"A man has got to always treat me like a lady, open doors, pull out my chair, you know, that kind of thing. And Paul's intuitive. He knows what I want, when I want it, and he's always ready.

"I guess I never loved a man the way I loved my work, which is hard to call work because I've always loved it so much.

"Paul is a part of my work because he loves my work and being part of it. He facilitates it, and he facilitates me."

Mae could be very quiet, and she valued what she called "quiet time." She didn't like being alone very much, she told me, but she did like having someone around who was present but quiet.

Sometimes, she said, she wasn't in the mood for conversation, especially "just making conversation. I like to talk when I want to communicate.

"But it's nice sometimes just to have someone around you can speak ordinary with when a thought turns up.

"And I don't like to have anyone talk at me, either, just to fill silences. Paul is perfect, because he's my person to be quiet with. A person to be quiet with is harder to find than someone to talk with."

. . .

When we went out, Mae and I sat in the backseat of the car while Paul sat in the front seat. He wore a chauffeur's cap with his suit rather than a uniform.

Arriving at our destination, Paul would leave the driver's seat and rush around to open the door for Mae. She never moved until he had opened the door, and he knew just how to help her out so that she made the most graceful exit from the car.

Mae entered a restaurant holding his arm. She walked as though she were on a red carpet, on her way to a grand event even when we were going to eat chop suey.

Inside, he pulled out her chair and spread her napkin on her lap. Then he sat down and became her friend and dinner companion, as we enjoyed our chop suey.

There was a small lamp on the table. Mae moved it to one side. Then she moved it to the other side. "We don't want to sit with an unflattering light on us, do we, dear?" she explained.

"Do you know my idea of a wonderful time?" Mae asked me. "Sex and chop suey."

"Together?"

"No, not at the same time. The chop suey tastes better after.

"Chop suey restaurants stay open late, and if they close, you can always go the next night. Chop suey, sex, and my career. My work was the most fun. Sex was second best. I didn't want it when I was working. Well, maybe that's going too far. I wanted it, but I refrained because I wanted to save my sexual energy to put into my work. You've gotta conserve your sex energy in order to do your work. You know, honey, you want to be sure and do that, too. It's the same energy.

"When I started to write or did a picture, I stopped all my sex activities. Sex divides your mind. The sex drive is behind everything creative we do. The stronger the sex drive, the stronger the desire to create. When an architect designs a building, he puts his sex drive into creating that building.

"People who want one thing more want every thing more. It's part of the same drive. But there are moments to slow down. I don't like a man that's in a hurry. 'I like a guy what takes his time.'

"Perhaps men could be divided into two kinds," I said, "those who take their watches off, and those who leave them on."

Mae brightened. "Say—I like that. You know, maybe you *could* learn, honey."

I noticed that Mae was watching me as I ate. "You have nice manners," she told me. "You chew nicely." I said it was a lovely compliment and one I'd never received before.

"You chew the way a lady chews, which is very important. If she doesn't chew right, it shows she isn't a lady. What you don't want is to chew like a cow chewing her cud. My model for the way I wanted to eat was my mother. She was so refined. She had come from Europe, and her family chewed in a refined way.

"So many people don't understand how much of their lives they spend chewing. It would be amazing if we could count the hours. We all do it, and we usually do it in the presence of other people. We don't think about it any more than we think about how we walk, putting one foot in front of the other.

"I've always paid a lot of attention to how I put one leg in front of the other. I have the most distinctive walk in the world. With chewing you don't want to be distinctive. You want to be *in*-obtrusive.

Mae showed great enthusiasm over the fortune cookies, not for eating them, but for the fortunes each contained. The owners of the restaurant, wanting to please her, brought extra cookies so she could choose among the fortunes. She read out loud to us the ones she liked most, and tucked them neatly into her small clutch bag. She was always attentive to our fortunes, too, and when Paul and I read ours out loud, she was pleased if we had good ones.

"When I was a child, maybe four or five, I sat at the kitchen table looking in a hand mirror to watch how I looked when I chewed."

After the meal, as we left the restaurant, Paul's chauffeur ritual was repeated.

Whenever Mae and Paul went out to a gala back-tie evening, she hired a limousine. Then Paul was her escort riding in the backseat with her.

Once when Paul and I were alone for a few minutes, he nodded toward her bedroom as we waited for her to return.

"This is why I'm here," he said. "My purpose in life is to protect Miss West. I was just a roustabout, and she chose me. I've been blessed."

Paul said she gave meaning to his life, that before she "chose" him, he had sometimes felt "lost and depressed," but afterward, he knew his life had meaning. He said that he would give his life without a second's thought, protecting her, that he would hope to die first. But then he said that he wanted to be there for her. "Miss West is the love of my life," he told me.

"Paul always carries a gun," Mae said, "and he keeps his license up to date. Partly it's for the diamonds, and partly it's to deter kidnappers.

"If you don't think you're valuable, how can you expect anyone else to think you're valuable?"

Mae rarely picked up the phone. It was usually Paul who answered calls. He told me he did that not to keep strangers from Mae, but to keep away some "friends." Strangers were easy and did not present a problem, but he was concerned about guarding her from contact with so-called friends he believed were not good for Mae.

He judged whether they were "suitable for Miss West or not" by the effect they had on her at the end of the conversation—whether she was "happier or less happy." Some of them, he felt, intentionally enjoyed trying to depress her. "She's naturally upbeat, and some people envy her the life she lives and that she never got old."

According to Paul, some of these people acted stupidly and wanted to talk about illnesses and funerals of mutual acquaintances, or they wanted to gossip. "Miss West never cares about gossip. She only cares about talking about herself, and I don't think that's gossip."

Paul told me he had had a dream since he was a boy. "It wasn't anything to do with muscle building. I wanted to see the world. I wanted to go around the world and preferably travel by ship, because I enjoyed being on water," he said. "It seems strange, but sometimes I feel more secure on water than on land.

"Miss West does not like long trips or ocean voyages, so I don't mind, because her happiness is my first consideration, my whole consideration."

The only time she ever showed any annoyance with Paul was when he came between her and sweets. Mae took her chocolates, candied fruit, and chocolate cream pie seriously.

Dan Price remembered a night that he had dinner with "Miss West" and Paul and "the affair of the baked potato."

"Everyone enjoyed the great meal," Price told me, "especially Miss West. She particularly relished a very large baked potato which she filled with butter and ate with obvious pleasure.

"When the dessert menus were presented, Mae was really studying hers carefully.

" 'Paul,' she said, 'I can't decide which dessert to have.'

" 'Don't worry about it, Mae,' he said, 'you won't be having any dessert tonight. Not after that meal you've just eaten, especially after that big potato you consumed.'

"While it meant Mae didn't get everything she wanted, especially sweets, it was clear she didn't mind Paul's proprietary, take-charge attitude. It showed her how much he cared about her. His tone was kind, if controlling. Mae always said she liked a strong man."

It may also have reminded Mae of her mother's attitude toward healthy foods. Mae had told me, "My mother was a health nut, and Paul's one, too." It was Paul who did all the shopping and all the cooking for the meals the two of them ate at home together. Mae said, "He's my monitor."

Mae and Paul were not vegetarians, and he cooked roasts and steaks. She said Paul was a wonderful cook. He did curried chicken, a recipe of the Sri's, and sole fresh from a fish market, a specialty. They had guests in for drinks and snacks, and went to restaurants with friends, but when they ate at home, it was just the two of them, unless Tim stayed into the evening.

"When the waiter arrived," Price continued, "well aware of her usual preferences, he said, 'Let me tell you, Miss West, about some of our special desserts tonight. We have a delicious chocolate pie with a buttery cookie crust, chocolate cream éclairs, dark and white chocolate mousse, and a hot fudge sundae.'

"Miss West responded, but she didn't look the waiter in the eye. She spoke to the tablecloth. 'No thank you. I don't want any dessert.'

"When the waiter, who had seemed surprised, left, Mae asked Paul, 'Why didn't *you* just tell him I didn't want any dessert?'

"He said, 'I didn't feel I had to lie for you.' "

Paul declined dessert. So did Price, who years later said he had been looking forward to it and who told me, "I certainly wasn't going to eat dessert in front of Miss West and torture her."

"I'm very anxious that Paul is well taken care of—free and independent—if I should go first," Mae told me, "A very important psychic told me that I'd live to be 115 years old, that it was a sure thing. He said I wouldn't change at all, and I'd look twenty-six till I died. Well, maybe that was a little exaggerated. I'll probably look twenty-eight.

"But I said to Paul, in case this psychic got it wrong, 'We've got to have a plan for you.'

"And he said, 'No, Mae, there's no way you can do anything for me. I've had the perfect life with you. I couldn't have wanted more, and there isn't anything for me without you. Without, you, I don't want to be around.'

"Can you imagine that?" Mae asked me. There was a tear in her eye. "Like I told you, I never cry," she said.

"You know why Paul and me have a good time together? We have fun. There's no better reason to be together than because you *want* to be."

"Would getting married ruin everything?" I asked.

"No, I don't think so," she answered. "But who knows? When something is perfect, I don't believe in tampering. There's a saying that if a thing ain't broke, don't fix it.

"I asked Paul if he wanted to marry me. You might say I proposed. He said, 'I'm happy the way it is, Mae.' "

Paul helped her to be Mae West for the world until the end. He helped her to believe she was still Mae West for herself and her own happiness. He was able to do this because *he* believed it.

Mae was looking forward to her eighty-seventh birthday. She believed that her very first birthday with her loving parents had started the trend in the right direction. Ever since, she had always enjoyed her birthday. There were no plans, but she knew Paul would think of a way to celebrate, and it seemed she always enjoyed everything more on her birthday.

They would probably go to Man Fook Low's for dinner, maybe with a few friends. There would be a birthday cake in the afternoon at home at the Ravenswood, something chocolate, possibly with milk chocolate cream between the layers and a dark chocolate frosting, maybe with chocolate cream roses. Paul knew what she liked, and he would permit her to indulge for the special occasion, though not to excess. Mae could count on Paul to be watching over her diet, even on her birthday.

She knew that Paul would have several birthday gifts for her, each beautifully wrapped. He understood how Mae loved opening packages, ripping off the ribbon, tearing the paper. It almost seemed it didn't matter much what was inside. Mae already had everything she could ever want. She had come to the realization that "a girl can only wear so many diamonds, and if you have all you could ever wear, no use collecting any more. Well, unless something really *great* turned up ..."

Mae never believed in resisting temptation. She knew from experience, however, that the greatest diamonds never turn up on schedule for a birthday or a special occasion. You have to accept them on *their* schedule.

The value of the gifts from Paul didn't matter. It was the thought and that she knew he was always thinking about how to make her happy. He didn't think about himself. Making her happy made him happy. And what a great body he had! She knew she'd been very lucky in life.

Eighty-seven wasn't old, not the way *she* was. She didn't feel even half that age. "You're young as long as your health is good," Mae said. "You're the age of your health." Mae believed the psychic who had told her she would live to be 115 in unchanging health, looking the same. She certainly wasn't going to start to worry until she passed 100.

On August 10, 1980, Mae fell out of bed, hitting her head. She appeared stunned.

Paul carried her to a chair in the living room. He spoke to her, but she didn't respond. He called her doctor.

It seemed that Mae had suffered a concussion, or a mild stroke. When Mae didn't get better, Paul agreed that she, *they*, would go to the hospital. He took a room adjoining hers. He registered them as Mr. and Mrs. Paul Drake.

The story that Paul gave out to the press, when word got out, was that Miss West had told him that she had been dreaming about Burt Reynolds when she fell out of bed. When he asked her if it had been a good dream, she had answered, "What other kind of dream could I have had about Burt Reynolds?" Paul's story was perfectly in keeping with the public image of Mae West.

The problem was Mae hadn't told him anything. She hadn't been able to speak at all.

Paul thought Mae would find the story funny as soon as she recovered. He hoped she would recover soon.

As it turned out, it *had* been what was called a mild stroke, but it had paralyzed her tongue. She could neither speak nor eat. Paul hoped Mae would recover in time to enjoy the birthday cake he had ordered. He knew she was looking forward to it.

"She looked very well, pretty much the same," Tim Malachosky, who was at the hospital, told me. "She seemed to be aware of our presence, Paul and me. It was clear our being there made her feel much better, so that made *me* feel better. It was just terrible to see her there in the hospital."

Paul put the huge bouquet of perfect roses into the two largest vases Mae had in the Ravenswood apartment. There was no vase large enough to contain so many. Carefully, he cut the stems in the hope they would last long enough to welcome Mae home. He took the beautifully written get-well letter from Elizabeth Taylor that had accompanied the roses with him to the hospital.

He knew the letter and gift would cheer Mae. Even though she generally wasn't a fan of cut flowers, Mae liked Elizabeth Taylor. Paul showed the letter to Mae and he read it to her. He wasn't certain how much of it she understood. He preserved the letter carefully for Mae's recovery. The roses probably couldn't be saved, no matter how much he clipped the stems and changed the water, but he would tell Mae about them.

Mae showed some improvement. She began walking short distances. She was more responsive and aware, though she did not regain her ability to speak. Paul was permitted to take her, with the assistance of a nurse, for a drive to the beach.

On September 8, she had another stroke, this time paralyzing one side of her body. She was moved to intensive care.

When she was able to leave intensive care and return to her private room, Paul brought records of hers to play. She seemed to enjoy hearing herself singing. He had a projector brought to the hospital so she could see her films.

"She knew we were there," Tim said. "She would smile at me, and I would sit there for hours holding her hand."

Doctors were called in for consultation. Paul sought the opinion of other doctors. When no one could offer anything positive, he turned to psychics, healers, and mystics. A few were allowed to come to the hospital, but to no avail. An afternoon of chanting produced no results, except that some of the patients in rooms nearby complained.

Tim recalled the sad moment when the doctors agreed there was little hope.

"I'll never forget when they said there wasn't anything else they could do in the hospital. They just said to Paul, 'You can take her home.'"

At first, Paul's spirits rose. He interpreted the news that he could take Mae home as hopeful, but quickly realized the truth.

There was nothing more that could be done for her.

A hospital bed was brought to the Ravenswood, and three full-time nurses were employed. Paul never doubted that Mae would recover and speak with him again.

He had one persistent and nagging fear, however, which he shared only with his closest friends. In spite of his comparative youth, wonderful health, and athletic prowess, something could happen to him, an accident that would prevent him from caring for Miss West.

When they left the Good Samaritan Hospital November 3, 1980, Paul was certain that being in her own environment, which she so dearly loved and in which she felt so secure, would be just what she needed for her recovery.

Tim recalled the experience as though it had just happened.

"I remember Paul and I took her back to the apartment, and she was in a wheelchair. We took her through the lobby and up in the elevator.

"I opened the elevator door, and Paul lifted her out of the chair, and he carried her in his arms to the door. Her expression changed as soon as she saw the door of her apartment. When the door opened and she saw the inside, her eyes lit up, and she glowed. She hadn't looked happy like that since she had left the apartment.

"Paul carried her to the bed with its silk-satin sheets and propped-up down pillows.

"I brought up a movie projector, and I put *She Done Him Wrong* on. We put her where she normally would sit, and as soon as she came on screen, she pointed. She knew it was her.

"She couldn't communicate much. Her right side was paralyzed. She couldn't talk at all. We had to feed her through a tube to her stomach, which was very difficult for her, I'm sure. She didn't complain. Even though she couldn't speak, she could have conveyed her unhappiness and discomfort, but she never did that. She put on a brave front to make it easier for us.

"It was very sad, and it took me a long time to get over it. I guess I never will completely. We always had that hope that someday she would rally and get back to normal. It didn't happen."

Despite the mental and emotional frustration she must have felt, as one of the most expressive persons of all time suddenly unable to communicate, Mae radiated good nature and acceptance for those who cared so greatly about her, but she was gravely ill.

On the morning of Saturday, November 22, 1980, Mae's doctor arrived and told Paul that Mae would not survive the day.

Paul was forced to recognize and deal with loss of hope. He had shared twenty-seven years with Mae. He tried to think what Mae would want. He hadn't prepared for the day because it had been something he couldn't bear to think about. Paul tried to reach a minister they knew, but he couldn't find him. There was no time to lose. He located a Catholic priest they knew who was nearby, and he came immediately.

He prayed and blessed her. Mae seemed to hear the words and was peaceful.

Within minutes after the priest left, Mae was gone. Paul kissed her goodbye. She died sitting in her favorite white satin chair where she often sat in her bedroom.

Despite his sense of numbness, his overwhelming grief, and his wish to deny the truth of what had happened, Paul went to the phone, remembering to call the friend who was going to cook a Thanksgiving turkey with all of the trimmings and send it over. He thanked her and told her not to prepare the turkey. They wouldn't be needing it.

Paul pondered what Mae would have wanted: a large public funeral or a small private one? They had never discussed this subject.

According to Tim, who helped with preparations, it had been Paul's original intention to organize a grand-style funeral. He felt Mae should have the largest funeral Hollywood had ever witnessed. It should be unforgettable, like the legedary Valentino funeral.

He knew that Lil would have wanted something public, with pomp and extremely stylish, but Mae was private, and such a public ceremony might be a violation of her privacy. Though he couldn't hear her voice telling him what she wanted, he made the decision to have a private funeral. Mae's agent at William Morris was given a list of people to call, and Paul called a few of Mae's closest friends himself.

Although Mae was to be interred in the family mausoleum at the Cypress Hills Cemetery in Brooklyn, the funeral service was held in Los Angeles at Forest Lawn. The service was not open to the public and was by invitation only.

Because the illness hadn't shown on her face and she looked lovely, Paul decided there could be an open casket. Her makeup was carefully and expertly applied by a cosmetician Mae favored. Paul knew that Mae would have been pleased. Tim remembered "Miss West looking years younger than her age, and not as if she had been sick at all."

"Frankie and Johnnie," "Easy Rider," and other music Mae had enjoyed and included in her personal repertory, but not generally played at a funeral, was heard.

The officiating pastor said of Mae, "Goodness had *everything* to do with it."

She was dressed in a white gown trimmed with pearls and rhinestones. Her hair was done in the style of *Sextette*.

The eulogy was written by Kevin Thomas. Producer Ross Hunter delivered the eulogy. He referred to "the tender love story" of which

Mae had been a part for more than a quarter of a century, thus recognizing Paul and their relationship.

Hunter said the more she concentrated on Mae West, the more she gave to others. Her importance in changing attitudes of men and women toward women's sexual needs was a concept to which she had greatly contributed. Perceptively, it was stated "the Mae West character had never wanted anyone to feel sorry for her, and she wouldn't want them to start now."

Robert Wise, Edith Head, and Joan Rivers were among the invited mourners.

Beverly West came alone and remained in the limousine, too distraught to enter and be with the other people. On the floor inside the car, empty bottles could be seen.

Immediately after the funeral, Paul and Mae's friend, Dolly Dempsey, who had come from San Diego to help during Mae's illness, traveled with Mae's body to Brooklyn, where Mae would rest with her mother, her father, and her brother.

Though Mae had never wanted to discuss the subject, and had said that she knew she had a long time ahead before she needed to make any plans, she did tell Paul that when the time came, she wanted to be placed in the family mausoleum in Brooklyn, which Mae had purchased when her mother died.

In Brooklyn, two priests and a bishop delivered a blessing. While Mae did not consider herself a Catholic, she enjoyed a friendly relationship with the Catholic Church. She had generously supported good works and projects of the Catholic Church.

In November of 2007, Joan Rivers spoke with me about Mae West. We were in the ballroom of Rivers's Upper East Side townhouse apartment, just around the corner from Fifth Avenue.

"Mae came to dinner at my home in California a number of times, and I was happy to invite her and have her there with us, but she had two conditions that we had to accept. We always had to have dinner by candlelight, and she had to sit in a certain place at the table, so everyone would see her from a certain angle. I always did that. She would tell stories, and we were happy to have her.

"Then, one Thanksgiving, not long before she died, but none of us thought she was *ever* going to die, Paul called me.

"He said Mae didn't have any family or friends who were celebrating Thanksgiving dinner, so would it be possible for Mae to join my family and me for Thanksgiving dinner. I wanted to say yes, but I knew it would mean our family would have to sit in candlelight all during the meal. I made some excuse about how we already had too many people, that I regretted it, but I just couldn't do it.

"And I've regretted it every since.

"Mae died just a short time after that. So, I couldn't ever invite her to a Thanksgiving dinner again.

"I felt I wanted to go to her funeral. I thought there would be a tremendous number of people going, that it would be a grand-style Hollywood funeral.

"I was shocked when I arrived. It wasn't a big event at all. There were only a few members of her family and some friends. Where were all her fans?"

Rivers told me that she remembered Mae saying to her and to others:

" 'When I go, you'll be surprised . . . '

"Mae didn't like to use the word 'die.'

"We all wondered what she meant. Some people thought it meant she was going to leave them something in her will. Jewelry? Some of us thought she meant she was going to be paying visits.

"She'd always said she believed she would be able to do that.

"Well, we waited, but nothing happened, and it's been a long time now."

The last time Mae and I spoke, she asked me, "Are you gonna give George [Cukor] a good report about me?"

"Of course, and it will be the truth."

"I don't usually go on talking so much," Mae said. "You know, honey, I see something men must like about you. You're a brilliant listener!"

As I gathered up my things to leave, she reminded Paul, "Did you give her the bag?"

Paul handed me a small cosmetics bag that contained a bottle of baby oil, a box of powder, and a new lipstick in a light pink shade.

"Don't forget, dear," she said, "the baby oil has to be warm and put on by a man—all over."

Then Mae reached out and clutched my arm, saying, "Honey, there's something I want to tell you before you go.

"You know, my diamonds I told you all those men gave me? I wanted you to know—I bought some of them myself."

Chronology

Stage Appearances

1900–08 Amateur appearances

1908–09 Hal Clarendon stock company

1909–10 Burlesque circuit

1911 *A La Broadway*

1911 *Vera Violetta*

1912 *A Winsome Widow*

1912–17 Vaudeville tours

1918 *Sometime*

1919–21 Vaudeville tours

1921 *The Mimic World of 1921*

1921–22 Vaudeville tours

1922 Act with Harry Richman

1922/25 Vaudeville tours

Mae West Plays

1926 *Sex*

1927 *The Drag*

1927 *The Wicked Age*

1928 *Diamond Lil*

1928 *The Pleasure Man*

1931 *The Constant Sinner*

1944 *Catherine Was Great*

1946–47, 1952 *Come on Up* (uncredited)

1947–48 *Diamond Lil* British tour

1948–51 *Diamond Lil* revivals

1954–59 Las Vegas Nightclub Acts (touring)

1961 *Sextette*

Unperformed plays

1921 *The Ruby Ring*

1922 *The Hussy*

1930–31 *Frisco Kate*

Films

1932 *Night After Night*

1933 *She Done Him Wrong*

1933 *I'm No Angel*

1934 *Belle of the Nineties*

1935 *Goin' to Town*

1936 *Klondike Annie*

1936 *Go West Young Man*

1937 *Every Day's a Holiday*

1940 *My Little Chickadee*

1943 *The Heat's On*

1970 *Myra Breckinridge*

1978 *Sextette*

Radio and Television

1933 *The Rudy Vallee Show*

1937 *The Chase and Sanborn Hour*

1949–50 *The Chesterfield Supper Club*

1958 The Academy Awards Ceremony

1959 *Person to Person* (not broadcast)

1959 *Dean Martin Special*

1960 *The Red Skelton Show*

1961 *Mister Ed*

1968 *A Night with Mae West*

1971, 1972 Armed Forces Radio Christmas shows

Books

1930 *Babe Gordon (The Constant Sinner)*

1932 *Diamond Lil*

1959 *Goodness Had Nothing to Do with It*

1975 *The Pleasure Man*

Index